Samish, Arthur H
The secret boss of California; the life and high times of Art Samish, by Arthur H. Samish and Bob Thomas. New York, Crown Publishers [c1971]
192 p. 22cm.

1. Lobbyists--California. I. Thomas, Bob. II. Title.

THE SECRET BOSS OF CALIFORNIA

THE SECRET BOSS OF CALIFORNIA

The Life and High Times of Art Samish

by ARTHUR H. SAMISH
and BOB THOMAS

CROWN PUBLISHERS, INC., NEW YORK

To Merced, Carolyn, and Jo Anne, with love

Library of Congress Catalog Card Number: 75–151022

Printed in the United States of America

Published simultaneously in Canada
by General Publishing Company Limited

CONTENTS

CHAPTER 1

Reflections in the Window of Suite 916 of the Kohl Building, San Francisco 94104

I'VE NEVER GROWN TIRED OF THE VIEW, NOT IN THE YEARS I HAVE occupied this office. How could I, when I can gaze down at the fairest city of them all and see so many things that bring back memories?

Over there on Telegraph Hill I can see Coit Tower poking up through the late-afternoon fog. Mrs. Coit had the tower built to honor the brave men who fought the Fire of 1906. I was here then, though I was just a boy, a mere boy.

That big beauty of a building down the street is the new headquarters of the Bank of America. Whenever I see it, I think of old A. P. Giannini, who built that bank into the biggest in the world. Old A.P., bless his Italian heart, loaned me the money so I could make my first million-dollar deal. He and I were great pals. I used to meet him coming around the corner on Montgomery Street and we'd stand and talk for hours while the cable cars clanged up and down California Street.

Looking out the window I can see a dozen billboards. Now they're advertising beers and breads and bottomless bars, but once I had them plastered with the photograph of Elmer Robinson. I got him elected mayor, too. I did it out of friendship because I didn't give a damn who was elected mayor of San Francisco. Or United States senator, either. The only ones I cared about were the senators and assemblymen of the legislature, those darling boys who made the laws that affected my clients.

Around the corner down there on Sacramento Street is Jack's, where I've enjoyed hundreds of fine meals—you can guess by my size that I'm a fellow who likes his vittles. Jack's has been in business over a century, and it seems as if Louie Lurie has been eating lunch there that long. Louie owns this building I'm in and a flock of others in the neighborhood, and he and I go back many years. Just today I saw him at his usual table in Jack's and he told me: "It's been fifty-two years, Artie. The first time was in the Palace Court of the Palace Hotel in 1918, when we got together with Harry Chandler of the *L.A. Times* and Joe Knowland of the *Oakland Tribune* to figure how we could get Sam Shortridge elected United States senator."

So many memories.

Then as I look around this office I can bring forth a flood of memories, too. On the wall facing my desk are bound volumes of laws passed by the California state legislature over thirty years. Many of those laws I wrote, or had written for me. Even though I never held office.

But I knew those who did. *I'll say* I knew them. Knew some of them better than they knew themselves. Locked in the big safe in my outer office are the black books I kept on every senator and assemblyman. My staff and I found out everything there was to know about the lawmakers, and I mean everything. It all went into those black books. Come election time, they could prove mighty handy.

In that outer room you'll find photographs of my staff at office parties. We had a lot of parties, because that's the way I think life should be. I had a big staff in those years—my office occupied two floors in this building and the penthouse as well.

Now they're all gone, and it's quiet here. Too damned quiet.

On the wall of my office you can see two oil paintings of clowns. It's no secret that I love clowns. Some of my critics claimed that I was a clown myself. I don't deny it. Clowns are lucky people. They can hide behind their funny masks and enjoy themselves by making other people laugh.

My credo was always: Raise hell and have fun. That's why I'm writing this book.

I thought about it for a long time. Years ago Gene Fowler said he wanted to write my story. Later, Eugene Burdick wanted to do the same thing. But I held off, and by the time I made up my mind both Fowler and Burdick were dead. So I decided to tell my story to Bob Thomas. Like me, he's a native Californian and he knows the state. And didn't he write a pretty good book about another rogue, Harry Cohn?

The reader might ask why I am finally telling my life story. It's because my life has been quiet for too long. I feel like raising hell and having fun one more time.

CHAPTER 2

In Which I Make an Immodest Reply to the Reader's Question: Who the Hell Is Arthur H. Samish?

YOU WOULDN'T NEED TO ASK THAT QUESTION IF YOU HAD LIVED IN California during the 1940s or 1950s. Or elsewhere, for that matter. During that time I became quite a famous character—some said infamous. I won't argue the point.

I never ran around getting publicity for myself; in my business it was usually better not to have any. But newspaper guys were my pals, my buddies, and if they asked me something, I'd give them an answer. A good answer.

One time a reporter asked me how I was getting along with the governor. "I am the governor of the legislature," I told him. "To hell with the governor of California." *That* gave the reporter something to write about.

My habit of talking turkey with reporters brought me into the national picture in 1949. First there was an article in *The Nation* by a nice fellow named Carey McWilliams. He called it "The Guy Who Gets Things Done," and he wrote: "It would be extremely difficult to find, in the entire range of American politics, a more extraordinary political virtuoso than Artie Samish." You've got to like a man who writes like that.

McWilliams added: "Although Samish is known to everyone in California who is directly interested in politics, I would venture to guess that not one per cent of the voters could identify his name although he is, beyond all doubt, the political boss of the state."

After discussing my multifarious activities, McWilliams remarked: "From 1931 to the present time Samish has controlled a large bloc of votes in the state legislature. Control of this bloc is tantamount to control of the legislature, as this bloc usually elects the speaker of the Assembly, who appoints the committees. Majority control of two or three key committees carries with it, of course, the power to kill in committee or send out with a 'do-pass' recommendation most important pieces of legislation."

"The Guy Who Gets Things Done" created a stir, but it was nothing compared to the articles in *Collier's* magazine in August of 1949. They were written by an astute gentleman named Lester Velie. His title was, "The Secret Boss of California." I borrowed the title for this book. I hope he doesn't mind.

Velie began his articles by quoting from a University of California professor who was lecturing his senior class in political science:

> "It says in the book that we elect a legislature in California to make our laws for us. It says the legislature is responsible to the people. It also says that we elect delegates to political conventions, that we elect attorney generals and mayors and district attorneys.
>
> "Well, let's see. . . . There's a man in California today who holds no public office and is responsible only to the interests who hire him. Yet this man can push laws through the legislature or stop them cold. He named our attorney general. He elected the mayor of San Francisco and he told him whom to name for police commissioner. He has the power to make or break governors.

> "The man once delivered California's delegates to a Presidential candidate—Wendell Willkie. He is the most powerful nonofficeholder in California. Who is this man?"

None of the professor's students could answer. But Lester Velie did:

> The man who "controls the state of California" falls into no easy identifying niche. He is neither labor boss, oil king, press lord, financial nabob, nor rabble rouser of the Huey Long type. You can't even neatly tag him as the Boss Pendergast or Crump or Hague of California. Not for Artie Samish are the mildewed methods of these political Neanderthalers. He is *sui generis*—the only one of his kind. An original, both as a human being and a political operator. He is a political boss without a party.

Velie got a lot of quotables out of me. I told him I had "the damnedest Gestapo you ever saw," which was the truth, and that "I can tell if a man wants a baked potato, a girl, or money," which was also true.

I not only supplied Mr. Velie with quotes; I gave him a prize picture as well. When his photographer was taking some shots of me, I told him: "You want the real picture? I'll give you something that tells the whole story."

Then I produced a little ventriloquist's dummy, a cheerful hobo with white gloves and top hat. I planted the dummy in front of me and said, "That's the way I lobby. That's my legislature. That's Mr. Legislature. 'How are you today, Mr. Legislature?' "

I had another thought, "If you can get a long enough ladder and put it against the Capitol dome, you can get a picture of me unscrewing the gold cupola."

I gave that eastern fellow something to write about. Strangely enough, the best quote of the articles didn't come from me, but from Governor Earl Warren himself. Velie had a meeting with the governor, and he asked, "Who has more influence with the legislature, you or Artie Samish?"

Said the governor, "On matters that affect his clients, Artie unquestionably has more power than the governor."

You never saw such a whoop-de-do as followed those articles in *Collier's*. The whole state of California and part of the nation seemed to be up in arms about Artie Samish. You can read almost any political history of California and it will tell you that the Velie stories were the beginning of the end of political power for Art Samish.

Don't you think that I knew that? Why do you think that I talked so openly to Lester Velie?

My good friend Carl Greenberg, the astute political reporter for the *Los Angeles Times*, thinks that I had a kind of political death wish when I talked to Velie. That's a highfalutin analysis, but Carl might have a point there.

Why did I do it? Maybe I was looking for a way out. Maybe the fun had gone out of being "the secret boss of California." Maybe I just didn't have the heart for it any more. You must remember this: my mother had died about a year before. She meant everything to me, and she still does; I think of her every morning and evening of my life. The driving ambition that I had was to make sure that she was well taken care of, to repay her for the devotion she had shown to me. When she passed on, a lot of my ambition died with her.

The end of my career didn't come exactly as I had planned. After the *Collier's* articles, I continued in business as usual. I knew I could ride out the storm—I had always done so before. I had been through grand jury quizzes and special investigations and every other damn thing, but nothing had ever touched me. I was clean.

There was a lot of blah-blah-blah about what a bad guy Artie Samish was, but I went on, just as before. I didn't lose any clients, and I didn't lose any power in the legislature. I could still call the shots the way I wanted. Everything remained the same as the good governor had stated: "On matters that affect his clients, Artie unquestionably has more power than the governor."

I felt sorry for Earl Warren. He had taken a great deal of abuse because of the Velie articles. One of his pet projects was the establishment of a Crime Commission, and I saw to it that the proposal got through the legislature. That was my first mistake.

If the governor wanted to play around with a Crime Commission, that was all right with me; it was none of my affair. But then he appointed Warren Olney III as its chief counsel.

Warren Olney III. I had good reason to be sentimental about that name; it was in the law firm of his father that I got my start in politics. Naturally I felt no trepidation when I was asked to appear before closed hearings of the Crime Commission one Sunday at the University of California in Berkeley. All of my books and affairs were in order, I believed, and I was willing to help Olney in any way I could—within reason.

"Mr. Olney just wants to ask you one question," said his deputy.

That sounded easy. So I went over to Berkeley on that Sunday, and I was surprised at what Olney wanted to ask me.

"Do you know whether Bill Cody is a bookmaker?" he demanded. Bookmaking, of course, was illegal in California.

I didn't like the question. Of course I knew that Bill Cody had been a bookmaker in San Francisco, and so did Olney. But he wasn't a bookmaker *then.* Poor Bill was dying of leukemia, and I wasn't going to let Warren Olney make me say something that would cause Bill further grief.

"Mr. Cody is a very fine gentleman with a very fine family," I replied.

Warren Olney III became stiff and insistent. "All we want to know is whether Bill Cody is a bookmaker," he said.

"Mr. Cody is a very fine gentleman with a very fine family," I repeated.

Olney was becoming red in the face, and a recess was called in the hearing. I took a stroll outside and I ran into a member of the commission. "Keep going—you're doing fine," he said to me.

When the session resumed, Olney wouldn't let up. "I'm asking you if you know whether Bill Cody is a bookmaker," he said once more.

Again I replied, "Mr. Cody is a very fine gentleman with a very fine family." Then I pointed two fingers at Olney and told him, "And don't you try to put words in my mouth."

Olney never forgave me. Later Dwight Eisenhower was elected President, and he appointed Earl Warren chief justice. Warren's man Olney was named assistant United States attorney in San Francisco. Coincidentally, the Internal Revenue agents came to visit me. I had nothing to hide, and I showed them everything. They spent months and months searching for something to nail me with. Finally they found it.

The way I figure it, that little finger-pointing at Olney cost me a million dollars in lawyers' fees, fines, and tax settlements. It also cost me twenty-six months at McNeil Island Federal Penitentiary in Washington State. But you know something? I had fun there, too. I also raised some hell. I didn't care whether I got out of that place or stayed. I called it the Isle of Dreams.

CHAPTER 3

A Smattering of Information about My Early Life, as Much as I Can Remember; Also, My Introduction to Politics

YOU CAN UNCOVER ALL KINDS OF OPINIONS ABOUT ARTHUR H. Samish. You take the late Senator Estes Kefauver. I had some nice chats with him and his Crime Commission when they came to California in 1951. The senator from Tennessee said about me: "He is a combination of Falstaff, Little Boy Blue and Machiavelli, crossed with an eel."

That fine writer for the *San Francisco Chronicle,* Stanton Delaplane, once wrote that I was a sort of Sidney Greenstreet character.

I've been described in all kinds of ways. A fellow named Elmer Ritter Rusco wrote 523 pages about me for his Ph.D. dissertation at the University of California at Berkeley. He called it *Machine Politics, California Model: Arthur H. Samish and the Alcoholic Beverage Industry*. Imagine writing all that about Artie Samish!

Despite all the words that have been written and said about me, the real story has never been told. Until now. So now I'll begin, and I'll start at the beginning.

I was born on August 9, 1897, in the Boyle Heights section

of East Los Angeles. My mother had been born in Los Angeles. My father was a china decorator and a native of Austria. How he managed to come to the United States and to Los Angeles, I have no idea. I never learned much about him. I remember him only as a tall, good-looking man.

When I was three or four years old, my parents moved to San Francisco. It was some time later that my father disappeared. He just walked out one day and never came back. That's why I don't know much about him.

So there was my mother, left with a small son to support. She was a fine, gentle woman who devoted her life to me. Is it any wonder that I revere her memory? She is my religion, and to this day I feel that she has never left me. When I started in business, I adopted the name of Arthur H. Samish. Many people wondered what the middle initial stood for. I took it from my mother's name, Henrietta.

My mother and my grandmother and I were living in a house on Eddy Street between Polk and Van Ness when the big earthquake struck on April 18, 1906. It was something terrible. I can remember the Mechanics' Pavilion burning down, and I still can recall how the old City Hall was knocked down in an attempt to stop the fire. We lived in the last block to burn in the face of the fire, and, like a quarter million other people, we were without a home.

The only place we could find to stay was out in the Richmond district at Sixth and Clement. There was a relief station on the corner where we lived, and I would load food onto my coaster and carry it around to the neighbors. That was the only food they could get.

We settled on Clement Street for a while, and I did what I could to help out. Every Sunday morning I arose at three and rode the streetcar all the way down to the Ferry Building. I had an apple box with some wheels on it, and I pushed it the few blocks to the Examiner Building, where I picked up the Sunday papers. Then I rode the streetcar back out to Clement

Street and sold the *Examiner.* On a good Sunday I could earn a couple of bucks.

Our next home was at Fillmore and A Street, where we stayed a few years. Then we lived at Divisadero and Post, then on Hayes Street near Fillmore. I was in and out of grammar schools all over town. Mostly out. I was a hell raiser even then—I liked playing handball and having fun instead of studying. As a result, my grades were pretty poor, and I was always in trouble with the teachers.

Mostly, I was looking for excitement, and schoolwork wasn't very exciting. I can remember the thrill I felt when I saw Jack Johnson, the heavyweight boxing champion of the world. He was training in San Francisco for his fight with Al Kaufman in 1909, and every afternoon he drove past the Fremont Grammar School in his fancy automobile. He stopped and talked with us kids, and all of us marveled at his dude clothes and his flashing jewelry. Jack Johnson made quite an impression on young Art Samish.

My mother was running a boardinghouse, and that barely kept us going. Besides selling newspapers, I ran errands after school for the Riverdale Creamery and worked at other odd jobs. But that wasn't enough; I had to contribute more to the support of our small family. So I quit school in the seventh grade and never went back. I don't think my teachers shed any tears.

Later in my career, I found myself dealing most of the time with men who had university educations and law degrees. Not only dealing with them, but trying to keep two steps ahead of them. Me, Art Samish, who never finished the seventh grade. Do I regret not getting more education? Hell, no. I learned fast out in the world of business and politics. I taught myself to type, and I became pretty good at figures. Damn good, in fact. No, I have no regrets. I managed to outsmart a lot of guys who spent half their lives in school.

After I left school, I delivered milk for the creamery,

clerked in a grocery store, ran errands, did anything to help support my mother. My first real opportunity in the world of business came when I was hired as office boy in the fine law firm of Page, McCutcheon, Knight and Olney in 1913. Do you recognize the name Olney? Yes, that was the father of the Warren Olney III who helped prosecute me into the Isle of Dreams. Curious, isn't it, that the man who helped give me my start would have a son who wanted to ruin me?

I was pleased to be even a small part of the firm of Page, McCutcheon, Knight and Olney. They had a big office in the Merchants Exchange Building, and all of the lawyers were fine, upstanding men. I kept my eyes and ears open, trying to learn lessons so I could be as successful as they were. One of my best lessons came from a partner named H. L. Atkinson. I had been offered a job in another office but I turned it down, partly because I wanted to stay with Page, McCutcheon, Knight and Olney but also because I was expected to work from seven thirty in the morning until six at night. Mr. Atkinson wrote me a letter which I have kept all these years. He told me:

> . . . You must not shy at good jobs like that because they look hard—it is a confession of weakness unworthy of a strong, capable man. Say to yourself, "I can do anything that anyone else can do," and then do whatever comes to your hand, and do it a little better than the average. Think over it, study over it, and put your best effort into it, all the time.
>
> And don't let a little thing like long hours stop you. Everybody that gets anywhere has to work long hours. I am myself working longer hours than that, by choice. After working nine hours a day here, I study three more hours at night, and all day Sunday, only allowing myself two hours off on Saturday afternoon, and one Sunday a month. The really hard work is to get the job, and that is already done.

You must remember, Arthur, that there is any quantity of incompetent men, and only a few competent ones, comparatively speaking. The incompetent ones are looking for the soft snaps; lazy men; men afraid of an honest day's work.

Don't get into that class; those are the boys who never get anywhere. The boy who gets there is the boy who is not afraid, who tackles the hardest-looking jobs, and conquers them, and makes them easy to him. Then he is in the position to show the other fellow how to do it—to boss the job.

This period of hard work is only a stage of your existence, a part of your education. Go to it cheerfully. Be glad that it is hard, because it is only by the hard things that we develop.

If your mother is not very well, don't bother her about getting your breakfast. Get your own breakfast. I have done it for years—so do fully nine-tenths of the married men I know. You may want to get married some day; get used to it.

Now Arthur, you are a strong, capable kid; but your strength and ability are of no use to you unless you use them. And the more you use them, the more they develop. And don't think that it is all grind while you are developing; there are compensations along the way. You have felt the pleasure of doing things for people you like. There is a greater pleasure in doing things for the sake of the things themselves, a joy over a good job well done that can only be felt by the man who has done it.

Go get it, kid, and good luck to you.

You can imagine the impression that letter made on a sixteen-year-old boy who was just getting his feet wet in business. I was more than ever determined to succeed, and I was willing to work as hard as was necessary to do so.

But of course it wasn't all work and no play in the life of young Art Samish. I had discovered I liked girls and was gratified to learn that they liked me. I cut a pretty dashing figure, if I do say so myself. I was pushing up to six feet two, and I had a strong, athletic build. And I loved to dance.

San Francisco had a lot of social clubs during those times, and I joined one called the Kotycks Club. It had its own clubhouse—I remember helping to install the wood inlay that spelled out Kotycks on the dance floor. Every weekend the club held dances, and I had a marvelous time waltzing and foxtrotting around the floor with the girls in their starched linen dresses. I also enjoyed meeting other young San Francisco men.

One of the club members I became acquainted with was Edward F. Bryant, tax collector of the City and County of San Francisco. He was a fun-loving fellow, and he and I would collect the dimes and buy beer for the Sunday night dances.

"Where are you working now?" he asked me one night.

"I'm at Fireman's Fund Insurance, working for Charley Page," I told him.

"Why don't you come and work for me in the collector's office?" he said.

I accepted his offer, and it was another important step in my career: my introduction to politics.

I loved it from the start. I enjoyed hanging around the politicians' offices and listening to them try to outfox each other. I had two great teachers in those days: Eddie Bryant, the tax collector, and Tom Finn, who was sheriff. Between the two of them, they ran San Francisco politics. Every man who wanted to run for elective office had to clear through them. And they were fair men, Eddie and Tom. Everything was aboveboard and honest. Of course, politics is politics, and always has been; certainly there were favors passed out for those who were loyal. But it was all perfectly within the law.

I felt at home in this new world I had entered. I believed that if I applied the lessons that Mr. Atkinson had told me, my hard work and earnest effort would bring me success in the business of politics.

In later years, I never forgot that advice. And I never forgot my own humble beginnings. One night in Los Angeles, after I had achieved affluence and success, I felt the urge to return to the house where I was born. I drove over to Boyle Heights and after much searching, I found the right address on Michigan Avenue.

It was a modest little bungalow, timeworn but reflecting the care and pride of its occupants. I went to the door and was greeted by a broad-faced Mexican man. At first he was suspicious. But when I told him I only wanted to see the house where I was born, he allowed me to enter. He had a wife and an assortment of kids and they stared at me as I gazed at their neat little home. My heart swelled with memories.

"Thank you very much, my good man," I said as I left. "By the way, who owns the house now?" He told me, and the following day I arranged to pay his next six months' rent.

CHAPTER 4

The Losing Battle against Prohibition; Then, My Early Acquaintance with Sacramento and the Other Important Woman of My Life

MY TENURE WITH THE TAX COLLECTOR'S OFFICE OF SAN FRANCISCO lasted three years, and they were equivalent to a graduate course in political science at any topflight university. Ed Bryant remained a close personal friend, and I was afforded an intimate view of how the politics of a city government operated.

Then it was discovered that I was under age; not being a qualified voter, I was ineligible for employment in the tax collector's office. Bryant's deputy, Maurice L. Rapheld, took me to the office of Harry Rooney, who was the head of the Knights of the Royal Arch, an association of the important retail liquor sellers of San Francisco. The organization was extremely political in nature, since the leading saloon owners and liquor retailers of the city were closely allied with politics. I indicated my eagerness to join the Knights of the Royal Arch, and I was appointed secretary-treasurer.

I served during the war and afterward, when the move toward prohibition of alcoholic beverages was sweeping through the land. Naturally, the Knights of the Royal Arch aimed to do everything they could to combat the banning of liquor, and one of the members, Harry Keeler, was placed in charge of the California Wet Federation, which was formed to combat the Prohibition forces. When Keeler died, I was selected financial manager of the California Wet Federation, a position that provided excellent training for my future endeavors.

My chore was to direct men in soliciting funds from liquor dealers to fight Prohibition. That was a tremendous education. I was able to see large money going in and large money going out. We collected a barrel of money. But alas, the campaign was a failure. With a large percentage of the younger male population away in the war, the wave of sentiment for banning liquor prevailed, and the nation went dry.

The next move was to Sacramento, a most significant event in my young life.

I went to Sacramento with Maurice Rapheld, a good friend who was chief deputy tax collector and had a lot of connections in the state capital. He introduced me to Alexander McCabe, private secretary to Governor Hiram Johnson.

I loved that man McCabe. I love him to this day. To me, Alexander McCabe was the most accomplished and the most successful political expert in the history of California. He handled all of Hiram Johnson's campaigns for governor and later for senator, and he helped Johnson push through the most constructive, humane legislation enacted on our books.

Alexander McCabe took me under his wing and gave me an education in state politics. I couldn't have asked for a better teacher. One of my biggest thrills was observing at close hand the fight between the administration and the big business interests over the King Tax Bill. This was a proposal to increase the tax rate for major enterprises in the state, and naturally the companies were dead set against it. They used all the power they could muster to defeat the bill. But Alexander McCabe also exercised his political genius, and he was able to muster enough votes for passage.

Through McCabe and Martin Madsen, another secretary of Hiram Johnson, I got a job in the Division of Motor Vehicles at Eighth and K streets. I was living at Mrs. Vandegrift's boardinghouse on L Street, where the food was good and the price was favorable. The price had to be favorable, because I was earning $65 a month, and sending half of it home to my mother in San Francisco.

But I still managed to have enough left over, together with some savings, to squire the girls around town. Sacramento was an enjoyable place to live in those years. It was still a pretty small town, and it still had some of the informal charm of the gold rush days. There were dances and picnics and fairs to take pretty girls to, and I did. Oh, I was a pip! I could sweet-talk the girls and glide over the dance floor like Vernon Castle.

One girl in particular caught my fancy. She was a lovely young lady named Merced Sullivan, and her father was Dan Sullivan, the state printer and three-time president of the California State Federation of Labor. She was also working in the Motor Vehicle Department, and I took her out dancing and to the ice cream parlor afterward. Being a Sullivan, she had a fiery temper. One time after I had gone out with a couple of other girls, she came running across the park and hit me over the head with her purse. Bing, bing, bing! Just like that. I thought it was funny, but she didn't. I didn't see her for a while after that.

I worked hard in the Motor Vehicle Department and became a fast operator on the adding machine. It was an interesting department to be in, since this was the beginning of automobile registration in the state.

Another interesting aspect of the department concerned gold. Many of the big companies still used gold coin for payments, and they sent their applications for vehicle licenses in envelopes that were heavy with gold. These were placed in a tin basket with three sections, and the gold coins managed to accumulate in these baskets. And disappear. The gag we used to tell around the department was that the janitor's job was worth $500 to $1,000 a night.

I didn't know anything about money in those days, so I didn't know what was going on. I did notice that two department employees used to play and lose large amounts of gold coins at the cigar counters that featured the "26" game. Finally, Charles Keane, the auditor of the State Board of Control, tried to make an audit. There was so much money missing and so little chance of finding it that he simply threw up his hands in despair. So they just changed the system and started anew.

After a few months in Sacramento, I had been able to observe the political scene, and the area that interested me most was the legislature. That's where the laws were made and that's where the real power was wielded. So naturally I aimed in that direction.

I was fortunate to acquire a job as page in the assembly. I ran errands and did favors for the assemblymen, and they recognized that I was an ambitious young man eager to please. Next I was appointed assistant history clerk at five dollars a day, and then history clerk at seven dollars a day. That meant I was filing the goings-on for future history, and although I enjoyed observing the day-to-day happenings, I was eager to be more concerned with what was being done.

That opportunity came January 21, 1921, when I was appointed engrossing and enrolling clerk for the entire legislature.

That was quite a responsible position for a twenty-three-year-old fellow. Extremely responsible. The engrossing and enrolling clerk saw to it that legislation went through the proper procedures until it became law. The clerk corrected the bill after its second reading and before its final passage. If the bill was altered by the senate and sent back to the assembly, the clerk had to check every detail—spelling, punctuation, intent, etc. After passage by both houses, the clerk sent the bill to the printers, after which it was delivered to the governor for signing or veto. If it was vetoed, then the bill returned to the legislature for sustaining or overriding. When the bill was finally passed into law, the clerk delivered it to the secretary of state for filing and future reference in the archives.

I soon realized how important the engrossing and enrolling clerk could be. He had full control of any piece of legislation from its inception until it was delivered to the governor's office.

A friendly engrossing and enrolling clerk could be very useful to the governor. The clerk could help stall legislation until the last days of the session; then the governor had thirty days to sign or veto. His veto would be much more effective after the legislators had gone home.

So again I was earning valuable experience for my future career, not only with the legislature, but with the governor's office as well.

I hustled all over the capitol, getting acquainted with everyone. One of the young fellows I met was a young lawyer from Oakland named Earl Warren. He used to sit behind a desk as clerk of the assembly judiciary committee. He was an affable fellow with a pleasant smile, but nobody paid much attention to him.

After working as engrossing and enrolling clerk, I was appointed by the governor's office to the Division of Markets. This was a very important department that had been established to encourage the organization of cooperatives. Since California was primarily an agricultural state, it was important for the growers to achieve a fair price for their crops. Too much gouging by the commission men was going on.

I worked as a deputy and then I was appointed chief deputy of the fish exchange in the Division of Markets. I directed a staff of inspectors who checked on prices and made sure that the public was not being overcharged for fish by the merchants. The prices on everything from sardines to sharks were regulated. During this time I became acquainted with some of the wonderful Italian-Americans who had become fishermen in this country; many of them became my lifelong friends. I was easy on those boys. If they came up a bit short on halibut or salmon, I wouldn't make any trouble for them. They appreciated my consideration, and our friendship proved mutually valuable in years to come.

Now I was ready to begin my life's work. While other fellows made their way through high school and the university, I earned my training in a different school. I had matriculated in the academy of practical politics. The training period was over.

At the same time, I chose my partner for life. I used my powers of persuasion to convince Merced Sullivan that I wasn't such a bad guy after all. We were married in Sacramento on August 11, 1921, and some of her friends predicted a marriage to that wild young man, Art Samish, couldn't possibly last.

Somehow it lasted. In 1971, Merced and I mark fifty years together. She deserves all the credit. When you consider the shenanigans I have been involved in over a half-century, you realize what a wonderful woman she is.

CHAPTER 5

Professor Samish Delivers a Lecture in California Political History, Then Describes His Start as a Lobbyist

CALIFORNIA IS DIFFERENT FROM THE OTHER STATES OF OUR REpublic. It has always been different, right from its Gold Rush start. Being different is something that we Californians are proud of, but it confounds and confuses and frustrates out-of-staters. As long as I can remember, Easterners have considered California an outlandish place filled with daffy people. They still think that way, even though California now has the most population and hence the most power of any state in the nation.

The trouble with those Easterners is they don't know California the way I do. California politics may seem nutty to them, but there are reasons for everything that goes on. To understand the reasons, you need a knowledge of the state's political history, and that's what I aim to give you right now.

Don't worry—this won't hurt.

Being a vigorous, pioneer state that wasn't stuck with tradition, California started out to be progressive. As early as 1866 we had the first primary election law in the country, so that candidates could be nominated by the people rather than by conventions of politicians. In 1868 there was a state law providing an eight-hour day for public works contracts, and many other employers observed that standard.

But all of the progressive hopes of the state's founders were destroyed because of the railroad.

During the last third of the nineteenth century, big business was corrupting public life all over the country, but nowhere was that corruption so widespread as in California. The state was big and undeveloped, and the farmers and businessmen relied heavily on transportation. The Southern Pacific squeezed them dry.

For forty years, the Southern Pacific held California in its fat hand. The railroad grabbed land, charged high freight rates, controlled business, bought judges and owned the legislature. The man who became famous as wielder of the Southern Pacific's power was William F. Herrin. He was a smart lawyer who was head of the railroad's legal and political department from 1893 to 1910. He could make the legislature sit up, bark, or roll over and play dead. Mostly he worked through the Republican Party, but he didn't play favorites—he'd buy a Democrat as well. Sometimes in a campaign both the Republican and the Democrat would be Southern Pacific candidates.

Old Bill Herrin found his match in Hiram Johnson.

There was a great man, that Hiram Johnson. The greatest we've ever had in California politics. When he became governor in 1910, he took on that Southern Pacific crowd and licked them. During his administration, California enacted some of the most progressive and humanitarian statutes in the history of this land.

Look at some of the things that Hiram Johnson was able to push through: the referendum, which allowed the voters to veto acts of the legislature; the initiative, by which the people could initiate laws and constitutional amendments; the recall, with which voters could fire public officials, including judges; regulation of public utilities; railroad regulation; workmen's compensation; wage and hours laws for women and children; woman's suffrage; nonpartisan election of city and county officials.

Hiram Johnson also put through in 1913 the cross-filing system by which a candidate could run for office on the ticket of both parties. This was to have a profound effect on California politics.

Cross-filing weakened the power of the political parties in California. What happened then? I'll let Carey McWilliams tell you: "With party discipline at a minimum, a vacuum had been created at Sacramento which had to be filled; if neither the governor nor the political party chieftains could boss the legislature, someone had to undertake this function and that someone was Artie Samish. . . ."

How did I get started on the road to such a position?

My first lobbying job came to me quite by accident in 1922. It might have been 1923—somewhere around in that time. In my wanderings around the capitol I had become acquainted with Jesse H. Steinhart, a very able and qualified attorney from San Francisco. For some years he had represented the S&H green trading stamps and the United Cigar Stores, which had their own trading coupons.

Steinhart's opponent was Frank Connolly, the lobbyist for the independent grocers of California. The independents didn't like the competition from the chain stores which gave their customers trading stamps with each purchase, and Connolly tried to get a law passed at each session of the legislature to ban trading stamps from California. Each session he was able to get the law passed, but Steinhart was able to get the governor to veto it.

I guess Steinhart had become rich enough that he didn't want to go on working for S&H and United Cigar. He seemed to think that I was an energetic and ambitious young man, and one day he asked me if I'd like to take over as lobbyist for the trading stamps.

"Sure—what the hell!" I replied. I was game to try anything.

I was just a green kid, but I leaped right in and started to learn the business. I had already gotten to know the legislators in my jobs as page, assistant history clerk, history clerk, and engrossing and enrolling clerk. But now I was in a new capacity. Now I represented the coupon industry, and I needed to protect my clients. I had to know how the legislators stood on the trading-stamp issue. So I began talking to them. I had a little Studebaker then, and I drove it all over the state to see assemblymen and senators. I also called on the chain stores and trading-stamp people, the ones who were paying my salary. I convinced them to provide funds to help the campaigns of those legislators who were favorable to their cause.

That was to be the pattern for my future career as a lobbyist. First, organize the interest group and convince the members to contribute funds for their own interests. Then, spend the money wisely to elect those who would be friendly to those interests.

The system worked with my first clients. Never again did the legislature pass a bill against the coupon industry. Poor old Frank Connolly—I gave him and his independent grocers fits. There wasn't anything they could do to stop the trading stamps after I took over.

My achievement stirred up a lot of interest in this young fellow, Art Samish. A lot of people—important people—started coming to me for help and advice. I'd give it to them. But I was still learning, myself. I kept my eyes and my ears open at all times. I wanted to find out everything there was to know about the lobbying business.

CHAPTER 6

In Which I Discuss What It's Like to Be a Lobbyist and How I Made My First Million-dollar Deal

WHAT IS LOBBYING?

I looked the word up in my *Encyclopaedia Britannica,* and here's what it says:

"In the broadest sense lobbying is the attempt of individuals and groups to influence public policy while avoiding direct political responsibility. . . . A free society by definition is one in which all comers are free to voice their divergent opinions and to petition their rulers for a redress of grievances. These basic constitutional rights make lobbying both certain and, in its most desirable forms, highly visible and useful in democratic societies."

The article goes on, but that gives you the general idea. Lobbying has been going on for a long time, according to the *Encyclopaedia,* since it can be said that Moses "lobbied" the tyrant Pharaoh. So you see—my profession goes all the way back to Moses.

Certainly lobbying has been active in California since the earliest days. When the first legislature met in San Jose, away back in 1849, they called it "The Legislature of a Thousand Drinks." It seems that the candidates for offices in the new state government set up bars in an attempt to win favor with the legislators. One of the lobbyists was a state senator named Thomas Jefferson Green, who was trying to get himself elected general of the state militia.

At the end of each session, Green hollered, "A thousand drinks for everyone!" He kept it up until his fellow senators finally elected him general.

Green's technique might have worked in 1849, but it sure as hell wouldn't have succeeded in my day. Lobbying was a great deal more subtle. You couldn't expect to buy a vote with a drink or a steak dinner, although I paid for plenty of drinks and steak dinners. But that was just being friendly, that's all.

To me, lobbying was not just a lot of backslapping and gladhanding. It was a business. I made sure it was fun, too, but primarily it was a business.

Some people didn't think lobbying was legitimate. Every few years they'd come sniffing around, expecting to find some hanky-panky. They never found any with me. I knew what the law said about criminal lobbying; it's right there in the state constitution: "Any person who seeks to influence the vote of a member of the Legislature by bribery, promise of reward, intimidation, or any other dishonest means, shall be guilty of lobbying, which is hereby declared a felony."

Bribery? Promise of reward? Intimidation?

That was for amateurs. It certainly wasn't for Art Samish. My method of delivering votes was the soul of simplicity. It was merely this:

Select and Elect.

That was all. I simply selected those men I thought would be friendly to my clients' interests. Then I saw to it that those men got elected to the legislature.

Select and Elect.

In that way I made certain that the bills I wanted for my

clients won a friendly reception in the legislature. Sometimes an assemblyman or a senator might have disappointed me. Maybe he voted the wrong way on a bill I wanted. Too bad for him. I did my best to see that he didn't return to the legislature after the next election. And most times I was successful in that endeavor.

Select and Elect.

I didn't care whether a man was a Republican or a Democrat or a Prohibitionist. I didn't care whether he voted against free love or for the boll weevil. All I cared about was how he voted on legislation affecting my clients.

That was my job. I was being paid—and as the years went by, being paid a vast amount of money—to protect the interests of my clients. And I did so to the best of my ability. Judging from the results, that ability was more than adequate.

I wasn't alone in trying to influence legislation, not by any means. Sacramento was jammed with lobbyists for every legislative session. In 1949 the *San Francisco Chronicle* reported there were 364 registered lobbyists—and probably as many more who weren't registered. Being registered merely meant that you could appear before committees.

So in 1949 there were perhaps six hundred or seven hundred lobbyists in Sacramento, all trying to sway the votes of forty senators and eighty assemblymen. When you realize that each of those lawmakers was being paid one hundred dollars a month, you can understand why some of them might be swayed.

Naturally the legislators couldn't live on twelve hundred dollars a year. All had other sources of income, and they pursued their regular professions most of the time; by law, the legislature met only every two years (in time, special sessions made the period of service much longer than the writers of the state constitution intended).

Some of the legislators augmented their income by outright bribes from some of my lobbying colleagues, and occasionally they got caught at it. That was stupid, both on the part of the legislators and the lobbyists. There were other, strictly legal ways of adding to the income of the lawmakers and simultaneously making them friendly to your own organization.

Supposing the senator or assemblyman was a lawyer, as many of them were. Well, then you could see that the worthy barrister was hired on a retainer or received important cases on behalf of your clients. Or if Mr. Legislator engaged in the insurance business, you could assure him of some lucrative policies provided by your clients. It was all very simple.

Such practices were not uncommon with many of the lobbyists. Sacramento was swarming with lobbyists for every industry—oil, movies, gas, electricity, fishing, railroads, liquor, billboards, and so on. There were also lobbyists for every conceivable interest group—veterans, teachers, doctors, dentists, osteopaths, dog lovers, nudists. You can see why lobbyists were called the third house of the legislature.

In my early years in the third house, I was learning fast. My first really big break came in 1924, when Harry Regan and W. H. Pearson came to visit me. They were the owners of the Peninsula Rapid Transit Company, which operated bus service between San Francisco and San Jose.

"Art, the railroads are giving us all kinds of trouble," Harry said to me. "Do you think you can help us?"

"Well, I'd sure be willing to try," I told them.

I made a study of what their problems were. Mainly, they were getting clobbered by the Southern Pacific, which didn't like the buses competing for passenger travel. The S.P. had been pretty well discredited in Sacramento, but it was still strong in the little towns and cities where the railroad went through. These communities were convinced to place taxes on the bus lines. So a line like the Peninsula Rapid Transit might be paying taxes in Burlingame, San Mateo, Belmont, San Carlos, Redwood City, Palo Alto, and every other damn town it went through. That was a mess.

One little bus line couldn't fight the railroads. But if all the bus lines got together, they could take on the S.P. and beat it.

I started talking to other bus-line owners—O. R. Fuller, who had a fleet of white buses in his Motor Transit Company of Southern California; Tom and Howard Morgan, who ran a bunch of stretched-out Pierce Arrows out of San Francisco; Buck Travis, who owned a line from Fresno to San Francisco. And a bunch of others. I convinced them of the wisdom of my plan, and they selected Arthur H. Samish as secretary-manager of the Motor Carriers Association.

After the appointment, Dr. Samish began diagnosing the patient's problem. The bus lines had to get out from under the tax squeeze of the local communities. I was able to convince the legislature to pass into law Section 50¼ of the Public Utility Act. That made all bus operations in the state full-fledged public utilities and placed them under the full and complete jurisdiction of the Railroad Commission (later called the Public Utilities Commission).

My next move was to place an initiative proposal on the ballot to give the bus and truck industry—I was now representing the truckers, too—the right to pay 4 per cent tax in lieu of any and all other taxes. We had a fight with that one.

I tried to educate the voting public on the need for standard taxation for buses, pointing out that 1,700 small communities had no other public transportation besides buses. But the railroads wanted to crush the competition of the bus lines, and they campaigned against the initiative with propaganda and advertising. The measure was defeated by 70,000 votes.

Next time it was different.

I was going to beat the railroads at their own game. I convinced the bus owners to put up enough money for a first-class campaign. I hired a well-known cartoonist named Johnny Argens to draw a picture of a big, fat, ugly pig. Then I splashed that picture on billboards throughout the state with the slogan:

DRIVE THE HOG FROM THE ROAD!
VOTE YES ON PROPOSITION NUMBER 2

I also had millions of handbills printed with the same picture and message. During the last weeks of the campaign they were placed in automobiles in every city and town. You'll note that I always spelled out "Number"; I never used "No." 2 because the voter might get confused and think he should vote "No."

The campaign worked. Boy, did it work! Nobody likes a roadhog, and the voters flocked to the polls and passed the constitutional amendment by 700,000! This was an amendment which I had managed to get through the legislature; it taxed bus lines at the rate of 4¼ per cent and trucks at 5 per cent in lieu of any and all other taxes. Not only that. The measure also provided free license plates for the buses and trucks.

All because the voters thought they were voting against roadhogs. That had nothing to do with it. Now what son of a gun but Art Samish could have thought of something like that?

The Motor Carriers Association was naturally pleased with the results, and I was happy to remain as secretary-manager for thirty years. Not only did my association with the bus industry provide a handsome fee over those years; it also enabled me to pull off a deal that made me financially independent.

Toward the end of the 1920s, I could see a trend toward amalgamation of the bus lines into one giant firm, Greyhound. Many of the owners I had been dealing with in the Motor Carriers Association began selling their interests to Greyhound for huge amounts of money.

I said to myself, "Why don't you buy one of those lines and cash in on the bonanza?" It was a hell of an idea, but I had no money to put it over.

One day in 1929 I was sitting in my office in the Flood Building in San Francisco. I figured I'd better do something soon or Greyhound would buy up all the bus lines. So I sent one of my assistants down to get an option to buy the Pacific Auto Stages from Floyd W. Hatchett for $275,000. That took a lot of nerve, because I didn't have $275,000.

But I had this idea. Pacific Auto Stages was a going concern with a fleet of buses that ran between San Francisco, Palo Alto, and San Jose, and I figured Greyhound would need it. I went first to Herbert Fleishhacker at the Anglo Bank.

Herbert was a good friend of mine. Whenever I went into his office I threw a twenty-dollar bill on his desk, and he'd bring out a set of gold dice that he had and we'd shoot for it. After we rolled for the twenty, I told him my idea about buying Pacific Auto Stages.

"Sounds good, Art," he said. "Go outside and get the money."

That scared me off. I don't know why, but I figured to myself, This Herb Fleishhacker is pretty damn smart. Too smart for me, maybe. If he gives in so easy, I'd better watch out.

I said I'd let him know, and I went to see Art Smith, who was head of Yellow Cab Company.

"I got this deal going, Art," I told him, "and I need help. If you'll help me put the deal through and help me manage the bus line, I'll cut you in on it."

Sure, kid, I'll go along with you," Art said. Why shouldn't he? He had nothing to lose.

Still I had no idea of how to swing the deal. Finally I decided, what the hell, I'll go see A.P.

I told you how A. P. Giannini and I used to meet on the street corner and talk for hours. I was just a kid, and he was a big man of finance, but he seemed to think I knew the political situation and he liked to talk to me. I went to see him and told him about my dream of buying the Pacific Auto Stages.

"I'll give you the money," he said.

I waited until the very last day of the option, and I made

a date to meet Hatchett on a street corner with my agent, Jack Goldberg. Right there on the street I handed over the money in $10,000 bills. Eleven of them—$110,000!

Here I was thirty-two years old and president of the Pacific Auto Stages. It was a dream come true.

I did things with that company. My competitors were my old pals, Regan and Pearson, who had brought me into the Motor Carriers Association. Their Peninsula Rapid Transit covered the same fifty-two miles of route, and we both had our own stations and ticket sellers.

I told Regan and Pearson, "For Christ's sake, let's fire some of the bastards and combine facilities. We can have one bus station instead of two and share the expense." They agreed, and we both cut costs. In addition, I owned the lease on the Fifth Street Terminal in San Francisco, and I collected 8 per cent on all tickets sold by the other bus lines.

Pretty soon I had run my profit from thirty-five cents a car mile to sixty-five cents a car mile. Then I was ready for my big move. I asked Regan and Pearson to give me an option for their Peninsula Rapid Transit Company, and I took the package to Tom Wilson at Pacific Greyhound. He bought the whole shebang for more than a million dollars.

I had held the bus line for only nine months, and I was able to clear $290,000 with no investment of my own. But I didn't take all the money. Art Smith of Yellow Cab Company had helped me set up the deal and had advised me on how to run the bus line; then he died on January 29, 1930. Poor Art had been hard hit in the Wall Street crash of 1929, and it didn't look as if his widow Rosabel would be left with anything. Even though I had no legal obligation to do so, I decided to share the profits with her.

Twenty years later, I received a letter from W. Lansing Rothschild, who became president of Yellow Cab in San Francisco after Art's death. Rothschild said what I did was "one of the most extraordinary instances of magnanimity, unselfishness, integrity of character, idealism and loyalty to friendship ever to come to my attention and which is rarely seen in these days. You credited half the gain, or $145,000, to the estate of Arthur O. Smith which otherwise would have been a very meagre estate for the benefit of his widow Rosabel.

"In my long business career I cannot recall a similar situation where an individual, purely through a sense of loyalty and under no obligation of any kind, did such a splendid, generous, unpretending and unsolicited act. What you did then can never be tied."

CHAPTER 7

Governors Who Have Known Me

MY EXPERIENCE WITH GOVERNORS OF THE GREAT STATE OF CALIFORNIA goes back to Hiram Johnson. I've known them all, right up to but not including this current one, the actor. What do I think of him? Not much. Look at all the things he's promised, and look at what he's done.

Hiram Johnson, as I've told you, was a great, great man. I wasn't a lobbyist in Sacramento when he was governor, but I knew him over the years and helped in his campaigns for the United States Senate. The first governor I worked with was William D. Stephens. He had been lieutenant governor, and he became governor when Johnson moved to the Senate in 1917.

When Stephens ran for governor in 1918, I supported him. Like so many elections in those cross-filing years, the real battle was in the primary. Stephens was running against another Republican, James Rolph, Jr., the mayor of San Francisco. Stephens won the Republican nomination, and Rolph won on the Democratic ticket. But under the cross-filing law, Rolph couldn't run unless he was nominated by his own party. So Stephens was unopposed in the final election.

Stephens's lieutenant governor was Dick Carnahan, who

gave us a little trouble. As president of the Senate, he had the power to appoint committees. He didn't take a liking to having some of us fellows making suggestions as to whom he should appoint. So we took the goddam thing away from him. We had the senate set up its own committee on rules, with the power to appoint committees. That showed Carnahan a thing or two. He was an able man, but he just got too smart for his own good.

I liked Bill Stephens, and when he ran for reelection in 1922, I was his campaign manager in Northern California. Unfortunately there was a conservative tide that year, and the Republican nomination went to Friend W. Richardson, who campaigned for economy. Richardson was elected, and he cut the budgets for all the state services, including the schools. He said, "The schools must be put on a business basis; they must not only teach but practice thrift." That sound familiar?

Richardson didn't bother me, and I didn't bother him. I knew he couldn't last.

In 1926, I put my support behind Clement C. Young for governor. C. C. Young had taught at the University of California and then became Speaker of the Assembly and lieutenant governor. He was a fine man, an able man. After he became governor, he *ran* the state. He didn't fool around with politics. If anybody wanted something political, he came to see Alexander McCabe or Art Samish. Once you had McCabe's or Samish's okay, that was all you needed.

When C. C. Young ran for reelection in 1930, I handled the San Francisco campaign. That was a tough fight, because Young was up against Jim Rolph in the primary. Rolph was a whoopee dresser, and he attracted a lot of attention with his cowboy boots and fancy duds. Rolph won in a very close election.

Jim Rolph was sore at me for opposing him, but he got over it. One of my good friends was Dan O'Brien, who had been Rolph's chief of police in San Francisco. You know his son, George O'Brien, the movie star.

It was through Dan O'Brien that Jim Rolph was convinced

that I wasn't such a bad fellow after all. Before long I was just as friendly with Rolph as I had been with C. C. Young. Dan O'Brien and I had a lot of fun together. Rolph appointed him head of the Motor Vehicle Department, and he had a bill for the department that he wanted to put through the legislature. Well, I put it through all right. But then I put it in my pocket and wouldn't give it to anyone. For several days I walked around with that bill in my pocket. That just drove Dan O'Brien nuts. Those were the days when I was drinking, and I did a lot of crazy things.

Jim Rolph died in his last year of office, and he was succeeded on June 7, 1934, by Lieutenant Governor Frank F. Merriam. Later that year he ran for governor against Upton Sinclair, the writer.

I had a lot to do with getting Merriam elected. He asked me to set up his headquarters, and I did. I also raised a lot of money for his campaign, something like $200,000. Of course it wasn't hard to raise money, because a lot of the wealthy Republicans were scared as hell of Sinclair. I didn't have anything against Sinclair; I didn't even know him. But Frank Merriam was my man.

That was a hell of a mistake. Frank Merriam was a real faker, the bald-headed son of a bitch. If I had known what I found out later, I could have handled him. I learned later that he had been run out of Iowa for a phony insurance scheme or some damn thing.

Merriam gave me nothing but trouble. You take that Gilmore Exploration Bill.

Some of the independent oil companies had been buying up property at Huntington Beach, one of the big oil fields in Southern California. They figured it would be a good idea to drill out in the ocean, but the trouble was that the state figured it owned the ocean three miles out. So Earl Gilmore, Tom Simmons, and some of the other oilmen came to me and asked if I could get a bill through the legislature giving them permission to drill in the tidelands. I said I'd think it over.

CHAPTER 8

Demonstrating Why They Called Art Samish the Guy Who Gets Things Done

I FIGURE THAT DURING THE 1920s I WAS LEARNING MY TRADE IN Sacramento. By the 1930s I was ready to swing into action. And I mean swing. I had my offices in San Francisco, with a big staff in the Kohl Building. I also had offices in the Biltmore Hotel in Los Angeles. And when the legislature was in session, I operated from my suite in the Capitol Hotel.

I never went to the capitol, the way the other lobbyists did. I didn't need to. I had my Gestapo working for me. I knew exactly what was going on at all times. A staff of men and girls attended all the legislative sessions, including the committee hearings, and they reported to me.

Nobody knew more about what was going on in the capitol than I did. Not even the newspapermen. In fact, they came to me for information. Say the *San Francisco Examiner* or the *Los Angeles Times* had one reporter to cover all of Sacramento. The poor guy couldn't be everywhere at once. So when it got to be deadline time and there was a committee hearing he couldn't cover, he'd call me. I gave him the straight dope. No charge. Those newspaper boys were my friends.

By midnight I had a full report of everything that had gone on during that day and evening. Then I could plan my strategy for the following day. I didn't like surprises. For that reason I saw to it that a rule was passed by the legislature declaring that no bill could be heard in either house without two weeks' notice. In that way I could be prepared for any legislation that affected my clients. I didn't want a bill popping up before I had a chance to decide whether it was good or bad for our interests.

During the 1930s, more and more organizations were coming to me with their particular legislative problems. Usually Dr. Samish could provide a cure.

One day a man from a San Francisco law firm came to me and said, "Art, we've got a problem."

"Well, you came to the right man," I said. "What seems to be the trouble?"

"Our client, the American Hawaiian Sugar Company has built a structure worth thirty to forty million dollars near the Carquinez Bridge. We checked the title to the property and we found out that American Hawaiian doesn't own it."

"That's quite some problem. Who does own the property?"

"The state of California."

"I see. And what do you want the doctor to do about it?"

"Anything you can. We need help."

They sure did. American Hawaiian had this big plant there in the tidelands of the San Francisco Bay, where all the big ships docked with the sugar. And they didn't own the property. They would have had one hell of a time moving the whole shebang.

I went back to Sacramento and I had a bill introduced in the legislature giving the director of finance power to enter into a lease with the American Hawaiian Sugar Company for the use of that tidelands property. When the bill got over to the assembly, I had the stipulation put in that the lease should be for sixty-nine years. I don't know how I arrived at that figure; it just seemed like a good number.

That bill went through the legislature without a ripple. Not a ripple. I can assure you that the American Hawaiian Sugar Company was mighty relieved to have it passed. They expressed their gratitude in the form of a very large check for Dr. Samish's services.

Two years later, just so everything would remain safe, I introduced into the legislature a validating measure. That protected the lease from any future problems.

Was the legislature aware that American Hawaiian had already built a huge plant on that property?

I never concerned myself with whether the legislature was or wasn't aware of certain matters. My only concern was to take care of my clients. And I did.

In 1935, a Hollywood agent named M. C. Levee came to the doctor with a problem. It seems that Assemblyman Thomas Maloney of San Francisco had introduced a bill to make it unlawful for any employment agency to charge more than 7 percent of the first month's salary for getting people jobs. All the agents in the movie business were up in arms because they thought the law would apply to them. If so, that would ruin them, because they charged actors and directors and other talent 10 percent of all earnings.

The agents couldn't pay very much for the doctor's fee—only $5,000. But I agreed to take on their case.

No problem. Assembly Bill No. 403 got through the assembly, but somehow it got stuck in the senate judiciary committee. There it died a natural death.

Two years later, Mr. Levee came to me again.

"What's the problem this time?" the doctor asked.

"It's this Assembly Bill No. 1226," said the agent. "This time it specifically mentions talent agents and limits us to charging the same commissions as employment agencies. If it goes through, all the agents in Hollywood will be ruined. Can you help us?"

"Certainly I can. But it will cost double what you paid the last time."

Assembly Bill No. 1226 had its funeral in the assembly judiciary committee. Death was quick and painless.

Over the years I performed a lot of services for people in Hollywood who were concerned about legislation. I came to know all the studio bosses—Louis B. Mayer, Harry Cohn, Jack Warner, and so on. My particular pal was Joseph Schenck. He was a wonderful man, a real sweetheart. He and I spent weeks together at his big house in Florida. Whatever Joe Schenck wanted, I got for him.

During the 1930s a lot of the other states were going for Daylight Saving Time. Joe Schenck and other movie bosses were against it, figuring that the extra hour of sunlight would keep people from going to the movies. I took care of it. All proposals to introduce Daylight Saving Time to California were defeated. The state didn't get it until World War II, when the extra daylight was important to save electric power.

Another of my clients was the National Orange Show in San Bernardino.

Now you might ask why an orange show would need the services of a lobbyist in Sacramento. Very simple. I managed to put through a measure which provided that 5 percent of the state's income from pari-mutuel betting at the racetracks would go to the National Orange Show. In the 1937–1938 fiscal year, that amounted to $111,000. With that kind of money you can buy a lot of oranges.

I felt good about that. I drank a lot of orange juice, especially after I quit boozing. It seemed right that the racetracks should contribute to the orange industry. Especially after all that I had contributed toward improving the racehorse breed. Some newspaper stories claimed that I bet a million dollars a year on the horses. That was an exaggeration. At least I think it was.

I may not always have been lucky at the track, but I made it pay off in another way: by selling my services as a lobbyist.

After horse racing became legal in California in 1933,

there was a lot of legislation which was important to the new racetracks. Dr. Charles Strub, the man who ran Santa Anita, realized this, and he hired the right man to look after his interests in Sacramento. I represented Hollywood Park, too.

For several years I made sure that Doc Strub's bonanza at Santa Anita wasn't tampered with. The state's pari-mutuel take remained at the same rate, and no new tracks were authorized. Santa Anita was assured of no serious competition.

It would have stayed that way except for Doc Strub's attitude. One day I was enjoying myself out at his race emporium in Arcadia when a messenger came to tell me, "Dr. Strub wants to see you."

I went all the way up to his cupola on top of the stadium, and Doc Strub started dictating to me what he wanted done.

When he was through, I stared at him for a moment. "You know, Charlie," I said, "I don't like you. That's going to cost you a hundred thousand dollars."

"What?" he said.

"That's right—a hundred thousand dollars. I quit."

I cost him a lot more than that. All of a sudden there was a different climate in Sacramento for racetracks, especially Santa Anita. The legislature started passing laws for a bigger take of the pari-mutuel betting. New racetracks were authorized, providing more competition for the established ones. And the state began clamping down on the outside investments of Santa Anita.

Doc Strub knew when he was licked. He whined, begged, pleaded for me to come back.

"Artie, I need you!" he said. "I may have to close the track if you don't help me!"

He sent his attorney to dicker with me. I told him I wanted a hundred thousand dollars, just like I told Doc in his cupola. We dickered and we dickered, and I let them off the hook for fifty thousand.

Suddenly the climate switched back in Sacramento. Once

again Santa Anita got the kind of legislation it wanted, and Doc Strub could pack away his millions without undue interference.

Another one of my clients during the 1930s was a big diesel company. This was at a time when diesel trucks were just being introduced on the California highways, and the oil companies were worried about the competition from a cheaper fuel. Somehow a bill was introduced by one of the legislators to tax diesel fuel at the same rate per gallon as gasoline. Naturally diesel people didn't like that. So some of them hired me to do something about it.

It was a tough assignment. Any time you're up against the oil companies, you've got a job on your hands. But, as I learned early in the game, there's more than one way to skin a cat.

The bill was introduced in the assembly, and I managed to keep it there until the closing days of the session. It passed unanimously and then moved over to the senate. Culbert Olson, the senator from Los Angeles and later governor, handled its progress.

On the last day of the session, the bill came up for the vote in the senate. Senator Olson proposed inclusion of an urgency clause, which would have made the law effective immediately upon signing by the governor instead of the usual ninety-one days.

The senate passed the bill, but now it had to be reprinted with the urgency clause and returned to the assembly for passage. With the clock ticking away the final hours of the session, the bill was sent off to the printer. Under the law, the legislative session ended at midnight.

A messenger was sent to pick up the bill and deliver it to the assembly. But as midnight approached, Governor Merriam was addressing the assembly with a farewell speech in his usual dreary style. As he droned on and on, my good friend Charlie Lyons, the floor leader, also opposed to the bill, kept telling him, "You're doing fine, Governor; keep it up."

The author of the bill kept calling, "Mr. Speaker! Mr.

Speaker!" But he couldn't gain recognition, and some of his more playful colleagues kept turning down his hearing aid.

The messenger with the bill entered the assembly at 11:50, and he was intercepted by my assistant, Frank (Porky) Flynn.

"Young man, you must observe protocol," said Frank. "You never interrupt the governor when he is speaking."

And so the bill remained in the messenger's hand until the clock marked midnight. The Speaker, Ted Craig, pounded the gavel and announced, "This assembly is now adjourned, *sine die.*"

That was the end of the diesel tax bill, at least for another two years. It was a case of The Law That Never Became a Law.

CHAPTER 9

The Making of a Legislator, 1934

DURING MY ADVENTURES IN THE LOBBYING TRADE, I MET EVERY kind of legislator—teetotalers and drunks, wise men and fools, churchmen and atheists, family men and lechers. Some of them were real characters.

You take old Senator William Kehoe.

Now there was a rare bird. He represented Inyo, Mono—the real cow counties. You could drive for fifty miles in his district and not see a single human being. Or even an animal. He even represented Death Valley, which gives you an idea of how desolate his area was.

Kehoe had his district sewed up, and he kept coming back to the senate term after term. And every time the legislature met, he introduced the same measure.

You see, Indians formed a large part of his constituency, and naturally he was for the Indians. He believed Indians should have the same rights as other American citizens, and that included the right to take a drink now and then. Federal law prohibited the sale of liquor to Indians on reservations, and the senator didn't think that was right.

So at every session of the legislature Senator Kehoe introduced a measure that would permit Indians to buy liquor. It didn't matter to him that the federal law would have precluded such a measure. He still went through the motions of introducing his law and trying to shepherd it through committee and onto the floor. He was dead serious about it, and he got sore as hell when he lost, as he inevitably did.

At one session his fellow senators sympathized with his crusade and he managed to get it passed through the upper house. Then it went to the assembly, where it had a hearing before the public morals committee.

There it suffered a quick death. One of the Public Morals Committee members was Eleanor Miller, who was from Pasadena and about as strong a Dry as you could find. She voted against everything that had to do with the sale of liquor. Naturally she led the fight against the law that would have allowed the Death Valley redskins to purchase firewater.

Senator Kehoe fussed and fumed about his defeat. He vowed he would have vengeance against his enemies.

The opportunity arose at the same session. Assemblywoman Miller introduced a pest-control measure that would benefit only the citizens of Pasadena. It was a minor measure, and her fellow members of the assembly quickly passed it out of respect for the assemblywoman from Pasadena.

Then her bill went to the senate. As was the custom, she appeared before the committee hearing to advocate the bill. She was an elocution teacher, and she made an eloquent presentation, explaining why the state should lend assistance to her bug-plagued constituents.

Senator Kehoe gave her the stony eye throughout her speech. When she had finished, he took the floor. He rolled his own cigarettes, and for a few moments he was silent as he sprinkled Bull Durham over the paper, the tobacco flying all over the committee table.

"Eleanor," he began, "you voted against my law that

would have permitted the braves in my district to buy booze—didn't you?"

"Yes, Senator, I did," she replied. "I am firmly opposed to the selling of hard liquor to Indians."

"Eleanor," he continued, "I don't give a damn if the piss-ants eat up everything in Pasadena. I move that this bill be tabled."

"Second the motion!" yelled two or three of his fellow senators, and Kehoe lighted up his cigarette with intense satisfaction as the Miller Bill went down to defeat.

Of all the legislators I knew during my years in Sacramento, none was more endearing than John Pelletier.

He's quite a story. Put it in a movie and you might have trouble convincing the customers that it wasn't some script-writer's fantasy. But it's true, by God.

The whole thing started early in 1934, when I got a phone call from my man in Los Angeles, Bill Jasper. He had been talking to one of our most important clients, a brewer we'll call Ernie.

"What's up, Bill?" I asked.

"Ernie's got this crazy idea," Jasper said. "He wants us to run somebody against Woolwine."

"That's a crazy idea, all right," I said. "What does he want to do that for?"

"He's mad at Woolwine for some damned thing. He wants to throw a scare in him, to teach him a lesson."

"Did you tell Ernie we couldn't put out any dough for such foolishness?"

"Sure. I told him that. He's willing to lay out the money. This is a private thing with him. What'll I do, Art?"

"What'll you do? Ernie's an important man with us, isn't he? We have to satisfy his whims. Get him a candidate."

"But where? How?"

"I don't give a damn where you find him. Just get him a candidate. We'll satisfy the son of a bitch."

The whole thing smacked of insanity. This Clair Woolwine was considered unbeatable. He was a member of one of the oldest and most distinguished families in Los Angeles—his brother had been district attorney. The voters knew Clair Woolwine as a classy guy, and he was about the most meticulous man I ever knew. He got shaved twice a day. When he was drunk, he even got himself manicured twice a day. His assembly district was the 44th, which comprised downtown Los Angeles. In early California, that was where the elite lived. But as the city grew, the elite moved to the outskirts, and the downtown became slums. During the Depression year of 1934, the 44th district had a high percentage of unemployed, winos, and just plain bums.

Where the hell was Bill Jasper going to find a candidate to run against Clair Woolwine? The guy had won both Republican and Democratic primaries in election after election, and his political opposition was nil. Woolwine was a Republican, but as far as the voters were concerned, he was nonpartisan.

Bill Jasper is a resourceful fellow. He went down to the Grand Avenue headquarters of Upton Sinclair, who was trying to get the Democratic nomination for governor. Jasper went inside the place, which was a dingy old store, and he found about forty campaign workers tying up bundles of E.P.I.C. (End Poverty in California) literature for mailing.

Campaign workers! Hell, they were bums. They had been rounded up at soup kitchens and flophouses to wrap bundles for fifty cents a day. They were ragged and unshaven and dirty.

"Any of you fellows from the forty-fourth district?" Jasper yelled.

One tattered old-timer raised his hand. "I am," he replied. He was skinny as a rail, and his bad teeth made his jaw upswept like a ski jump.

"What's your name?" Jasper asked.

"John Pelletier."

"Are you an American citizen?"

"Of course I'm an American citizen," the man answered indignantly.

"Well, you talk with an accent, so I just wondered," said Jasper.

"I grew up in French Canada. But I was born in this country."

"Okay," said Jasper. "How'd you like to run for the state legislature?"

Pelletier looked at Jasper as if he was nuts.

"I mean it," said Jasper. "Come with me."

Jasper bought him a meal, which Pelletier ate like a starving man. Jasper learned that he was a French Canadian who had been born in Maine and grew up in Montreal. He returned to Maine and graduated from Bates University. In spite of his education, Pelletier never could make a go of it. His French-Canadian accent seemed to hold him back, and he dropped lower and lower on the social scale.

When Jasper picked him up, Pelletier was living in one of those big old crumbling houses that used to be on top of Bunker Hill. He and ten other guys shared the joint at twenty dollars a month. They came and went, and there was always a mulligan stew on the stove to feed them when they were hungry. Pelletier lived on the twelve dollars a month he got for country relief and whatever odd jobs he could find. Like tying up bundles at the Sinclair headquarters at four bits a day.

After he fed Pelletier, Jasper took him to my headquarters in the Biltmore Hotel. The little French Canadian was still dazed at what was happening to him.

"First of all, we gotta clean you up," Jasper said. "We'll burn those goddam clothes and get you a new suit. Look there . . ."

Jasper pointed out the window at a sign on the other side of Pershing Square. It was a Foreman and Clark store that advertised a man's suit for twenty-five dollars.

"Twenty-five dollars!" Pelletier said. "That's too much. I

know a tailor shop at Third and Spring that I sometimes deliver handbills for. I could get two suits for twenty-five dollars over there."

"Okay, let's go."

Jasper took the little man to the tailor shop and bought him the suits, as well as shirts, socks, underwear and everything else he needed. Then Jasper delivered Pelletier to the Luxor Baths at Sixth and Spring.

"Here's ten bucks," Jasper told the attendant. "Clean him up."

When Jasper reported to me what he had done, I had to bust out laughing.

"You crazy son of a bitch, Jasper," I said.

"Shall I go ahead and run him, Art?" he asked.

"Hell, yes. The man wanted a candidate to scare Woolwine. Okay, we got him. Sure—go ahead. We can have a lot of laughs with this one."

When Jasper got Pelletier washed and shaved and dressed up in his new suit, the guy didn't look half bad. Not really good, either, but presentable enough. The first thing to do was to get him filed as a Democratic candidate in the 44th assembly district. Jasper asked him, "What do you do?"

"What do I do?" Pelletier said.

"Yeah," said Jasper. "You gotta list your occupation on the ballot under your name. So what do you do?"

"Well, you know those jobs I do sometimes."

"Yeah, but we can't list you as a handbill-passer. What else do you do?"

"Well, I stay at home and read a lot."

"Good. We'll list you as 'researcher.' "

Next we needed some advertising for our candidate. Jasper asked him for a photograph of himself. The only one he had was one taken twenty-five years before when he was in college.

"That'll do," said Jasper. He combined the youthful-looking photograph with a shot of the state capitol and had a hundred thousand cards printed. Pelletier spent his days handing out the cards all over the 44th district. Jasper gave him ten bucks a day for campaign expenses. Also to live on. We had taken him off the relief rolls when he filed for the assembly. It wouldn't have been good publicity to have it known that our candidate was on the dole.

Pelletier went to Jasper one day and said, "You know, I used to sweep out a sign shop over on Third Street. One of the fellows over there is a friend of mine, and he says he'll make me some posters if I supply the muslin and silk screen."

So Jasper bought five hundred yards of material and soon there were posters all over the district advertising "Vote for John Pelletier for Assembly."

I'll be goddammed if the son of a bitch didn't win the Democratic primary! By a thousand votes out of about nine thousand!

Jasper telephoned me in San Francisco to say that the brewer had called him to thank him for scaring Woolwine. "Now the fun's over and we gotta elect Clair," the brewer said. He sent his personal check for $2,000 to cover the campaign expenses.

"But I only spent eight hundred," Jasper told me. "That leaves me with twelve hundred left over."

"So what?" I said.

"Well, I kinda got interested in the little guy," Jasper said.

"And you'd like to lay that twelve hundred on his campaign?"

"Well—yes."

"Why not? It's no skin off my ass. Go ahead and have your fun."

Jasper had his fun, all right. John Pelletier was elected assemblyman from the 44th district!

"Jesus, we got a wild turkey on our hands!" Jasper told me. "What are we gonna do now?"

"We're gonna make him a legislator," I said.

First of all, we had to fix his jaw. I sent him to see my pal, Painless Parker, who did a first-class job of rebuilding the jaw. I had Jasper go out and buy Pelletier a soup-and-fish, which he would need for the inaugural ball. And, because he didn't have a dime, I gave him the train fare to Sacramento.

On the night of the ball, I was in my suite at the Hotel Senator when a call came from Pelletier. He was in his room at the Berry Hotel.

"I'm in trouble!" he said.

"What the hell's the matter?" I said, expecting the worst.

"This goddam suit I'm supposed to wear," he said. "It's got no belt loops. How the hell am I going to hold my pants up? And this shirt is the goddamnedest thing I ever saw. It's stiff as a board and it buttons up the back."

"Don't worry," I assured him. "I'll send Jasper over to help you." Jasper went out and bought him suspenders to keep the pants up and showed him how to fasten a boiled shirt.

We managed to get Pelletier together, and he was sworn in as assemblyman of the Great State of California. He served out his term and got reelected. And reelected. In fact, John Pelletier was elected five times from the 44th district.

He wasn't a bad legislator at all. He had a degree of intelligence and he voted according to his conscience. Always he was for the poor, the downtrodden—quite naturally, because he was one of them. And why shouldn't the poor have their own representative in the legislature? I thought it was a dandy idea.

Assemblyman Pelletier had only one failing: he hated lawyers. He'd listen for hours as the attorney members of the assembly argued back and forth on the fine points of the law. Then it got to be too much for him and he'd leap up, not waiting to be recognized by the Chair.

"Mr. Speaker," he shouted. "There are too goddamned

many lawyers in this assembly! I am going to introduce a constitutional amendment which will limit the number of lawyers who can serve in this body."

Pelletier's service in the assembly did not change his way of life. He still lived up on Bunker Hill, though now he had a room of his own instead of sharing a house and mulligan with his cohorts. He spent his days walking around his district to speak with his constituents, picking up a meal here, a cigar there. I'd venture a guess that he was the only legislator in the history of California who lived on his hundred-dollar-a-month salary. To John Pelletier, that was plenty.

One day in 1945, Bill Jasper called me with sad news: John Pelletier had died.

"God rest his soul," I said. "I guess we'll have to bury him. Well, let's bury him in style."

Many is the time that I picked up the tab for the funeral of a legislator or one of his relatives. This time I wanted to be sure that John Pelletier received the grade-A treatment.

I just guessed he was a Catholic because of his French-Canadian background. So I took over St. Vibiani's Cathedral on Second Street and I ordered the full choir, the high mass, the whole works. All the dignitaries of the state government appeared for the services. So did John's ragged old buddies from Bunker Hill.

It was one hell of a show. I just hope that John Pelletier was up there somewhere, looking down and enjoying it all.

CHAPTER 10

In Which I Tell How Weak Beer and a Strong Hand Helped the Beverage Industry to Higher Profits and Lower Taxes

IN SEPTEMBER OF 1935 I BEGAN WHAT WAS TO BE A LONG AND profitable association with the California State Brewers Association. Profitable to the brewers. Profitable to Art Samish.

I really did a job for those boys. This will prove to you the kind of a job I did: as long as Art Samish represented the brewing industry, the tax on beer never increased. For twenty years it remained sixty-two cents a barrel—and there are thirty-one gallons to the barrel.

Taxes on everything else went up during those twenty years. Not on beer. Every time a proposal came up in the legislature to increase the beer tax, it somehow never got out of committee.

While I was in charge of the brewers' relations with the legislature, the tax on beer was the lowest in the United States.

I was able to perform other services for the brewers, too. For instance, I saw to it that the alcoholic content of beer in California was kept a 3.2 percent. Why? I'll tell you why.

Congress decreed that 3.2 beer is not intoxicating. So if a drink is not intoxicating, there's no reason why it can't be sold to adults in any kind of an establishment. Anybody in the state of California could get a beer license for ten dollars. Before long, there were 47,000 places with beer licenses. That meant that a lot of beer went over the counter.

Of course the beer wasn't very damn good—what do you expect of 3.2? But the customers didn't mind. Hell, this was back in the thirties, when Americans had been starved for beer for a dozen years. The California drinkers were glad to be able to buy any kind.

You'll make note of the fact that I represented the California brewers. That meant that I had to protect their interests against any out-of-state beers, even if they did make Milwaukee famous.

So I had the legislature put through a law that each shipment of beer into California constituted a new license and had to be taxed accordingly. Oh, I was rough on those Eastern brewers. I made it so the California brewers had a virtual monopoly.

That law was airtight, too. It went all the way up to the Supreme Court and it stood up. None of the big nationally advertised beers could get a foothold in California. Finally in the 1950s they started buying out the California brewers and building their own plants in the state. By that time I had to have the law repealed. It was too drastic.

One time Coors tried to come into California with a six-ounce bottle. We didn't like that competition. Besides, those little bottles could easily get into the hands of children. That wouldn't be right. So we managed to get through a law stating that the minimum size of a beer bottle in the state was eleven ounces. Good-bye, Coors.

Naturally such services were very valuable to the brewers, and they paid accordingly. My basic fee was $30,000 a year.

The brewers also contributed five cents for each and every barrel they produced. This went into an educational fund to be used as I saw fit. The amount of the fund came to around $150,000, and I put that money to good use.

I did such a good job for the brewers that other elements of the liquor industry saw fit to make use of my organization. My assistant, Frank X. Flynn, also represented the California Liquor Dealers Association and the wholesale dealers of Northern and Southern California. So we had virtually the entire industry united behind us.

That was the way I wanted it. Only by being unified could the liquor industry protect its interests. There were 50,000 liquor outlets in the state of California. I figured that through employees and relatives, each could account for an average of ten votes. If they could be educated as to what were the best interests of their industry, that would mean a half-million votes as a starter!

Not only that. Each retail outlet had contact with hundreds of customers. If those customers could be swayed to a certain candidate or issue, that would mean additional political power.

Not only that. Through the beer and liquor dealers and manufacturers, we had control of more than four thousand billboards— in the state. Those could be used to good advantage at election time.

Carey McWilliams analyzed my setup this way:

> What Mr. Samish has done is to convert the interest-group into a political machine which functions independently of the party. From the lobbyists' point of view, of course, this represents a distinct advance in the forms of political control. A party machine can be challenged at the polls but as long as Artie controls the interest-groups, his power is beyond dispute.
>
> Theoretically his power could be challenged by the interest-groups he represents but—and this is the key to

the structure of power he has fashioned—these groups enjoy, despite the costs, great advantages from his representation.

In the first place, the state takes over the function and also the expense of policing the particular industry against "unfair trade practices"—an enormous saving in itself. In the second place, each industry-group and each individual member is spared the trouble and expense of dealing with individual politicians.

After all, it was much more practical to have the state enforce the industry's trade practices. That's why I put through the fair-trade laws.

The beverage business could have been hurt by unfair competition. For instance, the Thrifty Drug Store chain had a wholesale liquor license. That allowed Thrifty to charge less for the liquor it sold. It was unfair to competitors. We had to see that Thrifty's wholesale license was taken away.

Still, Thrifty and other big chains could offer bargain prices on certain liquors or beers as loss leaders—to get customers into the stores to buy other things. That had to be stopped.

I did it first through the Board of Equalization, which had jurisdiction over the beverage industry in California. The board provided the price-posting regulations.

But then it appeared that this action by the board might not be entirely authorized by state laws. So I had to get the legislature to provide a law. No problem. The bill providing the system of price-posting in the wholesaling of beer was passed in 1937. The bill also made legal fair-trade practices for any alcoholic beverage. That stabilized the industry, and it stayed that way as long as I was in charge.

As guardian of the beverage industry's interests, I had to keep an eye out for the Prohibitionists.

Now you'd think that after the failure of Prohibition, the

Drys would have given up. Not at all. They kept coming back, trying to make inroads on the legal sale of alcoholic beverages. Oh, we had some walloping fights.

In 1936 the Drys came forward with an initiative constitutional amendment which provided: "Every city, town, county, city-and-county, or territory outside of incorporated cities or towns, shall have the power to regulate, zone or prohibit the sale of alcoholic beverages within its limits."

Local option. That was something that could have severely damaged the beverage industry. As soon as beverage control got out of the hands of the state and into local hands, that meant trouble. There would have been towns all over the state that the Drys would have been able to close up for liquor sales. We had to fight that.

And fight it we did. After all, Art Samish had been around Sacramento a few years; he knew how to work the initiatives and referendums.

When an odious measure was going to appear on the ballot, it behooved you to place an opposition bill on the same ballot. One would cancel the other out, or at least confuse the voters enough so that both would be defeated.

Something else I learned: it pays to be on the top of the ballot. I always liked to have my measure listed as Proposition One, Two, or Three—any higher number had much less chance of passing.

How did I get the high position? Well, I had a lot of good friends in Sacramento, and one of them was Frank Jordan, the secretary of state, the man who decided what propositions appeared where on the ballot.

So it was no accident that the Dry initiative was placed Number Nine on the 1936 ballot. Ours was Number Three.

I spent a lot of money to promote Number Three and defeat Number Nine. Both of them were rejected by the voters, so I accomplished what I was after—to lick local option.

The Drys didn't give up. They came back in 1948 with

another local option initiative. It ended up as Proposition Twelve on the ballot.

My initiative on the same ballot was Number Two. If both amendments had passed and mine received more votes, it would have repealed Number Twelve. Proposition Two provided that the state laws against public saloons would remain in force—California didn't allow out-and-out saloons; food had to be served in drinking places. One provision forbade serving unaccompanied women, except at tables. That helped get us the sympathy vote.

I put on a hell of a fight. I raised $750,000 from the big boys, the manufacturers and wholesalers. The big boys paid the bills and the little fellows did the work.

I sent letters to all 50,000 licensees telling them not to make any contributions. It was their job to get out in their own communities and rally public support against Prohibition.

Advertisements for our cause appeared in every newspaper in the state. Announcements were carried on every radio station. Billboards—I had them everywhere you looked.

I got a picture of a mother—the most beautiful mother you ever did see. She was wearing a gingham dress and holding a broom in her hand. The slogan said:

LET'S CLEAN THEM OUT—VOTE YES ON NUMBER TWO!

That didn't have a damn thing to do with the proposition, but it sure as hell attracted a lot of sympathy.

The campaign against Number Twelve was just as strenuous. And it worked. Number Twelve was defeated in all fifty-eight counties. It got the most votes of any measure on the ballot and the count was two and a half to one against it—2,598,815 to 1,085,941! More than a million people in Los Angeles County voted against it.

When you get such a high "no" vote for any measure, the

other propositions are going to suffer, too. Proposition Number Two was also defeated. But I didn't give a damn. I had only put it up to wipe out Number Twelve.

After that experience, I got sore at the initiatives. It had become too damned expensive to fight them. So I decided to do something about it.

I saw to it that the law pertaining to petitions was changed. Under the old law, the Drys could start taking signatures in 1940 and if they had enough by 1950 they could get their proposal on the ballot.

The new law made it tougher. A group could file a petition with the attorney general for $200, then get title from the secretary of state. Then the group had 150 days to get the necessary signatures, with the right to petition for an additional 90 days. To qualify for a position on the ballot, 8 percent of the total vote of the last state election would be required.

That made it terribly difficult for an initiative to qualify for the ballot. The expense of acquiring so many signatures in so little time was virtually prohibitive.

Which is why the beverage industry was never threatened by local option thereafter.

CHAPTER 11

Two Governors Try to Shoot Down Art Samish with the Philbrick Report, But Our Hero Has the Last Laugh, as Usual

AS YOU LEARNED IN THE FOREGOING CHAPTER, I TOOK GOOD CARE of my clients in the beverage industry. Very good care. Not only in legislative matters, but on the administration level, too. Some gentlemen who served on the State Board of Equalization were good friends of mine. So were those who served on the State Liquor Control Board. I watched after their best interests, and they watched after mine.

Every two years I would put through a legislative bill to provide salary increases for Board of Equalization employees. That was a very concrete way of showing my appreciation of their friendship.

But one year my plans ran counter to the philosophy of Governor Frank Merriam, a confirmed Prohibitionist. We had a confrontation that caused one of the biggest hubbubs of my career. And it didn't do his career much good, either.

One day I told the governor of my intention to put through the bill to raise salaries on the Liquor Control Board.

"I'll have to veto that bill, Art," Merriam told me. "You know I'm Dry, and I can't sign any bill that would help the Wets."

"You gotta sign it," I said.

"Can't do it," said the governor.

"Why, you bald-headed son of a bitch," I said, "I helped you get into that governor's chair. And I'll get your ass out of it, too."

Frank Merriam didn't take too kindly to what I had told him. He got behind a move by the state senator from Los Angeles County, Culbert L. Olson, to have an investigation of lobbying activities in Sacramento. On the last day of the 1937 session, the legislature authorized the investigation. I let Merriam have it—I had nothing to hide.

Merriam appropriated $50,000 to finance the investigation by the Sacramento County grand jury, conducted by District Attorney Otis D. Babcock. A private investigator was hired, a man by the name of Howard R. Philbrick.

I had a lot of fun with him. I knew he was bugging my office and my telephone. So every time I walked into my office, I said quite loudly, "Good morning, Mr. Philbrick." And when I answered the phone, I said, "Now listen to this, Mr. Philbrick."

They started to have those grand jury hearings, and they fooled around and fooled around until they finally got to the guy they were after: Art Samish.

I played a little cat-and-mouse with them at first.

The D.A., this fellow Babcock, issued a subpoena for me in Sacramento. I conferred with my attorney, John Francis Neylan, an old friend and one of the most distinguished men in California—he was the chief legal advisor to William Randolph Hearst. Mr. Neylan advised me not to appear, so I took off for San Francisco.

Babcock chased me down there and had me arrested by a county detective from Sacramento. It didn't bother me. I handed over a thousand-dollar bill as bail to insure my appearance in court.

So I went back to Sacramento and accepted another subpoena to appear. Not only was I happy to talk to the grand jury. I let them throw the proceedings open to the public, instead of talking behind closed doors, as with most grand jury hearings.

So there was Art Samish in the spotlight, appearing before eight hundred spectators in the county supervisors' hearing room. I put on a good show for them.

Of course I knew all along that Frank Merriam was out to get me. He was up for reelection that year, and I was doing my best to give him trouble by backing his lieutenant governor, George Hatfield, in the primary election. Merriam won, as I expected, but the race damaged his chances in the final election.

I decided to let the public know what great buddies the governor and I had been. I turned over to the district attorney a couple of photographs which Merriam had enscribed to me—"to a pal, Art Samish." Naturally I showed them to reporters first.

I also produced some letters in which Merriam had thanked me profusely for the help I had provided in the 1934 election.

Merriam had provided the money to hire not only his gumshoe Philbrick but a special prosecutor, George M. Naus. It was this Naus who questioned me at first. Whenever he asked me a question, I answered him by beginning, "My good man . . ." No matter how nasty he became, I still replied, "My good man . . ."

That drove him nuts. One night at the Hotel Senator he accosted me and said, "Mr. Samish if you continue saying 'My good man,' I shall have to take offense with you."

The next day he asked me the first question on the stand, and I replied, "My good man . . ."

I had fun with the district attorney, Babcock, too. While the grand jury hearings were going on, Babcock was up for reelection. I happened to hear of a young man just out of law school who seemed like a good candidate for prosecutor. Almost overnight, signs appeared all over Sacramento:

HONEST MCDOUGAL FOR DISTRICT ATTORNEY

That really burned up Babcock. Almost got him defeated, too. One day when I was on the witness stand, he snapped at me, "You know a whole lot about McDougal's campaign, don't you?"

"If I had only had two or three days longer, I would have known more," I told him.

"But you didn't do it," said Babcock.

"No, but two or three more days and you wouldn't have been standing there as district attorney."

I really clowned it up. As I was watching the proceedings, I felt I was missing something. All those investigators and prosecutors came into the supervisors' chambers with their files and briefcases and notebooks, and I didn't have a thing. I decided I had to take care of that.

My good friend over the years was Walter King, who traveled with me all over the country and entertained me and my friends all the time. Walter was a piano player, one of the best, and a handy man to have around.

"Walter," I said to him, "we're going down to the bottom of K Street and buy ourselves a couple of suitcases. Then we're going to fill those suitcases with bricks and newspapers, and I want you to carry them into the grand jury hearings every day."

That's just what he did. Each day I appeared with Walter, and he placed the two suitcases on the chair in front of me. Then I put a legal pad on top of the suitcases. Every time Babcock or Naus asked me a question I didn't have the answer for, I wrote a very elaborate note on the pad and said, "I'll get that answer for you."

Everybody eyed those suitcases with great interest, believing that I had some secret papers inside.

When the grand jury hearing was all over, what do you suppose happened to Art Samish?

Not a damned thing. I wasn't even mentioned in the grand jury report. Of course it didn't hurt that I had three friends on the jury. Two were gentlemen that I had happened to meet in a bookmaking parlor. The other was a very important banker of my acquaintance.

Right in the midst of the grand jury investigation came the election for governor.

This time old Merriam was facing a tough opponent, Culbert L. Olson, who had been state senator from Los Angeles County. The Democrats were riding high in 1938; in fact, they would have won the governorship in 1934 if the public utilities and the other big interests hadn't been so dead set against Upton Sinclair.

I didn't give a damn about Olson, but I didn't want to see Merriam reelected, either. I had warned him that I'd help get his ass out of the governor's chair, and I did.

Merriam was a Dry, and he had sponsored a piece of legislation against the liquor industry. Naturally it didn't pass; Doc Samish saw to that. And I made sure that my clients realized that Merriam was no friend of theirs. I printed up a facsimile of that Dry bill, plastered Merriam's face on it and sent the circular to every one of the 50,000 liquor retailers in California. They got the message.

The investigation of Art Samish didn't end when Frank Merriam was voted out of office.

Merriam's sleuth, Howard Philbrick, had compiled a 185-page report about the findings of the investigation. It became known as the Philbrick Report. It almost didn't become known at all. Governor Olson sent it in a message to the legislature, and it was printed in the April 4, 1939, issue of the *Senate Daily Journal.* But then certain members of the legislature didn't like the way Mr. Philbrick had acquired some of his information. Not only had he bugged Art Samish; Philbrick had even placed a microphone in the bedchamber of the Speaker of the Assembly and his wife!

The senate ordered the April 4 issue of the *Journal* destroyed and reprinted without the Philbrick Report. But then Governor Olson ordered 15,000 copies printed at his office's expense.

And just what did Mr. Philbrick report about the nefarious Art Samish?

Here are some excerpts:

> Most of the lines of inquiry, at one time or another led to Arthur H. Samish, a relatively young San Francisco man who calls himself variously a public relations counsel, a legislative representative and "a guy who gets things done."
>
> If all investigative roads led to Mr. Samish, it was only natural. For he was unusually modest when he registered in the Senate lobby list as the representative of the Motor Carriers Association, San Francisco. Investigation showed that he actually was a lobbyist for motor carrier, railroad, liquor, racing, theatrical and other interests.
>
> Mr. Samish was the prototype of the lobbyist—and the envy of droves of his financially less successful competitors in the business of selling influence. Between 1935 and 1938, a total of $496,138.62, all of it from interests concerned with legislation, flowed into the many bank accounts of Mr. Samish. Investigators never presumed to believe that they had established a record of all of Mr. Samish's income from bank records, from testimony dragged from his evasive lips, from income tax reports he produced after fighting through the State Supreme Court and from corollary investigation. . . .
>
> As California's arch-lobbyist, Mr. Samish represented all of the methods used in part or in full by members of his

trade—campaign contributions to lawmakers with a lavish hand; fees to lawyer-legislators; cultivation of State departmental and legislative personnel with money or favors; knowledge of the mechanics of legislation and of the human frailties along the path.

The end and result of Mr. Samish's operations has been best phrased by Mr. Samish himself, in one of his infrequent candid comments: "I'm the Governor of the Legislature. To hell with the Governor of the State!"

Mr. Philbrick went on and on about the misdeeds of Arthur H. Samish, but all his words didn't prove a goddam thing. Nothing happened. Art Samish remained in business as usual.

But look what happened to Frank Merriam.

The old bastard was out of a job. He tried to go on being the Number One man in the Republican party in California, but I did something about that, too.

In 1940, a lot of the young Republicans in California were enthusiastic about the candidacy of Wendell Willkie for the presidential nomination. Former Governor Merriam was still the titular head of the Republican party in California, and Willkie was too progressive for him. He was in favor of a solid conservative, Robert A. Taft.

I didn't give a hoot about presidential politics. But I enjoyed doing anything to knock down Frank Merriam.

That chance came when the State Central Committee met for its convention in Sacramento. The night before the meeting, I was in the lobby of the Hotel Senator and I greeted a number of my friends on the Republican Committee. Among them was Ted Craig, whom I had known as Speaker of the Assembly. He seemed down in the dumps.

"What's the matter, Ted?" I asked.

"It's this race for State Central Committeeman," he said. "Willkie is coming to Sacramento for a speech tomorrow night, and we'd like to have a committeeman who would be for him.

But old man Merriam won't allow that. He's going to shove his own man down our throats."

"Well, you're not going to let the old son of a bitch get away with that, are you?" I said.

"Who the hell have we got to oppose Merriam's man?"

"How about that kid from Orange County—Tommy Kuchel?"

"Tommy's a nice guy, but he doesn't have a chance."

"I'm not so sure. Why don't you have a chat with Tommy? If he's willing to go along with it, you let the ole professor go to work on your problem."

Tom Kuchel, who was a twenty-nine-year-old assemblyman, said he was willing, and so I started making some calls. The key man was Jerry Seawell, the senate floor leader, He held the proxies for about one-third of the delegates who didn't come to the convention.

I decided to give Merriam the business. I called Jimmy Simms, an appraiser for the Board of Equalization who sometimes did some odd-job moonlighting for me. Jimmy had a child in the local high school, and I told him to recruit a hundred students at two bucks a head and send them to the gallery in the senate chambers, where the Republicans were to meet. They jammed the gallery and we instructed them to boo every time Frank Merriam's name was mentioned. Whenever Thomas Kuchel was mentioned, they were to cheer.

Everything went as planned.

Frank Merriam arrived and my small army of mercenaries hooted and hollered until his bald head turned lobster red. He made the nominating speech for his own candidate for state central committeeman, and the boos continued.

After a couple of seconding speeches, the chairman said, "Are there any more nominations?"

Senator Ralph Swing, one of the most respected members of the legislature, arose and said: "Mr. Chairman, Assemblyman Lyons has a name to place in nomination."

Charlie Lyons made the nomination speech, and every

time he mentioned the name of Tommy Kuchel, the youthful audience cheered as if he were the latest singing sensation. Ralph Swing seconded the nomination, and the clerk started to call the roll for voting.

Old Frank Merriam's bald pate turned even redder as delegates he had counted on voted for Thomas Kuchel. Then came Seawell, who cast his proxies for Kuchel. Merriam stalked out of the meeting, and his stooge made the motion to cast a unanimous ballot.

That night Tom Kuchel led the delegation to greet Wendell Willkie on his arrival in Sacramento. Tom later became state controller and then became a fine United States senator.

Frank Merriam? He slunk back to Long Beach and was never heard from again.

CHAPTER 12

In Which the Professor Tells of His Modus Operandi in Sacramento and Recounts a Tale or Two

OH, WE HAD SOME HIGH TIMES UP THERE IN SACRAMENTO.

And we got a hell of a lot of work done, too.

In those years, the legislature met only every other year. On the first Monday of January of the odd-numbered year, the legislators convened for three weeks of organizing and introducing of bills.

Then they adjourned while the bills were being printed. On the first Monday in March, the senators and assemblymen returned to take up the legislation. They usually adjourned in time to beat the Sacramento heat, in June or July. They didn't meet in the even-numbered years, except for special or budget sessions.

There were no frills in those days. Only the Speakers and the committee chairman had offices; the rest of the legislators worked from their desks on the assembly and senate floors. If they wanted to write letters, they had to get a girl from the stenographic pool for an hour or two.

Look at the California legislators today.

Each of them has a big suite of offices, a receptionist, a

private secretary, a field man, a state car with $125 a month for gasoline, and God knows what else.

Now the legislature meets for almost ten months a year every year. But I swear that the old legislatures accomplished more in eight to ten months than the present ones do in twenty.

Of course, in the old days the legislators had the advantage of the efficient services of Arthur H. Samish and his associates.

I worked just as hard as the senators and assemblymen. Harder, in fact. They only had to watch over their own areas of interest. I had to keep an eye on the whole damned legislature!

That meant a twenty-four-hour day.

Sometimes I would get up at seven to breakfast with a senator before he went to the capitol. By eight, some of the committees were already holding their meetings, and the telephones started ringing with reports from my Gestapo.

My agents were everywhere. Not a single important meeting could be held in the capitol without one of my representatives being there to observe the happenings. They either telephoned the news or came to Samish Alley in the Senator Hotel and delivered the report in person. I had four big adjoining rooms, so I could have people waiting for me in each one. I didn't like my own agents to know each other; I knew their reports would be franker if they preserved their anonymity.

Throughout the day I received visitors both big and small: legislators and state executives, brewery owners and bartenders, newspaper publishers and bootblacks. All received the same Samish hospitality. A buffet served lobster, shrimp, caviar, and other goodies. I ran the best-stocked bar in Sacramento. And neither I nor my two chief aides, Frank Flynn and Bill Jasper, ever took a drink!

I seldom left the suite during the day, since I didn't want to miss any of the reports that were coming in. I received them not only from my own agents. I also had a crew of volunteers. A clerk here, a secretary there. Such people could be very helpful in picking up bits of information about senators who were planning to change their votes or assemblymen who needed convincing.

Naturally I rewarded these informants in my usual beneficent manner.

Sometimes I went out to dinner, but if important committees were meeting in the evenings, I stayed in the suite, always working in my robe for comfort. Then after I was through with business, I descended to the senate lobby and enjoyed the social intercourse with the legislators, lobbyists, and whoever else might be passing by.

Vigilance was the keynote of the Samish operation.

I had to be aware of what was going on at all times; that was the only way I could properly service my clients. Most of the time I relied on the reports of my staff or of my unofficial army of intelligence agents. On rare occasions I visited the scene of action myself.

One time at the close of a legislative session I was vitally interested in a transportation bill that affected my clients in the trucking industry. I decided to pay a call to the assembly to listen to the debate on the measure.

I stood at the back of the chambers and listened with approval as Bill Hornblower of San Francisco spoke in favor of the bill which he had been helpful enough to introduce. Bill, bless his heart, was the soul of eloquence as he enumerated the merits of the measure.

Then Bill gave the floor to my good friend Charlie Lyons of Los Angeles. To my dismay, I heard Charlie start to castigate the bill.

I couldn't believe my ears. Charlie had already expressed his willingness to support the measure. But then I realized from Charlie's excess of eloquence what was happening. He had enjoyed a couple of nips too many, and he didn't recognize the bill was one that I favored.

I hastily wrote out a note to correct him. An assembly

page delivered the slip of paper. Charlie Lyons glanced hastily at the message and without a second's delay declared to his fellow assemblymen:

"Now that I have told you the bad things about the bill. . . ."

His midstream switch was noticed by no one else but me, and he proceeded to issue a ringing defense of the bill, which passed the assembly with scant opposition.

Booze could sometimes be a problem in the orderly passage of legislation.

On one occasion the assembly was coming up for a vote that was crucial to my clients. I expected the count to be close, and I was relying on the support of an assemblyman who had expressed his willingness to go along with the bill. But as the vote approached, he was nowhere to be found.

"We've got to have him to swing this vote." I said to my assistant, Bill Jasper. "Go find him and bring him to the capitol."

Bill was a reliable fellow, and he hunted for the missing assemblyman in all his favorite haunts, which were mostly bars. Finally Jasper decided to try the fellow's hotel room. Sure enough, there he was, awash in Irish whiskey.

When he saw Jasper, he started crying.

"What's the matter?" Jasper asked.

"It's me uncle," the assemblyman sobbed, the whiskey causing him to speak in a brogue. "One of the foinest monsignors in all of Ireland, he was, and now he's dead."

"I'm very sorry to hear that," said Jasper. "Is there anything we can do with the services?" It was my custom to help bury the departed of any of the legislators.

"No, no, thank ye anyway," said the assemblyman. There's nithin' we can do for him now. And what a foin broth of a man he was. See here."

He thrust a newspaper clipping toward Jasper. The monsignor was indeed a handsome though stern-looking man, according to his photograph in the Dublin paper. Jasper read the glowing obituary, and then he happened to notice the date of the clipping. The uncle had died six years before.

Jasper continued to extend his sympathy, but he managed to maneuver the grieving nephew back to the assembly floor in time for the vote.

There were other causes of absenteeism.

At the closing of one legislative session, I had been shepherding a bill through the two houses. Not an important bill, but one which would please a certain client. I had been keeping a close eye on it, simply because I made it a habit not to lose on a bill, important or not.

I felt confident about this particular measure. It had passed the senate with no important opposition. Now it faced the assembly, and my research had shown that I was assured of forty-two votes, two more than were needed for passage.

On the night of the vote, Bill Jasper took a reading on the assemblymen and reported back to me that two important supporters were missing. Let's call them Ernie and Bill.

"Where the hell are those bastards?" I said. "We need them."

I did some sleuthing and found out where Ernie and Bill had gone. They had taken a couple of girls on a voyage of the *Delta Queen*, a steamboat that made an overnight trip between Sacramento and San Francisco.

"I'll get 'em back," I swore, and I sent word to the assembly for a Call of the House. The author of a bill under consideration could make a Call of the House to insure that the present members could not leave while the absent ones were being sought.

I called my friend Bill Dwyer, who ran the *Delta Queen* and the *Delta King*, and he told me the boat's schedule along the Sacramento River. Then I had the sergeant at arms call the highway patrol and tell them to dispatch a couple of officers in a car which would meet the *Delta Queen* at the next drawbridge.

The highway patrolmen arrived in time to board the

steamboat and haul off the two assemblymen. With sirens screaming, the patrol car hurried back to Sacramento where Ernie and Bill cast their affirmative votes for my measure.

Afterward I thanked the two men for interrupting their trysts, and I told them: "I'll have Frank Flynn drive you to San Francisco before the *Delta Queen* docks. I'd hate to have those two girls arrive with no one to greet them."

CHAPTER 13

Some More Examples of How to Get Things Done

CULBERT OLSON DIDN'T GIVE ME ANY TROUBLE AS GOVERNOR. HE was a good man, an honest man, and while I wasn't very close to him, I got along fine with a number of his appointees. His director of finance, George Killion, was an old and good friend of mine.

As I've told you before, it didn't matter to me who was governor. The legislature was the important thing in my method of operation.

Here's a story that will show you how I operated. Parker Maddux, who was president of the San Francisco Bank, came to me with a problem. During the Depression, the bank had foreclosed on a lot of mortgages. The State Banking Act provided that a savings bank had to dispose of its foreclosed property within five years. Now real estate prices were still very low in the 1930s, and the banks would have to dispose of their real estate at depressed rates.

"Under the law, we'll have to get rid of between thirty and forty million dollars' worth of real estate," Maddux told me. "That would mean a substantial loss."

"Do you want the doctor to represent you?" I asked.

"Yes, I do," he said.

So I went to work on his problem. The solution was very simple: one word had to be substituted. All I had to do was change the word "five" to "ten" in the banking law.

I had the entire State Banking Law printed up—it came to a volume big enough to kill a rat with. In amending a law, you have to italicize the amended portion, so the word "ten" appeared in italics. Now you wouldn't expect anybody would be able to find one italicized word in a volume several inches thick. But just in case somebody did, I had the law amended a second time so the "ten" wasn't italicized any more.

The new version sailed through the legislature unanimously. I can assure you that Mr. Maddux and the San Francisco Bank were very grateful. With the change of one word I saved them about twenty million dollars.

Another of my clients in the 1930s was the American Potash and Chemical Corporation. That was a company that operated a huge plant at Trona, California, for the production of potash and borax.

American Potash hired me to see that there was no severance tax placed on fluid taken from the ground. That could have meant a lot of expense to the company. I spared them that expense. No severance tax was ever voted by the legislature.

I did a few other errands for American Potash, including the securing of a low license plate number for the general manager of the Trona plant. That was just one of my many services.

It wasn't until after World War II that I discovered whom I had been working for. It was revealed that American Potash had been owned by the German government. So my boss all through those years had been Adolf Hitler!

Of course I didn't know it at the time. I was pretty particular whom I worked for. Not everybody could hire the services of Art Samish.

Once a fellow named Preston Tucker came to me. He was a big-time promoter who wanted to get permission to sell interests in his Tucker Corporation to investors in California. But the California Division of Corporations didn't look too kindly on his venture. That's why he tried to enlist Art Samish.

"I'd like to get permission to sell my stock in California," he said to me. "They tell me you're the man who can swing it for me. Will you take on the job?"

I sized this Tucker guy up in a hurry.

"No, I'm not going to take on the job," I told him. "I don't want anything to do with you. I don't like any lovin' stock hustler who goes around selling phony issues to unsuspecting mothers. Why, you might even sell that lovin' stock to my own mother!"

I got rid of him in a hurry. And the California Division of Corporations refused to let him sell the stock. It was a "fraud upon the purchasers," they said.

A couple of others who got the bum's rush from me were the Allen brothers.

Willis and Lawrence Allen had been promoting a pension plan which had the slogan "Thirty Dollars Every Thursday." There were a lot of old, retired folks in California and many of them were hurting financially in the 1930s. So when the Allen brothers came along with the promise of providing the old folks with thirty dollars every Thursday, those people joined the organization.

The Ham 'n' Eggs movement, as it was called, became very powerful in California politics. The Allen brothers got an initiative proposition on the ballot, and they wanted me to help them put it over.

"Get the hell out of my office before I throw you out," I told them. "I don't want nothing to do with a couple of bastards who are taking money from poor mothers so you can get rich!"

The Ham 'n' Eggs initiative lost in the election, I might add.

On another occasion, I had the pleasure of refusing an offer from the mighty showman Cecil B. DeMille.

The director of *The King of Kings*, *The Ten Commandments*, and other epics had cast himself in the role of political martyr. For many years he had appeared on a radio program called *Lux Radio Theater*, for which he was paid $100,000 a year. One day he received a letter from the radio actors' union asking him to contribute one dollar for a fund to help defeat Proposition 12, which would have forbidden the closed shop in California.

DeMille didn't want to pay.

He found himself in a dilemma. To stay on radio, he had to belong to the American Federation of Radio Artists, which had made the dollar assessment compulsory for all members. But DeMille was also a millionaire and a conservative, and he didn't believe in the closed shop for unions.

DeMille refused to pay the one dollar, and he got thrown out of the union and off the air.

Proposition 12 was defeated, but DeMille wouldn't quit. Through some of his conservative friends, he managed to get a bill before the legislature which would have prohibited the closed shop in California. That's when I entered the picture.

One of my acquaintances at the racetracks was a successful Beverly Hills lawyer. DeMille was one of his clients, and the lawyer was helping him promote his antiunion measure.

The lawyer telephoned me to enlist my help.

"Art, you've got to do this for us," he said. "If this bill doesn't pass, we'll hold you personally responsible."

That kind of language didn't work with Art Samish.

"No one gives me ultimatums," I told him. "Now let's see you try to get that lovin' bill through."

The labor unions had just about given up hope of beating the bill. But that was before I decided to give them a helping hand. Suddenly legislators the DeMille forces had counted on for support had second thoughts. The assembly voted the bill down, fifty-four votes out of eighty being registered against it.

That was the biggest victory the unions had ever known in the legislature. C. J. (Neil) Haggerty, who represented the American Federation of Labor in Sacramento and later became the AFL lobbyist in Washington and a regent of the University of California, gave me the nod.

"This ought to show who controls the state of California," said Haggerty.

Time after time I helped Neil get what he wanted in the legislature, including workmen's compensation. I was always for the working stiffs. I told my staff, "They're the ones who buy our beer."

Sometimes my rich clients would complain because I helped labor.

"What the hell's the matter?" I replied. "Are you afraid your stockholders are going to get a nickel less in dividends? Share it with the people who buy your product!"

My services for labor were rendered without charge. That's the way I operated: those who could afford to pay for Art Samish would do so—and pay dearly. Those who couldn't—hell, I worked for nothing, if it was for someone or something I believed in.

Paul Smith was a good friend of mine. He was a brilliant man and a fine newspaperman; he was editor of the *San Francisco Chronicle*. One day he called me up and asked me: "Can you get a resolution for One World through the legislature?"

"What the hell is One World?" I asked.

He explained that it was something Wendell Willkie had started. It concerned a world federalist union or some damned thing. I didn't know what it was all about, but if Paul Smith believed in it, that was good enough for me.

The One World resolution went through the legislature without a word against it. California became the first state in the nation to favor a world federalist union.

I did a lot of other jobs that nobody ever heard about. Back in my early days in Sacramento the lobbyist for the University of California was Robert Gordon Sproul, who later became president of the university. He was succeeded by Luther Nichols. Both of them were fine, upstanding men, and they sometimes had trouble getting the legislature to appropriate enough money so the university could grow into the great institution it is today. I gave them help whenever they needed it, and I didn't ask anything in return.

There were many things like that that I did for people. Somehow those things never got written up in the Philbrick Report or magazine articles about Art Samish. Not that I gave a good goddam.

Just one more example and then I'll quit telling you what a nice man I really am.

I came across a letter in my desk drawer the other day. It was from my old and dear friend Marco Hellman, one of the great civic leaders of San Francisco. He told me he had come across a book of interviews conducted by the University of California School of Public Health.

A man named Lawrence Arnstein was telling about the trouble in getting legislation for child care centers. Neil Haggerty of the AFL told Arnstein that the only man who could get the bill through the legislature was Art Samish. Arnstein arranged an appointment with me through Sam Lilienthal, the head of a grocery chain.

This is what Arnstein told about our meeting:

"He turned out to be a man who used to come into our woolen business. When I saw him I said, 'Are you the man who used to come in to Arnstein, Simon and Company to buy clothes from Freddy Pratt?' He said, 'Yes; are you the man who was head of that business?' I said, 'Yes.'

"He said, 'What did you want to see me about?' I told him I wanted to see him about the child care center bill, because it was held up by Senators Swing and Hatfield and we needed their votes.

"He said, 'I'll see what I can do.' I said, 'Don't you want me to tell you what the child care centers mean to the Community Chest and the PTA and the League of Women Voters and the labor unions and everybody I'm working with?'

" 'No,' he said. 'I don't care about that. As long as Sam Lilienthal wants me to do it, and you who used to be in business are doing this for nothing, I'll see what I can do for the kids.'

"Next day the bill came out of committee. He certainly did a good deed for the child care centers, because if it had been killed in the Senate Finance Committee, it would have been dead permanently. Since that time, the centers have become permanent."

Marco Hellman added: "Mr. Arnstein told me that the child care centers now take care of 350,000 children. I thought this would be of interest to you."

CHAPTER 14

How I Ran the Best-selling Whiskey Out of California; and Other Adventures with Lewis Rosenstiel

A LOBBYIST'S LIFE IS FULL OF SURPRISES. ONE DAY I WAS SURPRISED to get a telephone call from a Mr. Lewis Rosenstiel in New York. Now I didn't know anybody named Lewis Rosenstiel, but I was willing to talk business with anyone. I soon learned who Mr. Rosenstiel was, and we ended up doing a whole lot of business together. A whole lot.

When I went to work for a client, I found out everything I could about him. What I learned about Lewis Rosenstiel was impressive. He had been born in Cincinnati in 1891 and at the age of seventeen went to work sweeping the floor of his uncle's distillery in Kentucky. Naturally the liquor business was ruined during Prohibition, but Rosenstiel knew that liquor would be legal again and he planned accordingly. He bought an unused distillery in Schenley, Pennsylvania, at a bargain price. Other distillers didn't want the expense of holding onto their stocks of whiskey, so Rosenstiel bought up their supplies, again at bargain rates. This was a real smart fellow.

When Repeal came in 1933, Rosenstiel's Schenley company was in the best position of any distiller. He had more aged whiskey than any of them, and Schenley's profits were enormous.

But Lewis Rosenstiel wanted more profits, and that's why he called me.

"Mr. Samish, I'm very much concerned about that Anti-discrimination Law in California," he said. "It could be very damaging to our profit structure in your state. Do you think anything can be done about it?"

"Mr. Rosenstiel, you came to the right man," I told him.

The law he was concerned about had been enacted to protect California wines and other beverages. It provided that if other states levied special taxes on California wines and liquors, California would reciprocate with taxes on those states' wines and liquors.

I saw to it that the law was changed so Schenley products would not suffer. Mr. Rosenstiel was pleased and impressed, and he hired me as public relations counselor for Schenley. I was paid $36,000 a year, plus $18,000 a year from California Vineyards, which he owned.

But it was more than a business arrangement. Lewis Rosenstiel and I became close friends. I mean close. So close that he sent me the key to his house and said it was open to me at all times. I staged birthday parties for him. I knew all four of his wives. One of them was the niece of Harry Cohn; she had been married to Beldon Kattleman and later became the wife of Walter Annenberg, Ambassador to Great Britain.

I was so close to Lewis Rosenstiel that I was convinced he would never desert me. That was a mistake.

I performed a great many services for Rosenstiel. During the war when cigarettes were scarce, I convinced him to give away packages of cigarettes to soldiers. On each package was the statement, "Compliments of the Schenley Company." Thirty thousand packs of cigarettes a month were given to servicemen, and a lot of friendship was generated for Schenley.

Schenley went into the wine business in a big way in 1940,

and I was responsible for it. I made it my business to find out everything that was happening in the beverage industry. One day I heard that Lucien Johnson was sick. He was the man who ran Cresta Blanca, a fine old company that dated back to the earliest days of California wineries. With the war going on in Europe, I knew that there would be a demand for domestic wines.

Here's how the rest of the story was related in *Fortune* magazine:

> The fact that the unaggressive Johnson was ailing and open to offers was known to, among others, Arthur Samish, No. 1 California lobbyist, retained by Rosenstiel to handle Schenley's public relations on the West Coast. Figuring that Schenley Import, the company's high-toned subsidiary, would soon have trouble importing anything, Samish had what he terms "a fool idea." He called his client and asked, "How'd you like to buy your company a winery?"
>
> Rosenstiel was not taken aback. Unlike most distillers, he is voraciously interested in everything from chemistry to a corporation's social obligations. Long enthusiastic about finding byproducts and sidelines, he told Samish to organize his thoughts and call him the next day. Samish got an option from Johnson and did so.
>
> "How'd you like to own Cresta Blanca and the eight gold medals?" he said.
>
> "What the hell are you talking about?" asked Rosenstiel, who had never heard of them. Samish had hardly explained before he was flying east with the option. Schenley bought Cresta Blanca for $280,000.

That purchase put quality California wines on the map. There had been a lot of cheap wine on the market, but the good wines had not received much national attention.

Rosenstiel spent two million dollars making Cresta Blanca a famous brand. He put on a coast-to-coast radio program on which the words Cresta Blanca were spelled out with a musical accompaniment. The other distilleries took notice. National Distillers bought Italian Swiss Colony, Seagram bought Paul Masson, Hiram Walker bought Valliant and Son. So enthusiastic about wine was Lew Rosenstiel that he then shelled out $6,400,000 for Roma, the biggest wine producer in California.

California had the Gold Rush in 1849. The Wine Rush came in 1940–1942. And I'm the guy who started it.

Another service I performed for Lewis Rosenstiel never got written up in *Fortune* or any other publication. That was The 10 High Caper.

One day I received a telephone call from Rosenstiel in New York. "Artie, I've got something important on my mind that I want to discuss with you," he said. "Come back here."

Well, when the big man calls, the little man jumps. So I grabbed a plane and went to New York to confer with Mr. Rosenstiel.

I met him at his office, and he said to me, "Artie, I'm very much concerned about Harry Hatch."

"You mean the president of Hiram Walker?" I said.

"Yes. He's a mean man. I'd like to see something done about him."

"What would you suggest?"

"Well, he has a whiskey called 10 High, and it's the biggest seller in California."

"Tell me something about it."

"It's a thirty-six-month-old whiskey . . ."

"That's all I need to know. You leave it to me—I'll take care of Mr. Harry Hatch."

On the plane going back to California I figured out my strategy. When the legislature came back into session, I had one of my friends in the assembly introduce a bill which provided that all whiskies sold in the state of California had to be at least four years old and all blends had to be at least 20 percent four years old.

I shepherded that bill through the legislature in my usual manner. First it was referred to the Assembly Committee on Public Morals, where it was passed unanimously. I guided it carefully through the second and third readings and then the passage by the assembly. Then the same process was repeated in the senate.

The bill zipped through the legislature without a whisper of opposition. Governor Olson vetoed it, but his veto was overridden. The Drys loved the bill; for once I had them on my side. They'd vote for anything that curtailed the liquor industry. The others thought it was a good bill because it protected the quality of whiskey.

After all, I was looking out for the public's interest. It just happened that the public's interest coincided with that of Lewis Rosenstiel.

I didn't learn until later that Schenley owned the great bulk of four-year-old whiskey in the United States.

So 10 High was run out of California, which then was consuming 27 percent of the nation's whiskey; 10 High returned later in a different form, but by that time it had lost all its prestige in California.

CHAPTER 15

How I Kept the California Liquor Industry Honest, Happy, and Healthy

WHILE I WAS PERFORMING ERRANDS FOR MR. LEWIS ROSENSTIEL, I was also watching over the interests of the entire liquor industry. And if I do say so myself, I was doing a bang-up job.

A few years ago there was a seminar on alcohol at UCLA, and a professor from the Yale University Institute for Alcoholic Studies gave out the statement that California has the best liquor laws in the nation.

That was no accident. I myself put through all those laws.

Not only that. I saw that they were enforced, too.

By God, I did such a good job that I even had the WCTU on my side!

As long as I was running things for the brewers, they remained in financial health. If you don't believe me, consider then and now.

Then—the standard price for a six-pack of beer was $1.20.

Now—you can buy a six-pack of beer in California for $1.10. Everyone knows how the costs of labor, materials, and taxes have risen, so you can see how much less profit the brewers are making.

Then—there were sixteen local breweries in California.

Now—only two remain. All the others have gone broke or have been taken over by the eastern companies. And many of the big companies have been hurting, too.

I operated on the theory that only by regulation and enforcement could the alcoholic beverage business thrive and prosper. Cutthroat competition could have been ruinous. So I put through the fair-trade laws to protect wholesalers, distributors, and retailers. All of them make a profit in California, and they always have.

But look what happens in states that don't have fair trade. New York, for instance. When the fair-trade laws were in effect there, a liquor license could have been worth $250,000. Then the state removed fair trade and the license is worth virtually nothing. The liquor business started competing so fiercely that it was tough for anyone to make a profit.

Then there's another problem that other states have: moonshining.

What causes illegal stills? High taxes on liquor. Many of the states, particularly in the South, taxed liquor so heavily that moonshining became an industry. Not in California. I kept the taxes so low that illegal stills became as rare as Hollywood virgins.

I kept an eye on everything and left no loophole unplugged. One year Bill Jasper had driven up to Sacramento with a friend, and he told me of stopping at a roadside stand in Kern County. The place had a big sign in front that advertised: "Eastside Beer on Tap."

Jasper's friend ordered a beer and had to spit it out. When he asked about the beer, the waitress told him it wasn't really Eastside; the boss just tapped whatever he had on hand and in this case it was an inferior brand.

"That's very naughty of him," I said to Jasper. "We can't have that sort of thing going on in this state."

And so I had a law passed to change that practice. The

spigot on every barrel of tap beer had to carry the name of the beer that was contained therein. California was the first state to pass such a law, and virtually every state in the Union followed suit. Canada, too.

You know those miniature bottles of liquor that you can buy for souvenirs? I love them. I've got what may be the largest collection of miniature liquor bottles in the world—six thousand of them.

But though I like to collect them myself, I know that those tiny liquor bottles are not good for the industry. They can get into the hands of minors too easily. Girls can hide them in their purses, boys can slip them in their pockets. So I had them banned from California.

I convinced the industry it was good business to keep liquor from minors. The rules against sales of intoxicating beverages to those under the age of twenty-one were clearly spelled out and rigidly enforced. On occasion a friend of mine would call me to report that a bar owner had been caught serving drinks to minors. Could I do anything for the man?

"Let the son of a bitch go to jail!" I replied.

That was my attitude toward any request for leniency from the law enforcers.

"Artie, I've got a problem," a tavern owner would tell me. "The Board of Equalization man came around at two thirty in the morning and he saw my bartender serving drinks. Can you fix it for me?"

"No!" I'd tell him. "You can sue the clock company if the clock showed before two and it was really two thirty."

Never once did I intercede with the liquor law enforcers for any of my fifty thousand clients.

I took pride in those laws. I passed through a bill that assured that liquor could not be sold in "close proximity" to schools and churches. The "close proximity" was left in general terms because each case had to be considered individually. For instance, you couldn't deny a liquor license to the Biltmore

Hotel in Los Angeles because the Unitarian Church was across the street. But in general the law was applied wisely to prevent bars and liquor stores from being too close to schools and places of worship.

I mentioned about the Women's Christian Temperance Union.

We got along fine. More often than not, the laws which I advocated and pushed through the legislature were also favored by the Temperance ladies. The WCTU had a lobbyist in Sacramento during the legislature sessions, and I always maintained good relations with the representative.

One time the WCTU lobbyist asked me if I couldn't get a job for her husband.

"Why, certainly, dear lady," I told her. And her husband soon found employment as an investigator for the Greyhound Lines.

The lady was most appreciative, and we became even closer friends. One stormy day she was complaining about her health. "I don't like this rain," she remarked. "It chills me to the bones. I lie awake at night and shiver."

"What you need," I told her, "is a little taste of brandy before retiring."

"Brandy?" she said. "That's liquor, isn't it?"

"Some may think so. I consider it medicinal."

"In that case—I might try it."

I went to the liquor store at Tenth and K streets and bought a bottle of Martell brandy and presented it to her. The next day she told me, "My, that certainly did the trick." Every ten days for the rest of the legislative session I had one of my secretaries supply her with another bottle of brandy.

My work in California did not go without the notice of the liquor industry in the rest of the land. On occasion I was consulted for problems elsewhere, but I must admit that I was not too successful in operating outside of my native state.

The reason for this was strictly personal. California was my territory. I ran things the way I wanted. When I went outside the state, I suddenly found myself confronted with committees and conferences and all manner of pussyfooting that corporations and associations fall victim to.

I am reminded of an industry function at the Waldorf-Astoria Hotel in New York. I was invited to attend and give counsel at a conference at which high members of the liquor industry were discussing their mutual problems.

For five hours I listened as the talk went back and forth about this problem and that. Finally the chairman turned to me and said, "Mr. Samish, do you mind saying what you think of our ideas? Do you have anything that would add to our discussion?"

I rose to my feet and gazed over the gathering of well-groomed, handsomely attired executives.

"Gentlemen," I said, "I have to be honest in my beliefs and conclusions as to what you have been discussing here today. I don't expect to be very popular with what I am going to tell you. But you asked for it.

"I have summed up this little gathering as a group of pompous brown-noses osculating the posteriors of your bosses. You are afraid that something might be advanced which would cut you off from a payroll. No work is being done."

Attendance at that meeting convinced me to resist any overtures to extend my activities to a national level. I was thoroughly content to restrict myself to the state I knew as well as any man alive.

My knowledge of the state and its beverage industry helped further the financial fortunes of Arthur H. Samish. On occasion I not only served the industry; I became a part of it.

On one occasion I got mad at Lewis Rosenstiel and I decided to show him a lesson. Through my contacts in the liquor business, I heard that National Distributor Brands was up for sale. That was a liquor company that distributed some of the best-selling whiskeys—including Rosenstiel's hated competitors—from San Jose to San Francisco.

I bought the company and renamed it Better Brands. I did a hell of a business and gave Schenley some tough competition in the Bay Area. Then I sold out to Seagram's at a handsome profit.

On another occasion I heard that the distributorship for Anheuser-Busch was up for grabs in San Francisco and Santa Clara counties. I went back to St. Louis and had a grand time being entertained by Anheuser and Busch. When I came back to California, I had the distributorship in my pocket. They *gave* it to me.

I sold their beer for a few years and made a nice piece of change. Then one day Gussie Busch called me from the Mark Hopkins Hotel and said he wanted to see me. I went over to see him and sold him back the franchise. Besides the profits I had earned, I pocketed a tidy $75,000 for my efforts.

Success in the liquor business is due in large part to the people you know, and I knew everybody. I knew more people in the state of California than any man alive.

One of my great and good friends was George Stout, the state liquor administrator of California. But don't get the wrong idea. George was a very honorable, straightforward, classy, decent kind of a guy. A real gentleman. He advised me on a number of things, and I gave him my counsel, too.

But I never asked him for any favors. I expected him to administer the liquor laws without preference to anyone—and he did.

George Stout was a sweetheart. In 1949, he was the host of the annual National Conference of State Liquor Administrators when they had their convention in San Francisco. He invited me to address his fellow members, and I was pleased to do so.

I told the distinguished visitors that it was high time that the alcoholic beverage industry of America "embark upon a campaign of offense to insure its perpetuation as an integral part of the economic and social life in America."

I explained how the professional Drys had brought every screwball and fanatic they could hire or subsidize into California for an all-out drive for Prohibition. How we secured a half-million signatures to place an opposing proposition on the ballot. How the big boys paid the bills and the little fellows did the work. How we carried the message to the public in every newspaper and on every radio station in the state of California. How we took over billboards and passed out handbills to warn against the Prohibition threat. And how we won the fight overwhelmingly.

"I think our public relations organizations must be something more than a fire department called in to put out a fire already started," I said. "We must not wait until we have been attacked to tell the public that our industry is a true cross section of the American religious, social, and economic life."

In outlining our own aggressive policies for the industry in California, I delivered my basic platform:

1. A reasonable margin of profit
2. A good night's sleep
3. Doors open in the morning
4. Impartial but just enforcement of all laws and regulations without favor to any individual.

At that time there were rumors in the trade that I was being considered as a top advisor in the national industry. I replied to that:

"Right here and now I want to go on record that I am very happy here in California. I am not interested in the best apartment on Park Avenue and all that goes with it. I say as emphatically as I can that I want no part of directing national policy.

"I hope this assertion will destroy once and forever any

report anyone may have heard in the past or may hear in the future that I am trying to play coy about accepting an invitation to go East. The industry is a big army and has enough brass hats. What we need is more people willing to do a job."

Just to emphasize my point, I closed with this statement:

"I'm sorry I won't be here to listen to the golden-tongued orators of the industry expound their paucity of ideas in a diarrhea of words. I'm sorry I won't be here to listen to butter-mouthed representatives of the bosses attempt to justify their junket to the Golden Gate.

"I really would like to hear their sycophantic fawning; their veiled insinuations; their oblique references to my remarks today.

"I am going back to Sacramento where the legislature is now meeting to do the best job I can for our California industry and our California people."

CHAPTER 16

Personal Notes Concerning Arthur H. Samish, Esq.

THE 1940s WERE BUSY YEARS FOR YOURS TRULY. MERCED AND I had two beautiful homes, one in San Francisco and a big spread down the peninsula. We had parties for two hundred, three hundred people, and I'd really put on a show for those folks. Always my dear mother was at the parties, and she loved to have people around.

When the legislature was in session, my home was Room 428 of the Senator Hotel, right across the street from the capitol. I had a big suite, and the icebox was always full of steaks and beer. I arose about eleven in the morning and studied reports from my staff about what was going on that day. There were about ten of them, and I'd give them their assignments.

Throughout the day and evening, they reported in to me and I'd be on the phone with clients and contacts all over the state. All over the country, in fact.

By eleven in the evening I finished my work and I went downstairs to the lobby of the Senator. There I'd be available to all comers until 4 A.M. If a senator had a problem with his campaign for reelection, I'd figure out how to help him. An assemblyman might stop by to ask my opinion about a piece of legislation. Judges, commissioners, cops, secretaries, reporters, clerks—I'd talk to them all. Bookies, too. I always kept a wad of bills in my pocket, just in case I had a hunch on a football game or a horse race.

I'd chat with my fellow lobbyists, men like Walter Little, who represented the railroads; Vince Kennedy of the retailers; Charlie Stevens, who lobbied for oil; Elmer Bromley, the power companies; Lynn Peterson, the American Legion and Eastside Brewery; Bob McKay, the teachers. They were all my buddies, and I'd give them advice when they asked for it.

We had a hell of a lot of fun. Every year I handed out membership cards to the other lobbyists. I figured we should be organized, just like everyone else. So I printed up cards that read:

California State Federation of Labor
— A.F. of L. —

This is to certify that

____

is a member in good standing of
LOBBYIST UNION NO. 1
for the regular session
of the California Legislature

The card was signed by Arthur H. Samish, President, and C. J. Haggerty, Chairman of the Executive Committee. Haggerty actually was the lobbyist for the AFL, and he went along with the gag.

On the other side of the card I had printed:

> OUR SLOGAN
>
> Government of the People, by the People, for the People, and with the People's Money
>
> OUR AIM
>
> To make the rich poor and the poor rich, divide the wealth and multiply income, tax the untaxed and untax the taxed, add the surtax and subtract the mistax, an acre of beans for every family and a garage to store them in sacks supplied by the State.

At the end of every legislative session we put on the legislative ball. The thirty-five biggest lobbyists in Sacramento contributed $100 apiece to put it on, but it was really my baby. I had Kent Redwine, who lobbied for the movie studios, send a bunch of stars up from Hollywood to put on the entertainment. The ball was held in the Governor's Hall at the state fairgrounds.

All forty senators and eighty assemblymen attended with their wives. The governor and the heads of departments were invited, too. And Art Samish had charge of the seating arrangements. Those who were friends got ringside seats in front of the entertainment. Those who had failed to display their friendship found themselves seated behind a potted palm.

During the war I pulled a stunt which gave me a lot of satisfaction.

You'll remember that liquor was in short supply during the war. This made it tough on soldiers and sailors who might have weekend passes and wanted drinks to have parties with. They often ended up paying black market prices or buying rotgut because they couldn't find good liquor.

So I established Military Bottle Shops. One was right in the Senator Hotel in Sacramento, three in Oakland, one at Vallejo near the Marine base, one in San Francisco, a couple in Los Angeles. Only military personnel could buy bottles, and they paid the regular price, nothing extra.

How did I get the liquor in those rationed times? I got it. I told the distillers they had to supply cases. If they didn't come through, I'd advertise to the trade that they weren't cooperating. They came through.

The stores stayed open only from five to eight in the evening, and the soldiers and sailors would be lined up around the block to get in. The other liquor stores squawked like stuck turkeys, but that didn't bother me any. I wasn't making any money from the shops.

I gave the management of the shops to deserving people. The president of the Military Bottle Shop at Tenth and K streets in Sacramento was Tony the newsboy. A fine young man, Tony. He was devoted to his mother, who worked in a cannery to help support them—Tony was crippled. After I gave him the shop, his mother was able to quit her job, and she and Tony were set up for life.

There were others, too. Frances the chambermaid, who had taken such good care of me when I was sick at the Senator Hotel. Harry Hansen, who had been fired by McKesson and Robbins. Walter King, my pianist—I gave him a shop in Oakland.

I used those Military Bottle Shops for public relations. I remembered how the Prohis had used the First World War to make the country go dry. Each shop featured copies of news stories about bootlegger wars with the slogan "It Can't Happen Here." And each soldier and sailor was asked to sign a sheet with the following statement:

"We the undersigned members of the Armed Forces express our appreciation to distillers and wholesalers cooperating in maintaining this fair-price source exclusively for the benefit of servicemen. We trust our purchases of alcoholic beverages may continue and will not be prevented by any Prohibition Law."

When the legislature wasn't in session, I was traveling a great deal of the time. I loved to move around the country, see new places, make new friends. It was good business for me, too. My interests weren't confined to the state of California; it paid for me to know businessmen and politicians elsewhere.

Wherever I went, I liked to have fun and frolic around me. That's why I often took Walter King along. Walter was master of the piano, and he could liven up a convention of undertakers. Walter never knew what to expect when I gave him a call. One day I told him to bring his whole band to the airport at San Francisco. When he and his seven musicians arrived there, I told them we were going to Alaska. The governor was having a shindig, and I wanted them to supply the music. We had a great couple of days up there.

My travels during those years took me all over. To Florida, where I stayed with Joe Schenck. To Hot Springs, Arkansas, for the baths. To Louisville for the Kentucky Derby.

I spent a great deal of time in New York, visiting Lewis Rosenstiel and other eastern clients. I even dabbled a bit in New York politics. Some of the liquor interests asked me if I could help the campaign of William O'Dwyer for Mayor. I was glad to. I gave him some advice on how to raise money and how to conduct the campaign. After the election I visited him at Gracie Mansion, and he expressed his gratitude.

I enjoyed the night life in New York City, and one of the places I frequented was the Copacabana. Jack Entratter, who ran the place, became a good friend, and I decided to help him out. Like every other night club during the war, the Copa was having trouble getting liquor. I saw to it that five hundred cases of I. W. Harper bourbon were delivered to the Copa.

There was one thing people couldn't understand about me. Here I represented the liquor industry and I was around parties all the time. But I never took a drop myself.

That wasn't always so.

When liquor was forbidden during Prohibition, I decided I needed it. I tossed down quite a few gallons of sour mash whiskey in my day. I drank because I liked to drink. No other reason.

But when liquor became legal again, I quit drinking. I'll tell you how it happened.

Tom Wilson, who was president of the Alaska Steamship Company, had a job he wanted me to do. It seems the United States government had appropriated some money to build a new ship to supply Alaska. Tom didn't want the competition. He asked me if I could do something about it.

I decided to go up there and look over the situation. So Doc Winkelman and I took one of Tom's ships up to Juneau, and we had a great time. We flew over to look at the glaciers, and I bought a camera and took pictures over everything in sight. I took more goddam pictures of those big dogs up there than you can imagine.

I also did some work for Tom Wilson. I calculated the number of ships that went in and out of Juneau and the other Alaskan ports, and the total indicated that more shipping wasn't needed. We sent a man off to Washington with the information, and the government changed its mind about appropriating money for a ship.

The time came for Doc and me to leave Alaska, and we decided to have a party on shipboard for all the friends we had made. Oh, it was a wild one. Tom Wilson was sailing back to San Francisco with us, and he brought to the party the governor's grass-widow daughter that he was sweet on. I was pretty damn stiff, and I pinched her cheek so hard that it left a black-and-blue mark. Tom was so mad that he wouldn't talk to me or Doc all the way back to San Francisco.

That's when I decided to quit drinking.

After I got home, I went to the Russian River near San Francisco Bay to sort of rest up. I took Walter King along, and he played the accordion while we canoed down the river drinking beer. I've never had a taste of alcohol since. Never missed it, either.

I quit smoking, too.

I used to smoke three or four packs of cigarettes a day. Then one day I was having trouble breathing, and I went to see Dr. Joe Zeiler. He examined me and said, "Art, you've got to cut down on the cigarettes."

"I can't cut down," I said.

"Well, you've got to, or your health is going to suffer."

"Okay, Doc," I said. I took the pack of cigarettes from my pocket and sailed it out the window. That was forty years ago, and I haven't had a puff since.

For about twenty years I had a Christmas ritual that I organized and carried out by myself. It took place at San Quentin.

I felt sympathy for the prisoners. I always used to say that the only difference between them and us is that they got caught.

Every Christmas I'd get together a truckload of goodies. I'd have thousands of cigarettes, cigars, candies, phonograph records, miniature photographs I had bought myself in Europe, turkeys, and other kinds of treats for the prisoners. I took along Walter King to play the piano, and maybe a magician or a comedian or a tap dancer to entertain. Also movies of the latest prizefights.

My caravan started out for San Quentin early in the morning, and we stayed all day, handing out treats to the prisoners, entertaining them, and even conducting a crap game or two.

When the day was over, I insisted that everyone leave the hall but the inmates. Then I told them they could write out any message to someone on the outside, and I would see that it was telegraphed that day. I hoped that they would send Christmas greetings to their mothers. But it didn't matter. They could send the message to someone else they loved—or hated. Either way, I would get the message through, and only I would read it.

After the party, I went back to my office in San Francisco and had the messages typed up for the telegraph office.

I always had a concern for the unfortunates in prison, and I visited other penitentiaries as well. I remember one time when I was looking around at Folsom, and I stopped to get a shoeshine from one of the colored prisoners.

Along came a big, red-faced guard, and he started bawling the bejesus out of the prisoner and calling him all kinds of bad names.

"Just a minute, my good fellow," I said to the guard, "there's no reason to talk so rudely to this gentleman."

"You keep outa this," the guard shouted. "This is between me and this stinkin' nigger."

"I don't like to hear that kind of talk," I insisted.

"Yeah? Whadda ya gonna do about it?"

What I did about it was to go back to Sacramento and look up the appropriation for penal institutions in the state budget. That guard's salary was stricken from the budget.

CHAPTER 17

The Warren Years Bring Continued Prosperity to the Art Samish Enterprises

IN 1942 CULBERT OLSON WAS DEFEATED FOR GOVERNOR BY EARL Warren, and that was all right with me. I was on Warren's side. I had known him since he was clerk of the Judiciary Committee, and I was just a little shaver in Sacramento. I followed his career as district attorney of Alameda County and as attorney general of California. He was a decent sort, with a pleasant smile and a hearty handshake. Earl was ambitious. But then show me the politician who isn't.

As governor, Earl Warren didn't give me any trouble, and I didn't trouble him. As a matter of fact, I would pitch in and help him when I could. Like when he tried to raise the gasoline tax so the state could build new highways. Naturally the oil lobby put up a terrific fight on that one. I helped the governor push the gasoline tax through.

Earl and I didn't always agree, and one time he vetoed a bill that I had been promoting.

"What's wrong with the bill, Governor," I asked him.

Warren gave a detailed analysis of his objections to it.

"All right, Governor," I told him, "if that's the way you feel about it, I'll give you another bill."

So I whipped up another version of the same bill and had it passed by the legislature and placed on the governor's desk for him to sign. Which he did.

Warren had it easy during the war years. California was booming with war plants and military bases, and the governor could play the hero by reducing taxes and still run up a surplus. He was so popular that he won both the Republican and Democratic primaries in 1946 and ran unopposed in the final election, the only governor in history to do so. That was a neat trick when you consider that Warren was a Republican and the majority of California voters were Democrats.

The Warren years were busy ones for Art Samish and his multifarious enterprises. Some of my assignments were extremely interesting.

Once I had the state of Nevada for a client. At least I presumed the state of Nevada was hiring me; I never asked questions like that. This big lawyer from Reno came to me, a man named Woodburn, and he said he was concerned about a proposed law that would have made it easier to get married in California. At that time there was a two-day wait, and the couple had to get blood tests and go through a lot of red tape. But if the same couple went to Nevada, they could get married right away. The Nevada wedding industry would have been ruined by the proposed bill.

I'm a man who believes in the sanctity of marriage. If the California law made quickie weddings more difficult, I was in favor of it. The proposed change in the marriage law was defeated. The state of Nevada—or whoever paid my fee—was extremely grateful.

Another of my clients was Philip Morris. I not only took good care of it, but the entire cigarette industry as well.

How? By keeping the cigarette tax out of California.

Three governors tried to convince the legislature to institute a cigarette tax. At one time Governor Warren argued that forty-one other states in the nation taxed cigarettes. But he wasn't able to sell the legislature. As long as I represented Philip Morris, California never had a cigarette tax.

Sometimes I didn't get paid for assignments. Take the Stoneson deal. This fellow named Stoneson presented me with his problem: he had a big piece of real estate which he wanted to develop for a huge shopping center south of San Francisco on the ocean side. But the state of California also had its eyes on the property and had started proceedings to condemn it for a college.

"I'll see what I can do," I told Mr. Stoneson.

It wasn't a pushover assignment, because the state was dead set on having the property for the college. When the time came for a vote on the bill, one legislator just happened to be absent. The bill died. Poor bill.

And so Stonestown was able to develop it into a shopping center worth millions of dollars. And how much did Artie earn for his efforts?

Not a dime.

Mr. Stoneson died shortly after the vote in the legislature. I hadn't asked for a retainer, but had expected to be paid after the job was done. I didn't fret over it.

There were a lot of times when I performed my wiles for no reward whatsoever. For instance . . .

One year a move was under way to legalize dog racing in California. Since none of my clients was involved, I didn't give a damn whether they raced horses, dogs, or mice in the state. But a lot of powerful people did.

One of them was my old friend Charlie Strub of Santa Anita. He was scared those doggies were going to cut into his take, and he wanted to make sure that the bill didn't pass. But he didn't know how to go about it because he knew I was mad at him. So he sent an intermediary.

Joe Schenck, who was the head of Twentieth Century-Fox, asked me one day: "How would you like a big diamond?"

"Now what would I want with a big diamond?" I asked.

"Doc Strub wants to give you one."

"He does, does he?"

"Yes, Artie. He wants you to do something about that dog-racing bill."

"You can tell Doc Strub what he can do with his diamond."

"Yes, I know you don't like him. But it isn't only the race-tracks that don't want dog racing, Artie. The picture business doesn't want it, either. It would keep people away from the theaters."

"Are you telling me that *you* don't want that dog-racing bill passed, Joe?"

"That's right, Artie."

"Then that sheds a different light on the matter."

I need not add that dog racing never became legal in California.

Such assignments were mere diversions in the life of a lobbyist. My base of operations remained the brewers and the liquor industry. They paid me handsomely, and I served them well.

I kept track of everything. All the liquor ads in the state came across my desk. If I found anything that I thought would reflect ill on the liquor industry, I had the advertisement killed. I watched all the newspapers in California. When I found evidence that the liquor industry was being poorly treated in the news columns and editorials, I lodged a protest. If the offenses continued, I pulled out the Schenley ads and any others I could influence.

My kind of operation required complete cooperation. For instance, the billboards. They were an important part of our campaigns for legislators and ballot propositions. Most of the industry gladly provided the use of the billboards during election campaigns. But there were a few backsliders. In those cases, I had photographs taken of the billboards which were not made available, and I circulated those photographs to all members of the industry. The holdouts came through.

They realized I was watching out for their best interests. There could be no doubt of it. One of my lawyers, Emile Hoerchner, counsel for the Brewers Institute, wrote every liquor law passed in the state of California.

Maintaining such control required a friendly atmosphere in the legislature. How did I achieve such friendliness? That gets us back to the Samish System of Politics:

Select and Elect.

CHAPTER 18

In Which I Reveal for the First Time the Samish Technique of Selecting and Electing

IN THE BEGINNING WAS THE FIVE-CENT FUND.

That was my base of operations, and what a sweet, lovin' thing it was! The brewers slapped that five-cent assessment on every barrel of beer that was brewed in the state of California, and they handed it over to Artie to do with as he saw fit.

I did right by them. I put their nickels to good use. They never questioned what I did with the fund, and I never told them. All they had to know about was the results. And when the industry isn't taxed, even when the state is going deeply into debt as it did some years, then you know that the Keeper of the Fund is providing results.

The selection of candidates was something I didn't leave to chance.

I told you about the black books I kept on every candidate. I mean I had everything about a politician in his book—the names of his clubs and fraternities, whether he liked Scotch or bourbon, his religion, family life, hobbies, and so forth. One of my secretaries did nothing else but clip and file newspaper stories which included every public utterance of every legislator and candidate for the legislature in the state of California. I included absolutely everything, including whether a man had been arrested for anything, even a traffic violation.

The black book was my Bible. It told me just how to proceed with each lawmaker, where his strong and weak points were, how he could be approached on matters concerning the interests of my clients.

Mainly, I depended on my Gestapo to feed me information. I couldn't be everywhere, and indeed, some weeks I scarcely stirred from my headquarters, Samish Alley in the Hotel Senator. The detail work was carried out by my staff, those bright and attentive people who attended legislative and committee sessions and reported back to me. When I had messages to impart to certain senators and assemblymen, I often sent them via my trusted aides, Frank Flynn and Bill Jasper. They performed ably as my pipelines to the capitol. They knew my desires so well that they could make field decisions by themselves. But the major policy could be set by myself alone.

The one great essential for my mode of operation was to see that the right candidates got elected.

This fellow Rusco who wrote his Ph.D. dissertation about me said in his paper: "Samish conducted his candidate campaigns with a degree of organization and sophistication which overshadowed the efforts of partisan organizations in the two decades in question [1930–1950]. He had better financing and a statewide plan of action, and he probably employed more experienced campaigners on a year-in, year-out basis than either of the major parties."

I can't argue with that. I did have a hell of an organization. The Republicans and the Democrats had nothing. The Hiram Johnson system of cross-filing and nonpartisan local elections kept party activity at a minimum. Every candidate was on his own. He needed help wherever he could get it. And he got it from Art Samish—provided the candidate had been selected by me.

Every two years—assemblymen faced election every two years; state senators every four—I put the Fund to work. I started at the Oregon border and worked down to Mexico, studying each assembly district and those senate seats that were up for election.

My two lieutenants did the legwork. Frank X. Flynn handled Northern California, and William Jasper operated in Southern California. I gave each of them a handy sum to begin with, say about $10,000, and they spread the money where it would do the most good. They dealt mostly in cash, because the candidates preferred it that way. We never asked for receipts.

The campaign contributions ranged from $250 to $1,500 in most cases. But if there happened to be a hot campaign where one of my selected candidates was running against a Dry, then the Fund might pour $10,000 to $20,000 into the fight.

I preferred to lay out the money for specific costs, so that I knew where it was going. A printing bill here. A headquarters rental there. The cost of a rally or radio announcements. That sort of thing.

The billboards were provided free of charge, courtesy of the brewers and liquor dealers. I kept the industry unified for maximum political results. Here is a copy of a letter I sent to the liquor retailers:

> To the Industry:
>
> As the time of the general election, November 7, draws near, campaigns of candidates for various political offices and initiative propositions will intensify.
>
> We urge you to make no contributions, make no commitments, permit no solicitation, financial or otherwise, for your support of any candidate or proposition.
>
> An industry-wide committee is now making a careful survey.

> This committee will report to the industry association of which you are a member.
>
> Every advantage you now enjoy in California has been made possible because a united industry stood solidly behind its leaders. . . .

When we decided on which candidates would be good for the industry, the retailers were notified. Letters were sent with the name of the assembly or senate candidate and the instructions: "We must contact our employees, our patrons, our families and relatives, our friends, and their friends and inform them of the urgent necessity for voting for this outstanding and excellent candidate. Let's make sure that our industry is protected!"

Sometimes we'd step right in and run a campaign for a candidate. Take the case of Hugh Burns.

Burns was running for the state senate from Fresno in 1942, and he seemed like a good man for our cause. "I'm not going to make a campaign contribution," I told him. "You're no good to me unless you're in Sacramento. So I'm going to see that you get there."

I assigned a bright young fellow, a man who later became a newspaper editor in Northern California, to be Burns's campaign manager. I paid the bills for newspaper ads, radio announcements, handbills. And Burns was elected.

We had ways of rewarding our friends and punishing our enemies. For instance, there was Senator Jack Metzger of Redding. I had helped him get elected and he seemed like a cooperative man. But after he became chairman of the Government Efficiency Committee, he started doing things that I didn't like. He was a smart aleck, and I told him, "You go on like this, Jack, and you're going to be defeated at the next election."

He went on like that, and he was defeated.

Senator Ralph Swing was a good friend over the years. He

was from San Bernardino, and I considered him the best mind in the legislature. A brilliant constitutional lawyer. But one year when he was chairman of the Government Efficiency Committee, he got in my way.

All of a sudden he wasn't chairman of the Government Efficiency Committee any more. I didn't make any move to defeat Ralph Swing in the elections, because I considered him too able a man. I was sure he would see the error of his ways.

He did. Ralph became his old self again, and we were pals once more.

Most of my candidates were Republicans. Some of my biographers have noted that I was a registered Republican and concluded that I possessed some party loyalty. Baloney. I never cared whether a politician was a Republican or a Democrat or a Whig. All I cared about was whether he was good for the interests of my clients.

It so happened during all the years I operated in Sacramento that, except for the Olson period of 1938–1942, the Republicans held the power. That's what I cared about—power. No matter which party it belonged to.

The peculiar politics we had in California kept the Republicans in power. The state senate was nearly always strongly Republican. The reason was simple: no county could have more than one senator. So the big urban centers which were predominantly Democratic had only one senator apiece. The cow counties, which leaned to the Republicans, had one senator apiece. A few of the smaller ones, like Inyo, Mono, and Alpine, were combined into one senatorial district. Those three had 15,000 residents in 1960, and one senator to represent them. Los Angeles County had seven million residents, and one senator to represent them.

Cross-filing also helped the Republicans.

In 1944, 90 percent of the candidates for the state senate won in the primary by taking the election in both parties. Eighty percent of the assemblymen also won their seats in the primary.

Republican campaigns were usually better financed and better organized than the Democratic ones. Also, Republicans were more apt to vote in the primaries than the Democrats.

Cross-filing was a great asset to the Samish System of Selecting and Electing. A great deal of money was saved by campaigning in only one election, rather than facing both the primary and the general elections. And it was easier to sway public opinion when a smaller vote was cast. In 1944, 86 percent of the registered voters cast their ballots in the general election, but only 56 percent voted in the primary.

Supposing I had a Republican running for assembly in a predominantly Democratic district. It might have been possible to see that a weak Democrat was nominated opposite him. Or maybe a number of Democrats, so the vote would be split and our Republican would win the Democratic nomination.

Naturally there was no problem about our man getting the Republican nomination. We wouldn't waste our time with that. We concentrated on the Democratic primary.

We could make our Republican look like a God-fearing, dues-paying Democrat. None of the campaign literature would identify him as a Republican. We sent circulars to the Democratic voters making him out to appear like one of them.

Chicanery was our middle name.

CHAPTER 19

Some More Adventures in the Political Trade, Including a Hello and a Good-bye to Mexicali Rose

ONCE IN A GREAT WHILE I TURNED MY ATTENTION FROM THE election of the legislature to campaigns for other offices. Not often. I didn't like to waste my time on unimportant things. The legislature made the laws that affected my clients, and that was my all-abiding concern.

In 1946 I got involved in the race for attorney general of California. This was because a couple of my "boys" wanted to run for it.

One of them was Fred Napoleon Howser. I gave him his start in politics when a liquor wholesaler recommended him to me for the assembly. I met Howser at the Elks Club in Long Beach, and he seemed to be a pleasant, able man. I backed his campaign, and in 1940 he was elected to the assembly. He remained grateful, and I maneuvered him into the chairmanship of the Public Morals Committee.

One day four of the five supervisors of Los Angeles County paid me a call. They were looking for someone to sponsor a bill that would raise their salaries. Not the usual way. They wanted to be appointed flood control commissioners in addition to their supervisor offices, and thus receive an extra salary.

I made it a firm policy never to accept a fee for legislation on behalf of a public agency. But I was always willing to offer advice to friendly parties.

"Why don't you get Fred Howser to handle your bill?" I suggested.

The supervisors accepted my suggestion, and their bill passed. On that same day, John Dockweiler, district attorney of Los Angeles, died. The county supervisors were charged with appointing a successor. Their choice: Fred Napoleon Howser.

Fred's middle name seemed just right for him, because he was always seeking more power. In 1946 he came to me and said he wanted to move up to attorney general.

At the same time Assemblyman Sam L. Collins of Orange County told me he wanted to run for attorney general. Sam was also one of my protégés, and I didn't want to disappoint him.

Howser or Collins?

It didn't take me long to figure out the answer. During Earl Warren's first term (1942–1946), California had had a very popular and able lieutenant governor named Fred Houser. I knew the voting public wouldn't be able to differentiate between Fred Houser and Fred N. Howser, so I told Howser that he should run for attorney general.

But what about Sam Collins?

"You can be Speaker of the Assembly," I told Sam. By God, that's what happened. Fred Napoleon Howser was elected attorney general, and Sam Collins became Speaker of the Assembly.

Later I had reason to regret both choices. When the going got rough, Sam Collins pretended he'd never heard of me. As for Fred Howser, I got him elected, but I didn't know he had all that funny money behind him. Some of his top assistants tried to muscle in on gambling rackets in the state, and they got caught at it.

Howser was in hot water, and he came to me for help.

I let him cool his heels outside my suite in the Senator Hotel for a couple of hours, then let him inside. I was having a nice, friendly lunch with thirty of the legislators, and I expressed my displeasure.

"What are you doing here, you lovin' bastard," I told the attorney general. "Don't ever let me see your lovin' face again."

Fred Napoleon Howser was wise enough not to try to run for attorney general again.

I hardly ever dabbled in municipal elections. Why the hell should I? The state makes the laws that affect the liquor industry, not the cities. I had long before removed the fangs of any local option threats. Municipal elections were only a playtoy for me.

In 1947 I did get involved in the election of Elmer E. Robinson for mayor of San Francisco. I had known Robinson since he had been a municipal judge, and I thought he would make a good mayor.

Letters went to tavern owners and hotel operators telling them: "You must vote. Your employees must vote. Your families must vote. Your friends and their friends must vote. Vote for Judge Robinson for Mayor."

Placards for Robinson were sent to every bar in San Francisco. Beer and liquor ads came down from billboards, and up went signs telling citizens: "Elect Judge Robinson Mayor of San Francisco." They did.

Since San Francisco was my hometown, I sometimes couldn't resist taking part in the local elections, even though the outcome meant nothing to my operations in Sacramento. Usually I became involved out of friendship, as in the case of Elmer Robinson.

Another good friend was George Schonfeld. George and I went way back to the Kotycks Club together. I had great admiration for George. He was a poor boy, just like me, and he had made his way up in the world the hard way. He had studied law and had been admitted to practice by the Supreme

Court of California; in those years a lawyer could get started that way instead of passing the bar. George was a damned good attorney. He was appointed deputy district attorney and then decided to run for judge. I told him I'd help him get elected.

The law establishment didn't like the idea of George's candidacy. Even though he was perfectly well qualified, the bar members didn't want a judge who hadn't passed the usual procedures for becoming a lawyer.

The Big Boys tried to put the squeeze on me. One of them told me: "Artie, pick anybody you want who's a graduate of the University of California, and we'll see that he gets the judgeship."

That's all I needed to make me more determined than ever to see that George Schonfeld got elected. I hired a radio announcer named Stew Stewart, who had a voice that could sell sand to Arabs. Stewart went on the air and told about how George had to study law while he was earning a living; he couldn't afford to go to law school. Then Stewart reminded his listeners of another young American who had to study law on his own because he couldn't afford to go to school, a fellow named Abraham Lincoln.

Oh, it was a grand fight. Not only the bar, but the entire political organization of San Francisco, headed by Tom Finn, was against George. But he won. After all, how could the citizens vote against Abe Lincoln?

The fellow who was defeated by George was Pete Mullins. Now I had nothing against Pete; in fact, I found him to be an affable, capable fellow. I ended up getting him elected, too.

It was at the Firemen's Ball, I remember. The Mullins sisters got me in a corner and asked if I would help their brother win a judgeship. I never could resist the ladies, so I agreed to support him. The race wasn't easy, because Pete was running against an incumbent. Nobody could remember when an incumbent had been unseated from the bench.

This particular incumbent was a man I didn't like, so I had an extra pleasure in removing him from office. It was a tough campaign, but Pete won.

One of my most interesting escapades with the political breed should be told with a musical background. A few bars of "Mexicali Rose," Professor . . .

The story begins in 1936. Down in a Los Angeles district there was a popular assemblyman named Ralph Evans. He decided not to run for reelection, and a number of would-be politicians scrambled to fill his position. Most of the lobbyists put their support behind one prominent party worker, and I went along with them.

But then, about ten days before election, my Gestapo brought me some information about this particular candidate which I found disturbing. I telephoned my Southern California man, Bill Jasper.

"We gotta dump the son of a bitch," I told Bill. "Talk to all the other candidates and find out which is the best man."

Jasper invited the other candidates to visit our office in the Biltmore Hotel. They were a scroungy bunch. One of them wanted to out-Townsend Townsend, the doctor who was trying to tap the treasury for pensions for old folks. Another one was hot for the Single Tax. Only the last candidate Jasper interviewed showed any promise.

"His name is Jack Tenney and he's a nice-looking guy," Jasper reported to me.

"Why is he running for the legislature?" I asked.

"He says he's only doing it because he wants publicity. He just passed the bar."

"He sounds okay. Know anything else about him?"

"Oh, yes—he plays the piano, and he wrote a song called 'Mexicali Rose.' "

" 'Mexicali Rose,' huh? I like that song. I'll come down there and talk to him."

I rode the Southern Pacific Lark to Los Angeles that night, and the next day I interviewed Jack Tenney at the Biltmore. He seemed like an affable fellow.

"What did you do before you studied for the law?" I asked him.

"I played piano in a whorehouse in Mexicali," he admitted.

I had to laugh. "Jack, you'll make a good legislator," I told him.

We went to work to get him elected. It so happened that the candidate who had lost my support also had the first name of Jack. So it was a simple matter to plaster Tenney's last name over the other fellows on all the billboards I had arranged.

This was 1936, when the popularity of Franklin Delano Roosevelt was at its peak. Naturally we had to cash in on that.

The other candidate had the official Democratic endorsement, but that didn't stop us. Bill Jasper had a newspaper friend who worked in the National Press Club Building in Washington, D.C. Bill sent his friend bundles of letters to be mailed from Washington in official-looking envelopes.

Every voter in the district got a letter from the National Democratic Committee in Washington endorsing Jack Tenney as the man to carry on the good work of President Roosevelt.

It didn't matter that there was no such thing as the National Democratic Committee (the party was run by the Democratic National Committee). It didn't matter that an assemblyman would have little to do with carrying on the programs of FDR.

What mattered was getting Jack Tenney elected.

We only had ten days, and we tried everything! We had painters stencil signs on the streetcorners:

ELECT PRESIDENT ROOSEVELT'S CANDIDATE—
JACK TENNEY

Jack Tenney won in a landslide.

He hardly knew what had hit him. He came to me in a daze and asked me: "What'll I do now?"

"What'll you do?" I said. "You're on your own now, Jack. I just want you to go up to Sacramento and be a good legislator."

He seemed like an eager fellow, and I saw to it that he drew some very important committee assignments. Very important. He was an eager worker, and he learned fast. He was developing into an astute assemblyman.

Except for one thing. Somehow he was getting his hands on bills that seemed rather questionable. One of the bills he introduced was a repeal of the Criminal Syndicalism Act. And there were others that seemed to favor the radical element.

Finally I asked him one day, "Jack, where are you getting these bills?"

"They come from constituents of mine," he told me.

"I don't think they're so smart. I think you should at least mark them 'Introduced by request,' so you aren't held responsible for them."

Tenney took the advice to heart, and he became more careful about the bills he took from his constituents.

After three terms in the assembly, Jack Tenney wanted to move up, and he filed for state senate from Los Angeles County. This was an important post; as the only senator from the county, he represented 43 percent of the state population. I still thought Jack Tenney was a reliable legislator, and I backed him in his successful campaign.

Something happened to Jack Tenney after he became senator. I'm not sure what the affliction was, but it might have been Headline Fever, a common ailment among politicians that can sometimes be fatal. In Tenney's case, it was.

Tenney got himself named as Chairman of the Un-American Activities Committee. He seemed to enjoy the position, and I thought it was a nice toy for him to have. I didn't care for the Communists, and if he was going to smoke some of them out, that was all right with me. None of that red-hunting business affected my clients' interests, and so I didn't pay it any heed.

For a guy who used to introduce bills that favored the leftists, Jack Tenney surely made an abrupt change. He saw reds under every bed. As a chaser of Communists, he made Martin Dies and Joe McCarthy seem like pinkos.

He completely lost all sense of proportion. I tried to kid him: "Catch any reds today, Jack?" He didn't think it was funny. He had become The Great Man.

He also became less and less cooperative in matters of legislation that I was concerned with. That was unfortunate—for him.

Senator Tenney continued with his investigations, and a lot of innocent persons were hurt by his shotgun blasts at political positions opposed to his. Many of them were in the movie business, where I had a lot of friends. The *San Francisco Chronicle* editorialized:

> . . . One of the Committee's troubles under Tenney's leadership was that it roamed and rambled into fields of character assassination and guilt by association which had nothing to do with overt subversiveness. Anyone who was in favor of overthrowing Tenney, as distinguished from overthrowing the Government, was likely to be hauled up and smeared by inquisition and innuendo. His methods have done more damage to the cause of intelligently combating Communism than almost any other influence in California. . . .

Jack Tenney had to go.

The opportunity came in 1949, when he issued a committee report that blasted everybody in sight. A bill was introduced in the assembly calling on the senate to remove Tenney as committee chairman. That night Tenney accused one of his assembly opponents of "being on sabbatical leave from the Communist Party." Obviously Tenney had flipped his wig.

Many of the legislators had been scared to fight Tenney because he would smear them as Communists. But when Speaker Sam Collins and Assemblyman Sam Yorty, both known anti-Communists, spoke out against Tenney, his goose was cooked. He saw the end coming and resigned as chairman. He was replaced by my good friend Hugh Burns of Fresno.

Guess who Jack Tenney blamed for his defeat?

Artie Samish, of course.

Tenney bellyached that Samish had succeeded in defeating his committee's program to curb Communism in California. All his loyalty oath bills had suffered death in the legislature and "there was no doubt what happened and who caused it to happen."

He didn't stop there. He introduced a bill to have me barred from the senate. Got it passed, too.

What a laugh that was! I never went to the senate. Why should I give one tinker's damn whether I was barred?

Jack Tenney hung around the senate for a few more years, but he was pretty much discredited. So much so that he decided to go back home and run for mayor of Los Angeles.

One of his sponsors was an acquaintance of mine named Maury Stravers. He visited me one day and made the flat statement that Jack Tenney was going to be elected mayor. The few hairs that I had left on my dome stood straight up in the air.

"I'll bet you one hundred dollars to one that Jack Tenney will not be elected," I told Stravers. "I'll also bet you that whoever loses this bet will have to push a peanut around the block of the Senator Hotel with his nose. And will have to run a hundred times around the lobby."

The confident Mr. Stravers accepted the bet. The voters of Los Angeles then demonstrated their wisdom in sending Jack Tenney down to inglorious defeat.

That left the bet to be collected, and I did it in grand style. The lobby of the Senator Hotel was decorated with banners and balloons. The place was jammed with people watching circus clowns do their stunts. A disreputable-looking piano player sat in the middle of the lobby playing "Mexicali Rose" on a beat-up old piano.

A running track had been laid out on the perimeter of the lobby. A doctor was in attendance—anyway, I had a fellow dressed up in operating clothes. For the bet-losing Stravers I supplied a running uniform of red-flannel underwear.

A gun went off, and Stravers started his run. After ten laps he took a dive, and the "doctor" gave him first-aid treatment. I excused him from the peanut pushing, out of the tenderness of my heart.

It was a grand show, enjoyed by everyone present. Mr. Jack Tenney, who was not present, did not enjoy it. But then, his enjoyment of life had soured somewhat after he decided to take on Art Samish.

Not much was heard from Jack Tenney after that. But then, I suppose he could always go back to playing "Mexicali Rose" on the piano.

CHAPTER 20

What the Doctor Did after Elections, and Some Public Recognition Thereof, Not Entirely Welcome

"OKAY," SAYS THE STUDENT IN POLITICAL SCIENCE, "SO YOU SElected and Elected. What happened after that?"

I'll tell you what happened after that.

The California legislature was a peculiar and complex institution, which nobody knew better than Art Samish. Legislators came, legislators went. They had their term or two, or ten. But always they were subject to the whims of the fickle voters. Only Art Samish remained. I had studied the legislature from my earliest days as a page, and I knew what made the mechanism work.

I also knew how to work the mechanism.

The organization of the legislature was a matter of great delicacy. First and foremost, there was the selection of the Speaker of the Assembly.

Consult almost any book on California politics and you will learn that the Speaker of the Assembly is ranked second only to the governor as the most powerful elective officer in the state. One expert wrote about the Speaker: "His power to control and direct legislation exceeds that of any other elective officer in the legislature."

Why is he so powerful? Because he appoints all committees and their chairmen, except for the Rules Committee, for which he appoints only the chairman. He also has the very important power of referring all bills to committee.

During my years as a lobbyist, I usually managed one way or another to assure myself that the Speaker of the Assembly was a friendly sort. With that friendship assured, it was quite natural for me to have the friendliest of representation on the committees that were important to my clients. Those committees were:

Public Morals: It had jurisdiction over alcoholic sales, racetracks, cigarettes, and other matters in which I had an interest.

Revenue and Taxation: Here originated the levies on such industries; hence it was vital for me to have friendly members.

These two were the main committees I cared about. But on occasion I would have legislation of a different nature which I wanted to promote or impede, in which case I would look into the membership of the corresponding committee.

The senate was a slightly different matter.

As I told you earlier, the lieutenant governor originally held the power of committee appointments. But my experience proved that procedure left too much to the element of chance, or political disaffection. So the appointment power was taken away from the lieutenant governor and placed under the control of a Senate Committee on Committees.

The two senate committees which were most important for my purposes were:

Governmental Efficiency: The counterpart of the Assembly Committee on Public Morals, with jurisdiction over liquor, racing, and so on.

Revenue and Taxation: Same as in the assembly.

Aside from assuring friendly committees, there were other safeguards. It helped to be friendly with the sergeants at arms, who could be accommodating about hurrying a piece of legislation through the procedure of the legislature. Or slowing it down, if necessary.

My kind of operation required knowing what was going on everywhere, at all times. My operatives attended all committee sessions and legislative meetings. In addition, all of the legislators spoke from microphones at their desks. These were fed into the Speaker's office. By rigging a telephone line into the Speaker's office, an outsider could listen in to what was happening on the assembly floor at all times.

Some of my critics have claimed that part of my power was in my control of the press. That's pure nonsense.

I had a great many friends among reporters, editors, and publishers, too. I even did a good turn for Mr. Hearst once, when he was worried about a harbor at Santa Monica. But I never counted on any newspaperman to "protect" me.

My attitude toward the press was to be as open as can be. I didn't give a goddam what they said about me. I knew some of what they printed was going to put me in a bad light. That didn't bother. I was courteous and nice to them at all times. Those reporters were darling boys, all of them.

I didn't go looking for publicity. In my line of work, it was sometimes just as well not to have any. But I didn't shy away from publicity, either.

So I wasn't unhappy in 1949 when Carey McWilliams came out in *The Nation* with his story, "The Guy Who Gets Things Done—Artie Samish, California's Uncrowned King." How could anybody object to being called a king, crowned or uncrowned?

There had been other articles about Art Samish before, but this was the first to attract nationwide attention. Here's how McWilliams analyzed the Samish methods:

The general pattern of Artie's operation is clear. When asked to represent a special interest group, his first step is to organize a trade association. The trade association, usually the alter ego of Arthur H. Samish, then retains Arthur H. Samish as its "public-relations counselor." "There is no difference," Artie once said, "between Arthur Samish and the Motor Carriers Association. I *am* the Motor Carriers Association."

Once he has a contract, Artie will obtain whatever legislation the association wants or repeal or amend obnoxious legislation. At this point the trade association usually decides that the services of Mr. Samish are indispensable. . . .

Artie, it should be noted, is a new-style political boss. Usually political machines are able to control the legislature by controlling the party. But in California both major parties have an extremely weak organization, and there are no party machines.

What Artie has done, therefore, is to convert the interest group into a political machine functioning independently of either party. From the lobbyist's point of view this represents a distinct improvement. A party machine can be challenged at the polls, but as long as Artie controls the interest groups, his power cannot be questioned. Theoretically the interest groups could dispense with his services, but it is easier, and probably cheaper, to deal with one master lobbyist than with a collection of party chiefs.

Each industry group and each of its members becomes a link in the political power of Arthur H. Samish. For example, there are 50,000 retail liquor outlets in California. The owners of these outlets are all political legmen for Artie; they are the "ward bosses" of his new streamlined machine.

In short, Artie uses the trade association as Pendergast once used a patronage machine. Patronage machines have a tendency to get out of hand—there are always minor rebellions, and the careerism of lieutenants can become bothersome—but Artie has no troubles of this sort. Most of the trade associations that he represents publish bulletins or journals, and Artie sees to it that the trade knows just as much as he thinks it should and no more about the industry's politics . . .

In the absence of party machines and given California's cross-filing system, he can nominate and elect candidates in many districts by the expenditure of nominal sums. He is very reluctant to make campaign contributions, for he knows the old California political pastime of running campaigns for a profit; he spends the money himself and thereby gets full value.

His power cannot be exposed, since the most powerful special-interest groups in the state are among his clients. For instance, Artie keeps up-to-the-minute files on the allocation of advertising space by his clients. If a newspaper becomes "unfriendly," the advertising can be promptly removed. Though Samish has been the undisputed boss of the California legislature for two decades, he has never been the subject of a newspaper exposé.

One of the keys to this man's influence is his ability to sell the police power of the state. California has been very active in regulating general business by statute. In 1907 it adopted an anti-trust act. Two years later the act was amended to provide that agreements and combinations are not illegal if their purpose is to insure a "reasonable" profit. The State Supreme Court then interpreted this provision to mean that manufacturers might set a price for commodities and require retailers to keep to it.

Finally, in 1933, the legislature adopted the Fair Trade Act, which put previous court rulings into the law and permitted firms suffering from price cutting to sue those which sold goods below the fixed price. This whole pattern of legislation developed earlier and has been carried further in California than in any other state, the marked instability of the state's economy having created a demand for all types of "stabilization" measures. Let a retailer cut the price of a bottle of bourbon by so much as a nickel, and his establishment will promptly be visited by state liquor officers. Artie, it will be noted, does not have to hold the retailers in line; the state does the policing.

But the real secret of Samish's astonishing political power is to be found in the economic diversity of California. Only New York can rival California in that respect. Where there are many interests to be served, there is always competition for favors. On the other hand, where a single interest is dominant, as, say, "copper" in Montana, the possibilities of political merchandising are narrowly limited. Agriculture in California is not "wheat" or "corn" or "cotton"; it is 214 different crops. "Banking" is, or was, Giannini versus the other bankers. "Medicine" does not mean merely "doctors and dentists"; it means osteopaths, chiropractors, naturopaths, Chinese herb doctors, and whatnot. Hence the fantastic "angling" which makes Sacramento a market where grapes and sardines, wines and race tracks, bid for power and preference. Other lobbyists do not waste time on the legislators: they deal directly with Artie. . . .

California's legislature really is a corporate state in which commodities, not people, are represented. Artie is the middleman between the business interests and the legislators; as he himself puts it, "I'm just a guy who gets things done." The power is really not in Artie; it is in a situation which he has learned to manipulate.

In his parvenu days Artie sported a belt with an enormous buckle on which the word ARTIE was spelled

> out in diamonds. Imagine a similar belt drawn tightly around the middle of California and you have an accurate symbolic representation of the power of Arthur H. Samish, California's nearly anonymous political boss.

The article in *The Nation* didn't affect me one way or another. The following month, *Collier's* came out with its stories by Lester Velie. After they appeared, Art Samish was no longer "nearly anonymous."

CHAPTER 21

Collier's Magazine Makes Art Samish the Not-so-secret Boss of California

WHEN LESTER VELIE CAME TO SACRAMENTO IN 1949, HE CAUGHT me at a good time to get his sensation-making story. I had been down in the dumps since my mother died. As I've told you, that wonderful woman meant everything to me. I could never repay her for the sacrifices she made for me, although I did everything I could to make her life happy and comfortable. It's a strange thing—after she died, I discovered she hadn't spent a lot of the money I had given her. I guess she figured that she could then help out if we were ever poor again. What a woman she was!

With Mother gone, I just didn't have the zest for the political chase that I had all those years. The thrill had gone out of it. I was getting tired of the twenty-four-hour grind of staying on top of everything that pertained to my clients. Maybe in the back of my mind I was looking for a way out.

Lucky for Lester Velie.

I knew he was coming. A friend of mine was Nate Gross, columnist on the *Chicago American.* He knew Louis Ruppel, editor of *Collier's,* and once a staff member of the *Chicago American.* The word passed along.

I had fun with Velie when he came to see me in Sacramento.

"I knew you were coming," I told him. "I also know what you've been studying about me. The Philbrick Report. The grand jury investigation. I know what you're going to do—you're going to chew my ass off."

Of course Velie protested that he wasn't planning to do any such thing, but he didn't fool me for an instant. I knew damn well what he was after. And, as long as he had come all the way across the country, I decided I'd send him back with a crackling good story.

Just in case he didn't believe how good my Gestapo was, I proceeded to tell him.

"I know what you've done since you arrived in Sacramento," I said. "You've talked to the governor, to the attorney general, to . . ." And I rattled off the name of every state official he had interviewed.

Velie's eyes kept getting wider as I told him about conversations he thought had been private.

"Now tell me this," I said. "Why did you ask the Board of Equalization whether I had taken George Stout to Florida and to the World Series?" George was the state liquor administrator.

"If you know about that, you must have a pretty good hold on that board," Velie remarked.

I didn't deny it. I even told Velie about conversations he'd had with senators and assemblymen, both in Sacramento and Los Angeles.

"You know," I said, "there's a politician waiting to see me right now. Right outside this office. He says you want to talk to him about me. And he's ready to swear that he hasn't seen me in two years."

I had a big laugh over that, and I told him, "You got to love me for telling you all this. You know, Artie's not such a bad kid."

I even told him how my Gestapo worked. I had twenty-five people stationed around the capitol, and they were truly undercover workers. Nobody knew they worked for me. In fact, they didn't even know each other.

Here's a story I told Velie:

A young man and a pretty girl were on my payroll as informants, covering legislative hearings. They became acquainted and he asked her for a date. She put that information down in her report.

The next time the young man reported to me, I asked him, "What do you mean by trying to date that young blonde in the senate chambers?" You should have seen the look on his face. He never had the slightest idea that the girl was working for me, too.

I gave Velie everything he wanted, and then some. And he printed it all. Boy, did he!

It was all there in his two articles, laid out in black and white. Running Fred Howser for attorney general. The "Road Hog" campaign. The brick-filled suitcases at the grand jury hearing. How I beat local option with the mother and her broom. The turndown of Cecil B. DeMille and Doc Strub. Jack Tenney and "Mexicali Rose." Of course I didn't give him everything. A lot of things he never knew about, because I was saving them for this book.

Lester Velie was even more overwhelmed by the Samish System than Carey McWilliams had been. Here are some of the comments about me in the *Collier's* article (which was reprinted in *Reader's Digest*):

> He has a master's grasp of the inner workings of the Legislature, knows its lawmaking machinery as intimately as, say, Toscanini knows the pieces in his symphony orchestra.
>
> To this chain of strength Samish has forged another link. It is California's Board of Equalization, a key state

agency which, his close friends as well as his critics will tell you, "is in the palm of Artie's hand" because Artie, the political powerhouse, can see to the election of its members.

The Board of Equalization administers the state liquor laws, and grants and revokes licenses. It has important discretionary powers over a wide range of taxes, and over assessments affecting vast corporations as well as sales taxes affecting small merchants. Its potentialities as a political pork barrel are second only to the state legislature. Samish can deliver both the board and the legislature.

All this came about because Samish is a practical man. Starting out as a lobbyist he found an easier way to persuade legislators than the method ordinarily employed.

Lobbyists usually perform the legitimate function of bringing their clients' interests to the attention of the lawmakers. Representatives of farmers' groups, teachers, labor and business interests have a recognized place in the state capitals and Washington. They appear before legislative committees and legitimately try to affect the shaping of legislation.

But Samish, a forthright and logical man, went right to the heart of his lobbyist's problem. The problem: to deliver legislation beneficial to his clients. Why bother with such chancy and indirect methods as marshaling arguments before legislative committees? Why not control the committees themselves?

Although he never got beyond the seventh grade in school and so never took geometry, Artie well knows the shortest distance between two points. The shortest distance to the control of committees and legislation is the control of legislators. Surest way to control a legislator: elect him. Artie Samish's system worked. . . .

Armed with a commanding block of votes, a friendly Speaker and key committees Artie is ready for all eventualities in the state legislature. But to deliver laws or kill them, Artie needs one more thing: insight and mastery of the obscure twists and turns, the detailed legal protocol by which a bill moves from the idea stage through the legislative hopper to become a law. This is known as *procedure.*

Listen to Artie:

"Procedure," he says, "is the secret of success around here. It's the one lovin' thing I know. There isn't a short cut around the place I don't know."

No one in California knows them as well. . . .

To get a bill through under normal procedure usually takes hearings, arguments, public debates, sponsors who are out in the open. Artie openly sponsors nothing. His is the power, *not* the glory.

"Samish never fronts for anything or anyone," says Samish.

Unlike a Hague or a Crump, against whom voters can occasionally rebel, Artie provides no visible target. How can you beat a man when you don't even know that he's there?

Operating in the shadows, he is so well hidden that it is only by patient and diligent sleuthing that an investigator can find that Samish is the man behind a candidate, the man who is masterminding a drive in the legislature, the man who's backing a referendum that means millions to some private interest or boosting a spate of laws that will work against a former employer. . . .

Samish rarely makes a political speech (although he can "stimulate 'em, bring 'em to white heat" when he tries). Even more rarely does he get into the papers.

And yet here is what three lifelong friends of Artie's, men whom I saw on Artie's own, earnest request, said of him:

One, a distinguished corporation lawyer—"Artie is a one-man Tammany Hall."

Another, a great California political strategist—"Artie

a political boss? Absolutely—he's more. More than any man in California, he can deliver the Legislature."

A third, a successful corporation lawyer and the author of a best-seller—"Artie's the real Governor of California. The Governor's only the Mikado. But Artie is the Great Shogun."

The man who is all these things will only describe himself as:

"Who, me? I represent industry. I'm a lobbyist, a public relations man."

This lobbyist label, like the stripe on a zebra, gives Artie protective coloration. It is the secret of why he remains California's secret boss. The zebra blends and disappears into a jungle backdrop. Artie blends into and loses his true identity as a political boss against a similarly lush growth—the lobbying at California's state capital at Sacramento. . . .

And there was more, much more. That fellow Velie didn't miss a thing, not a lovin' thing.

The trouble was, he couldn't tell when I was clowning. Like when I told him, "If you dropped a couple of bucks in the rotunda of the Capitol, you'd start a riot."

Or when I was having dinner with Velie and I hollered to the waiter, "Hey, Senator!"

Velie put it all down.

But it wasn't anything I said that had the biggest reaction from the *Collier's* articles. It was the answer that Governor Earl Warren gave when he was asked who had more influence over the legislature, the governor or Artie Samish.

The governor's reply:

"On matters that affect his clients, Artie unquestionably has more power than the governor."

CHAPTER 22

Open Season on Art Samish, and Other Hazards of the Political Life

AFTER THOSE *Collier's* ARTICLES APPEARED, YOU-KNOW-WHAT HIT the fan.

You never heard such a furor in your life. You would have thought I was a combination of Jack the Ripper and Attila the Hun.

I honestly was surprised. I knew the articles were going to have some sensations, but I never suspected that they would shake up the state from one end to the other. It wouldn't have been so bad if I had had a chance to review the articles before publication. After I had talked to Velie, I realized I had done a lot of clowning with him, as well as a lot of straight talk. Since he didn't know me well, he might not have been able to differentiate.

For instance, when I told him, "If you get a long enough ladder and put it up against the capitol dome, you can get a picture of me unscrewing the gold cupola."

A month before the articles appeared, I wrote him for permission to look over the articles "to make certain there will be no misunderstanding or that no wrong construction will be placed on the pictures or the text which might reflect derogatorily on the California legislature."

Velie and *Collier's* did not grant me that privilege, and the articles appeared in the issues dated August 13 and 20, 1949.

The state was in an uproar. Not just the state—the entire nation. Earl Warren was an important figure in national politics, having run for vice president in 1948, when the opinion polls elected Tom Dewey as president but the voters decided on Harry Truman.

Large numbers of legislators rose up in righteous wrath to denounce me and deny that they had ever so much as shaken my hand. I had defamed them and the legislature, they claimed.

Earl Warren was getting his lumps, too. A Republican representative from San Francisco said in Congress that *Collier's* had quoted Warren as saying I was more powerful than he was. The congressman added: "California can and must be relieved of this terrible stigma by the election of a Governor who will carry into effect the policies laid down by the late Hiram W. Johnson. . . . Would to God California could have another Governor fashioned after Hiram W. Johnson." To which I would have added: Amen!

Well, I was denounced here and denounced there, and denounced all over place. But, oddly enough, I did have a few supporters.

The *Sacramento Union* wasn't taken in by all the oratory, and it editorialized:

> The article in *Collier's* Magazine about "the man who secretly controls the state" is a disservice to California. It leaves the impression that constituted authority has broken down, and that a lobbyist, Arthur H. Samish, need only turn thumbs down or thumbs up on any undertaking and that he can determine its fate.

Arthur Samish is a powerful lobbyist, whose power stems from the fact that the people elect representatives to the Legislature who will do his bidding. When the people get tired of such a set of circumstances, they need only elect others, and the change will be brought about.

But Art Samish is not the menace that he was pictured to be in the article. There are greater menaces to the welfare of California, by far, than this lobbyist. There are, for instance, the sworn enemies of the Collier-Burns highway program who have dedicated their lives and fortunes to the destruction of the Governor and his administration; there is the gambling element in the State, which reaches into the statehouse and causes weak men to do their bidding, who are constantly undermining due process in an effort to break down law enforcement machinery; there are those who would destroy California's Constitution, and set up in its place and stead a more pliable document which would serve their own selfish purposes. There are men in the statehouse when the Legislature is in session who go about their own bailiwicks with pious mien and holier-than-thou expressions, but who sabotage measures to curb slot machines in California.

Samish is a lobbyist who represents special or vested interests, and he represents them well. There are other lobbyists to represent other interests, and if it were not Samish it would be someone else, for, under our system of government, business and industry and agriculture need protection from the lawmakers, and employ lobbyists or special representatives to afford that protection.

Collier's account of lawmaking in California is much like the tourist who spends two weeks in Europe and comes back with an expert opinion of what's wrong on the continent.

My favorite reaction to the whole uproar came from a man

I didn't know. He was M. S. Slocum of Pasadena, and he wrote this letter to the *Los Angeles Times:*

> In reference to the article in *Collier's* telling of the magnificent job Artie Samish is doing in Sacramento for his clients, it is our idea that we might make better use of Mr. Samish's exceptional ability. We propose the following:
>
> 1—That we, the people, hire Mr. Samish as our lobbyist at an annual salary of $1,000,000. He will henceforth be known as "the people's lobbyist." To those who may think that this proposed salary is too large, we would point out that if Mr. Samish saved his client—the people—in proportion to what he is now saving his present clients, he would be cheap at double the price.
>
> 2—We would further require that all lobbyists register with Mr. Samish, listing clients and submitting all bills that they wanted passed so that Mr. Samish could be sure that they did not conflict with the interests of his client—the people. These lobbyists would each pay an annual fee of $10,000 to the State, which would soon pay the salary of Mr. Samish.
>
> 3—As all bills would pass through the hands of Mr. Samish, the Legislature would only have to be in session a few days per year—just long enough to rubber stamp Mr. Samish's bills, a practice at which they have doubtless become proficient.
>
> 4—The Governor is quoted as saying, "On matters that affect his clients, Artie Samish has more power than the Governor." This clearly indicates that we would no longer need a Governor, thus eliminating his salary.
>
> This is just a sample of the advantages of appointing Mr. Samish as the people's lobbyist.

Now *that* was an assignment I would have relished. In fact, I would have done it for nothing.

Unfortunately, Mr. Slocum's proposal didn't get a hearing. The legislators were too busy ranting about what a menace Artie Samish was.

What was I doing during all this fuss? Business as usual. People didn't realize that the legislative portion of my job was only a fraction of my activities. I was still busy taking care of my clients' interests in other areas as well.

Naturally the reporters came around to see me, and I told them anything they wanted to know. Matter of fact, I accepted the invitation of the San Francisco Press Club to address the members about the *Collier's* affair.

"I got no apology for the articles," I told them frankly. "And I got no explanations. It would be easy for me to cop a plea and say that I had been misquoted. But hell, I wouldn't do that if any of *you* got me in hot water, and I certainly wouldn't do it to a fine reporter like Lester Velie. Ninety percent of what he wrote was true. The only trouble was that he had some preconceived notions about how California politics operate. And he used all his information to try and substantiate those notions of his."

I closed by saying:

"The people must wake up. I hope the *Collier's* articles will help wake them up. The legislators are now calling for an investigation of lobbying. I welcome it. I'll do everything I can to cooperate.

"But the investigation must be thorough. It must bring in all the representatives of special interests. If the result of the investigation is to eliminate all lobbyists—including myself—I'll be the most pleased man in the State. Because I would know that the people had won back their government."

I believed that. I wasn't clowning in the least when Lester Velie asked me point-blank: "How can the people get rid of you and others like you in California, Artie?"

He printed my reply at the very end of the articles:

"There is one way. The people must take more interest in the men they elect."

CHAPTER 23

In Which Our Hero Makes More Headlines and Invites His Inquisitors to Attend the World Series

IN THE AFTERMATH OF THE *Collier's* ARTICLES, THE MEMBERS OF the legislature were intent on redeeming their honor, for which I didn't blame them. They had been treated rather severely in the gospel according to Samish, as interpreted by Velie. I knew they would want to refute the *Collier's* stories, and I was willing to go along with them—up to a point. Beyond that point I wasn't willing to proceed.

The legislators were clamoring to conduct investigations, but that privilege befell A. I. Stewart, a Republican from Pasadena and chairman of the Assembly Committee on Governmental Efficiency and Economy. "It has been suggested," said Assemblyman Stewart, "by various citizens and State officials that it is the duty of this Committee to conduct an investigation of the subject matter of that [*Collier's*] article in general and of Arthur Samish, self-styled Governor of the Legislature, in particular."

I was willing. But, as I had suggested before the San Francisco Press Club, I felt the committee should have interrogated all the representatives of special interests, not merely the No. 1 target of the moment, Art Samish.

In typical style of politicians, the hearings began and ended with the appearance of Arthur H. Samish.

They were ready for me. Committee chairman Stewart had hired—without letting the other members know about it—a special counsel. He was Eugene D. Williams, who had been an assistant district attorney in Los Angeles and an assistant in the prosecution of General Tojo, who led the Japanese war against the United States. My God, you'd think I was a war criminal!

I reported for the committee hearing in the State Building in San Francisco on September 22, 1949. First of all, I insisted on reading a statement which I had prepared. I began by saying, "If the press and the public generally will not treat this matter as a short-lived sensation and go back to sleep again, the *Collier's* articles will prove one of the most constructive happenings in California's recent history.

"Some people seem to think I talk too much about politics, lobbying, and kindred matters. The fact is I have not talked enough."

Again I declined to say I had been misquoted, although I admitted my questioning of some of Velie's interpretations of my remarks.

"I have come here to talk; to answer questions you may want to ask about good government in California. But if this committee just wants to play politics; to make a Roman holiday; to let this inquiry degenerate into plain nonsense, I hope you will spare your time and mine. This is, or should be, a serious investigation. We should get down to cases about lobbying and public interest in representative government."

I went on to point out that nobody favored more rigid enforcement of the liquor laws than I did, and I added:

"I challenge anybody to show that my interest in the Board of Equalization has been other than an insistence on a strict but impartial enforcement of the alcoholic beverage laws and regulations. I have never asked a special favor or partial enforcement of the law for any client. But I have insisted that what is good for one must be good for all and must be in the public interest.

"By all means, let us keep an eye on lobbyists—all the lobbyists—even those who appear in the guise of public relations consultants and other phoney titles.

"Let us not be hysterical about it and let us not stop just with lobbyists and lobbying. Let us also inquire into the activities of the lawyer-legislator-lobbyists; those who have solicited and accepted or have been proffered and accepted employment from interests directly concerned with legislation."

That struck a nerve. A number of legislators, including some of those on the committee investigating me, sold their services to special interests as lawyers—and voted accordingly.

I told the committee that I was willing "regardless of what I have been in the past, to sacrifice myself to help make America safe for my children and for democracy—in short, to become the people's lobbyist."

"When did you decide that?" asked the committee counsel, Williams.

"A while ago," I said. "The public needs a good lobbyist."

"And who pays you for these beautiful thoughts—the brewers?"

"No," I said, "nobody pays me." I could see that he was out to get me, and I was on my guard.

Williams asked me whether it was true I could make or break a governor and boss legislators. "That's silly; you know better," I told him.

He asked whether I had the Board of Equalization members in the palm of my hand. I said I had never attended a board meeting, and I rarely went to legislative meetings because "lots of things that go on up there are 96 percent bull anyway."

Oh, I had fun with that fellow Williams. When I admitted I had made the remark about having my own Gestapo, he commented:

"Then you're the Hitler of California?"

"No, I didn't say so," I replied. "You may say so, Mr. Williams, but that doesn't make it true." Then I added: "Don't get funny with me. I'm trying to be cooperative."

Later he asked me about the remark that "I can tell if a man wants a baked potato, a girl, or money."

I replied that my political strength did not require the supplying of any of the three, but I added: "If you're in distress, Mr. Williams, I'll be glad to get you a baked potato."

I admitted that much of California's liquor legislation had been based on my ideas and that I had successfully campaigned against local option. But I tried to explain that a lot of the extravagant statements in the Velie articles were the result of clowning and nonsense.

Mr. Williams didn't have much of a sense of humor. He took everything seriously and even wanted to know if I had offered to unscrew the cupola on top of the capitol.

"I never had enough education to know what a cupola means," I told him. "I was just joking when I offered to climb a ladder to get some gold—if there was gold up there. We're all in the discovery business in California."

I blamed some of the statements about me on my old friend, "Philbrick the Bug." I repeatedly suggested to the committee that other lobbyists were worthy of investigation, especially Monroe Butler, who represented the millionaire oilman William Keck. Butler, who had an immense amount of money behind him, had been reported in *Collier's* as having entertained fifty legislators in his hotel suite in Sacramento.

But the committee wasn't interested in investigating the oil money that had been used to influence legislation in Sacramento. The members had found their whipping boy, Art Samish.

They had no notion of leading a full-scale investigation of lobbying, as I had suggested. As I feared, it was going to be a Roman holiday. So I treated it as such.

When the hearing was over, Chairman Stewart asked if I would be present when the committee held its meetings in Los Angeles.

"I'd be pleased to—as long as it doesn't affect the World Series," I told him. Then I had an afterthought: "Can I take the committee to the World Series?"

Chairman Stewart sniffed, "I'm not sure the committee would want you to do that in view of your testimony here today."

It was all very holier-than-thou, and the committee never held any more hearings, having acquired the headlines it was after. In December of 1949, Governor Warren called a special session of the legislature, and one of the nine points he proposed was: "To consider and act upon legislation relating to lobbying and other attempts to influence legislation."

The legislators were standing in line to introduce lobby-regulation bills, or, as one of them put it, legislation to "stamp out Samishism." Ten of the sixty-seven bills offered in the ten-day session were aimed at lobbyists, principally me.

Not only that. My dear friend, Jack Tenney, the sweetheart of Mexicali Rose, offered a resolution which began:

"Whereas, Arthur H. Samish in two widely published articles in *Collier's*, a national magazine, has boasted that he is the Secret Boss of California; and

"Whereas, The said Arthur H. Samish by his boasting statements has cast a slur and a shadow on the reputation and integrity of every member of this Legislature; now, therefore, be it

"Resolved by the Senate of the State of California, the Assembly thereof concurring, That the name of Arthur H. Samish and the names of his employees be stricken from the rolls of legislative representatives forever. . . ."

Forever! This incredible nonsense by that two-bit piano player managed to rush through the senate and the assembly with the swiftness of an express train. "Railroaded" is the proper term.

Reporters asked me what I thought of Tenney's resolution.

"This is just a little gesture from the man I discovered," I told them. "You know, I found him behind the Hall of Justice in Los Angeles. He didn't have a dime."

Just to demonstrate that the ban didn't upset me, I commented: "Thank heavens it has been proved I do not control the legislature. Now I can catch up on my Christmas shopping for my grandchildren."

The banishment didn't mean a damn thing to me. Not a goddam thing. I quote from an editorial in the *San Francisco Chronicle:*

> For self-righteous hypocrisy, ineptitude, and sheer futility, the sweeping exclusion of Lobbyist Arthur H. Samish and "all of his employees" from the legislative chambers—but forever!—sets a new mark.
>
> The legislators knew to begin with that "forever" was a stipulation well beyond their means to enforce. No Legislature can bind the succeeding Legislature to any course of action. "Forever," then, was pure window dressing; it had the ring of a revival parson banishing Sin from the earth, and we presume that was just how the lads wanted it to sound.
>
> In the next place, Samish—as every legislator knows—never comes into the Legislature itself. His bailiwick is the fourth-floor suite of the Senator Hotel, where the bulk of his work is done. Legislators come there, he doesn't go to them, and the business customarily is transacted over good liquor and a board groaning with lobster and canapes. We look for no diminution of the popularity of this traditional free snack bar for legislators.
>
> In the third place, the Legislature's action against Sa-

> mish dispensed completely with the ordinary rules of fair play. No charges were cited against him. He was not done the elementary courtesy of being invited to talk in his own behalf. Apparently the only basis for the action was the publicity Samish and the Legislature received in *Collier's* magazine, and a few legislators' red faces are hardly sufficient ground for this kind of action. . . .

The Chronicle was absolutely correct. Traffic continued at a steady pace down the fourth-floor Senator Hotel corridor that had become famed as Samish Alley. The booze remained the best in town, and the lobster and canapes were superb.

CHAPTER 24

The Collierization of California Lobbying, a Futile Gesture

THAT SPECIAL SESSION OF THE LEGISLATURE IN DECEMBER OF 1949 demonstrated the devious nature of the political mind. Governor Warren, in an obvious nod to his old acquaintance Art Samish, had told the lawmakers that "the honor of our State" had been assailed.

"Disreputable lobbying practices are impairing the efficiency of State Government and besmirching the creditable work of the vast majority of our legislators, officers and employees," declared the governor.

He said that he didn't want to interfere with honest lobbying, "but everyone around this Capitol knows the kind of lobbyist influence that is not helpful, that is not honest."

The governor presented a bill to the legislature which was a mixture of lobbying measures adopted by other states. Its provisions:

1. Registered lobbyists must report all financial dealings with legislators, the governor and lieutenant governor; this included campaign contributions.

2. All individuals, corporations or groups hiring lobbyists must file detailed accounts of such expenditures, including campaign contributions.
3. No lobbyist could be employed on a contingency basis—payment due only upon success.
4. No elective or appointive officer of the state can represent a client before any agency of the administration or legislature.
5. Those guilty of infractions of the first three provisions would be subject to felony prosecution.

The legislators gave lip service to the bill, but I knew damn well they wouldn't vote for it. It was like asking them to cut off an arm or a leg, or something even more vital. It was that Point 4 that bugged a lot of them. Many of the legislators were earning fancy fees by representing interests as lawyers. In fact, it has long been the custom for lawyer-legislators to retire from the senate or assembly and stay on in Sacramento as high-powered lobbyists and lawyer-representatives.

The legislators gave the business to the governor's bill. First of all, both houses took out the portion that applied to lawyer-legislators. They passed the bill, but the assembly provided a convenient amendment that made it apply to no one. Because of the different versions of the bill, it went to conference, but the assembly adjourned without even waiting for the conference report.

The legislature eventually passed not one, but three separate bills regulating lobbying. All three were patterned after the Federal Regulation of Lobbying Act. In fact, the legislators did such a poor job of copying that the word "Congress" had been left in the bills and later "Legislature" had to be substituted.

So Earl Warren had his choice of three bills, all of which he called "half a loaf." He signed the Collier Bill, and this led to the observation that lobbying in California had not been regulated but Collierized, because of the magazine and the bill.

The assemblyman who took credit for the bill was John L. E. Collier of Highland Park. He was not exactly a fan of mine. In fact, he had ranted to the newspapers that I was "the most sinister, unethical and corrupt stylist in the lobbying profession." I didn't think much of him, either.

Nor his bill. I wasn't upset by its provisions—hell, I could operate under it with no trouble whatsoever. What distressed me about the Collier Bill was that it was a sloppy piece of legislation.

It aimed to do two things: (1) require everyone receiving contributions or making expenditures for the purpose of influencing legislation to file monthly statements identifying contributors of twenty dollars or more and the recipients thereof; (2) require every paid lobbyist to register details of his employment and file monthly financial reports of contributions and expenditures over ten dollars, to name publications which printed articles at his request, and to identify the legislation he was hired to influence.

A lousy bill, and the legislature soon realized it.

In the 1950 special session of the legislature, a joint committee declared that the Collier Act was "inadequate and to a large extent unintelligible and ambiguous. . . . It cannot be clarified or strengthened without a complete rewriting."

The committee, headed by Tom Erwin of Los Angeles, declared that it had "sincerely attempted to study the entire matter in a calm and sensible manner, rather than give way to the hysteria which was generated in many minds following the publication of a certain magazine article." Guess which one.

The 1950 legislature came forth with the Erwin Bill, which tried to straighten out some of the nonsense that had been in the Collier Bill. As you might expect, the learned lawmakers wouldn't touch the matter of the lawyer-legislators with a ten-foot pole.

The Joint Committee declared that "only confusion can result from an attempt to cover, in a measure designed to regulate the activities of professional lobbyists, the subject of corrupt practices by some members of the electorate, and the subject of what activities a Member of the Legislature may properly engage in." Besides, the committee decided, "an attempt to cover so broad a field in one bill would be the surest way to insure its defeat by those who want no regulation of lobbyists."

So the legislature preserved the fat fees of its lawyer members. The Erwin Bill had four main provisions:

1. Disclosure of the employment of legislators by lobbyists or their employers.
2. Prohibition of "contingency" employment for lobbyists.
3. Establishment of a board of four senators and four assemblymen to register and regulate lobbyists and recommend improvements in the law.
4. Establishment of a code of behavior for lobbyists.

This code amounted to a Bill of Wrongs with which lobbyists would be measured for misbehavior. In fact, it could have been interpreted like the Ten Commandments:

Thou shalt register as a lobbyist.

Thou shalt abstain from acts designed to obligate legislators.

Thou shalt never attempt to deceive a legislator.

Thou shalt never introduce a "cinch" bill (one which is certain of defeat, but is introduced for ulterior motives—to impress a client, embarrass an enemy, etc.).

Thou shalt not seek employment except on the basis of knowing thy employer's field.

Thou shalt not create fictitious appearances of public support on a legislative proposal.

Thou shalt refuse to deal on legislative matters with a lobbyist whose registration has been suspended or revoked.

Thou shalt not claim that thou can control or obtain the

vote or action of any member or committee or the Governor of California.

Thou shalt not represent an interest adverse to that of thy employer.

Thou shalt keep records needed to substantiate thy financial reports for a two-year period.

That was the result of the legislature's Operation Samish, as the newspapers termed it. Big deal! The Erwin Bill passed both houses and was sent to Governor Warren, who called it "the lobbyist's own bill." If he meant me, he was off the beam. I had nothing to do with it. I didn't give a damn what they passed.

Warren signed the Erwin Bill, which had been greatly amended, and it became the law of the state.

How did it affect me?

Not at all.

Oh, perhaps I had to change some of my procedures. But I went on doing business at the same old stand, watching after the interests of my clients.

The hubbub over the Collierization of California lobbying ended without a conclusion. The whole point had been missed by everyone concerned. All the rules and regulations in the world wouldn't change the influence of lobbyists like myself in Sacramento.

There was only one way the situation would change. I gave the secret in the last paragraph of the *Collier's* articles.

Velie asked me how the people of California could get rid of me and others like me.

"There is one way," I told him. "The people must take more interest in the men they elect."

As long as the people of California paid only $1,200 a year to the men who made their laws, as long as most candidates were elected in the primaries, as long as most citizens didn't even know the names of their senators and assemblymen, then the people would not get rid of Art Samish.

CHAPTER 25

A Fatal Encounter with a Traveling Circus

IF YOU HAVE READ THIS FAR, THEN YOU HAVE BEEN ABLE TO RECognize the amazing survival powers of Artie Samish.

By God, look what I came up against! The grand jury investigation. The Philbrick Report. The *Collier's* articles. The assembly committee hearing. Banishment from the legislature "forever." The Collier Bill and the Erwin Bill, both of them aimed at Art Samish.

I survived.

Not only survived. I continued to flourish. My clients continued to contract for my services, and I served them well. My enthusiasm for the job was not the same since my mother died, but I kept the business going, partly out of habit, partly to spite my enemies.

It appeared that nothing could defeat me. But the fates combined with the Presidential Virus to bring me down.

What do I mean by that? I'll tell you.

The Presidential Virus is one of the rarest and most serious diseases known to man. It infects political bodies, and once it grabs a hold, it is almost impossible to cure. Look at Harold Stassen, a hopeless case.

Earl Warren was a victim of the Presidential Virus. He had been a popular governor of California, winning his second term unopposed in 1946. He had his eye on the White House, and he nearly made vice president in 1948. Now his sights were on the 1952 presidential election. His chances were helped when he won an unprecedented third term as governor in 1950.

But Art Samish was a source of embarrassment to the Guv. After all, he had admitted before God and everybody that, in matters concerning my clients, I had more power than he did. That wasn't good for his reputation. Not good at all.

Obviously Earl Warren had to do something to repair his image. His move for lobbying legislation was part of that. I suspect he also had some other ideas in mind. I told you in Chapter II about how I helped the governor get through the legislature his California Special Study Commission on Organized Crime. And how his man Warren Olney III, the son of one of my early mentors, tried to get me to squeal on a dying bookmaker. And how I infuriated Olney by pointing two fingers at him and telling him, "Don't you try to put words in my mouth."

Later Dwight Eisenhower became President, and Earl Warren was very close to the new Republican administration. So close that he was chosen chief justice of the United States. And who should become an assistant United States attorney in Washington, D.C., but my old friend Warren Olney. He had an old score to settle.

Olney had help from another politician who had been infected with the Presidential Virus. His name was Estes Kefauver, and he was a barefoot boy from Tennessee. He became United States senator and in 1950 embarked on a series of hearings of the Special Senate Committee to Investigate Crime in Interstate Commerce. Kefauver was chairman, and he found a brand-new way to become a national political figure: television.

Senator Kefauver became as famous as Lucille Ball and Arthur Godfrey in the early days of television. Viewers stayed glued to their sets as the drawling Tennessean took on the big and small fry of organized crime.

Like most successful productions, the Kefauver Committee went on a road tour, and naturally he came prospecting for headlines (and votes) in California. And naturally he subpoenaed Art Samish, who was everybody's favorite target of the moment.

I was the soul of cooperation. Investigators for the committee came around to see me, and I gave them anything they wanted. They couldn't have asked for a more helpful subject.

On March 2, 1951, I paid Senator Kefauver a call. I even arrived a half hour early for the hearings in the Post Office Building in San Francisco. With me was Harold Hoertkorn, my accountant, who brought along a couple of briefcases. This time I didn't have bricks in them; the senator had asked me to bring along my financial records of the previous ten years, which I was pleased to do. Also with me were my associate, James Rieden, and of course my old pal and piano player, Walter King. After all, I couldn't put on a show without having Walter there.

And what a show it was. Television cameras. Spotlights. A packed house. Reporters and photographers. I was determined to give them a good performance.

The senator was a very courtly Southern gentleman, and he greeted me with kindness and consideration. I extended the same to him. We shook hands and smiled at each other, and I assured him I would cooperate to the fullest.

I explained that I worked for the California Brewers Institute and "as long as we have the use of television, I'm going to sell some beer." So I told the audience how the brewers combined the grains and the hops and the whole process of beer making.

Senator Kefauver didn't seem so interested in beer making.

He wanted to know what my arrangements were with the Brewers and how I operated.

"I want to be very helpful with this committee and with you, Senator," I told him. "I have here a copy of a contract I made with the Brewers in 1935. I think you'll find it most interesting. Just one thing, though. I ask you to keep it to yourself. No one else has seen it."

The senator looked as if I had handed him a pinless grenade.

"Just a minute," he said. "This is a public hearing, and I don't want my fingers on anything confidential."

"In that case," I told him, "you can do anything you want with it."

The senator asked me to name my clients in 1949. I gazed at the ceiling for a long time, then replied, "I'll have to look at my records about that."

I looked inside one of the brief cases and then I told him my employers: the Brewers Institute, the Philip Morris Cigarette Company, Schenley Industries of New York, and the Motor Carriers Association.

"I've been working with the Motor Carriers for twenty-five years," I remarked.

What about the California Orange Association? It was apparent that the committee investigators had been studying up on me through the Philbrick Report.

"That was a nominal account I had for $5,000 ten years ago," I said.

And the Southern California Distilled Spirits Foundation?

"I confer with them on policy, but I receive no compensation from them."

The committee dwelled at great length on the Brewers' Five-Cent Fund. The committee had already learned some details about the Fund from James G. Hamilton, the Secretary of the Brewers Institute. During the previous six years the Fund had amounted to $935,943.19, which had been deposited in a special account in Crocker First National Bank of San Francisco. Hamilton said that I had complete control of that account.

Senator Kefauver asked him: "Now, when it comes up as to whether a proposed referendum is to be good or bad for the brewing industry, whether an election of a State Senator, a member of the Legislature or the passage of a bill in the Legislature will be good or bad, that decision is made exclusively and wholly by Mr. Samish?"

"That is my understanding, yes," said Hamilton.

The senator seemed very intent on finding out where the money went. I told him the checks on the Fund were made up in my office, sent to the Brewers Institute for signing, then returned to my office. Then I was asked what happened to the bank statement and the canceled checks after they were returned from the bank.

"I take a recapitulation—the bank statement and the canceled checks—and I throw them in the wastebasket," I replied.

That answer seemed to startle the entire committee. I was asked specifically about a check for $15,000 drawn for cash on October 3, 1950. That, I explained, was during the General Election when many checks for cash were spent to see that "honest, outstanding officials that subscribed to the temperate use of beer, wine, spirits and other things are returned to office."

Then we had this exchange:

Q. And where does the money go, sir?
A. It is expended.
Q. It is expended?
I nodded.
Q. And what does that mean?
A. Well, it is expended in connection with campaigns.
Q. And who gets it?
A. The cash is handled through me.

Q. You get the cash, then?

A. Yes.

Q. And what do you do with the cash?

A. We spend it. Make contributions and distributions. . . .

Q. Well, sir, we are not arguing policy with you. We are trying to find out where the money went, physically —whose hands it got into.

A. Well, it comes into mine.

Q. And then where does it go from yours?

A. It is given in contributions.

Q. To whom?

A. To different campaigns.

Q. Name one.

A. Well, I don't keep a record of that. I'd be glad to see if I could find it for you. . . .

Q. Now you have the money in your hand. You have $10,000. You are going to give it to the campaign committee. How do you do it?

A. I handle it. I have been doing it for a great many years.

Q. Do you handle it in cash?

A. Well, we pay bills sometimes. Sometimes we handle it in cash.

Q. What is wrong with writing a little check to the campaign committee?

A. I tell you what I decided after this situation—I told Mr. Hoertkorn, my accountant, "For your information, starting March 1, everything in that Fund is going to be by check. . . ."

Q. Is there a distinction between "cash" and "contributions"?

A. "Cash" and "contributions" are the same thing.

Q. Who decides whether it is to be a contribution or cash?

A. All of our contributions, with rare exceptions—once in a while we may make a check out if I don't happen to be around, or for what reason I don't know—but I would say that 95 percent of it is in cash.

We chatted about this and that and the other thing, and the senator seemed intrigued about my attitude toward money. I mentioned that I got a flat payment of $36,000 a year from Schenley.

"You must do a lot of work for them for $36,000," Kefauver said .

"Well, I do at times, Senator," I told him. "I do, but not always. I mean I am 'callable' when they want me."

I added that Schenley used to pay me $54,000 a year, but that had been cut down "because I was earning too much money."

It was a most pleasant conversation, as far as I was concerned. I enjoyed being on television, and I think I put on a hell of a show—my pal Joe Schenck said I gave an excellent performance, and he was an expert.

When I was excused after a full day's testimony, Senator Kefauver stood up and said very cordially, "Let me thank you for appearing before this committee."

"I must thank you, Senator," I told him. "I was glad to have had the opportunity to sell my beer."

I guess I made quite an impression on him, because later he gave out that quote I told you about earlier. His full comment was:

"In both personality and physique, Samish is a remarkable figure. Physically, he stands over six feet, two inches, in height, and must weigh better than three hundred pounds. He is bald with a monk's tonsure of gray fringe, and his face has the bland innocence of an *enfant terrible* about to light a giant firecracker under his nurse's chair. In manner, he is a combination of Falstaff, Little Boy Blue, Machiavelli, crossed with an eel."

A compliment, I guess. But Senator Kefauver was not so complimentary when he filed his committee report. He remarked about the Brewers' Fund:

"Mr. Samish was extremely vague as to exactly how this money was spent. He has no records to indicate what he has done with almost two million dollars which passed through his hands. He testified that he threw canceled checks and bank statements into the wastebasket.

"He made no reports to the Brewers Institute, though he was required by contract to do so. Most of the checks were drawn to cash and, according to Samish, the cash was 'expended in connection with campaigns.' It seems obvious that these sums were spent by Samish to elect candidates he could depend on or control."

The Kefauver Committee recommended that both the Justice Department and the Internal Revenue Service look into the affairs of Arthur H. Samish in connection with California Brewers Institute.

So there was Artie on the spot again.

Well, I had been there before, and I had always escaped. But this was the first time I had been up against the Federals.

The Justice Department came around and looked into my affairs and couldn't find any hanky-panky.

The Internal Revenue boys swarmed down on me, and I handed over the canceled checks and bank statements Senator Kefauver had been inquiring about.

"But you told the Senator you had thrown these in the wastebasket," said one of the agents.

"Sure," I replied. "But he didn't ask me what I did with the lovin' wastebasket. I just reached in and pulled 'em out."

For months, the Internal Revenue boys went over my records. They couldn't find a thing that wasn't on the up-and-up. It appeared Artie Samish had once more escaped the massive efforts to do him in.

But then, appearances can be deceiving.

CHAPTER 26

In Which the Famous Samish Luck Finally Runs Out

THOSE LOVIN' T-MEN LIVED WITH ME FOR TWO AND A HALF YEARS. I mean *lived with me.* They spent more time in my office than my secretary did. They asked me questions for three hours at a time. They traveled all over the country with me.

"You fellows want to study me?" I said to them one day. "Well, I'm going down to Miami for a while. Why not come along? I'll put you up at my suite. We'll live it up. What do you like? Sailing? Girls? Gambling? If you want to know how I live and have a little fun, too, come along and you'll really learn."

So the three of us went to Miami. But of course the Treasury men wouldn't stay in my suite. They put up at a smaller hotel. And instead of the usual Miami pleasures, they spent their time interviewing all my friends and trying to get the lowdown on Artie.

Poor fellows! By the time they finished with the case, they were so worn out that they had to go into the hospital, both of them.

I came to like those two boys—Jack Wilks and Charles Kisthardt were their names. I liked them even though they were trying to hang me. They were just doing their job, and I did everything I could to help them. I had nothing to hide.

The T-men probably would have given up if it hadn't been for my old friend Warren Olney III. He had been helped along by Earl Warren, first in the district attorney's office in Alameda County, then when Warren was attorney general of California. After Eisenhower became President, Warren became chief justice and his protégé Olney headed the criminal division of the attorney general's office.

Olney wouldn't accept the Justice Department's decision that there was "no provable violation of federal law" in the Samish case. Olney convinced the Internal Revenue Service to continue investigating me until something turned up.

And so the T-men continued on my tail until they thought they found something. And Warren Olney III flew from Washington to San Francisco to make sure that the proceedings got under way before the statute of limitations expired.

I had been so certain that I had done nothing wrong that I let the T-men inspect all my personal correspondence, which I really didn't have to show them. That's where they found the clue that led them to the Biow Company.

Milton Biow. The name makes me sick just thinking about it.

I first met the son of a bitch in early 1942. Only I didn't know then that he was a son of a bitch. Biow operated a big advertising agency and one of his accounts was Philip Morris, which I represented in California. Alfred Lyon, the president of Philip Morris, was in Miami Beach when I was visiting him. He telephoned Biow in New York and suggested that Biow come down to Florida and meet me.

We met at dinner in Lyon's house, and I soon learned why Biow was so eager to make my acquaintance. "I'd like you to help me get the Schenley account for my agency," he said.

Lyon assured me that Biow had done a splendid job in advertising Philip Morris. As a favor to Lyon, I agreed to put in a good word for Biow with Lewis Rosenstiel, the president of Schenley. And I did.

Shortly afterward, I met with Rosenstiel and mentioned what good work Biow had done for Philip Morris and suggested that Schenley might investigate the possibility of hiring Biow's agency.

That was that. I had nothing more to do with the negotiations, which turned out successfully for Biow. In early 1943 Biow went to Tucson to meet with Rosenstiel, and Schenley entered into a contract with the Biow agency. To me the affair had ended. I had simply done a favor for Mr. Lyon, for his friend Mr. Biow, and for Mr. Rosenstiel. I sought no compensation for any of them and expected none.

A year afterward, I was in Lyon's office in New York, and he said to me, "Milton Biow is so grateful for your help in getting the Schenley account that he wants to give you something."

"I don't need anything from Milton Biow," I told Lyon. "I get enough already from Philip Morris and Schenley."

"Yes, but he wants to give you something, anyway. You'd be foolish not to take it, Artie."

"Well, if he wants to give his money away, I can find ways to do it. Not for myself. But if he wants to make some political contributions and gifts to some friends of mine, I suppose there's no reason why I should stop him."

Later I talked to Biow himself, and he told me that he wanted to reward me for helping him with the Schenley account. I told him exactly what I had told Lyon: if he wanted to contribute to campaigns and to worthy friends, he was free to do so.

In late 1944, Biow asked me to meet with his treasurer, Morris Zinneman, which I did.

"I have some money for you and I want to make out some checks to cover it," Zinneman said. "Give me some names."

"Why don't you just make out the checks to me," I suggested.

"No, I can't do that," he said. "I don't want your name on the checks."

"Why not?"

"That's my business."

It seemed like a funny way to do business, but I gave him names of friends of mine and he filled out the checks. This went on for a period of years. I never knew what the amounts of the checks would be, or how often they would be issued. But the checks kept coming, and I kept giving them to worthy recipients. I was playing with someone else's money, and it was fun.

But the Internal Revenue Service didn't see it that way.

In 1953 the government charged me with evading $71,878 of income taxes because of thirty-four checks that had been issued by the Biow Company.

I still wasn't concerned. My whole life was an open book—I proved that by showing the T-men my correspondence and everything else they asked for. I hadn't used that Biow money for myself. It had gone to worthy friends and for political purposes. I didn't think I had anything to worry about.

I was wrong. I had misjudged the resolve of Warren Olney III to see that I was punished. And I didn't realize how far Milton Biow would go to cover up his own misdeeds.

After I had been hit by the suit, I subpoenaed the books of account of the Biow agency. That's when I realized something strange was going on. There was no Samish account. Instead, the checks that had been issued to the payees I suggested were listed as "radio time," "radio talent," "magazine payable," "newspapers," or "outdoor advertising." Curious.

Even more curious was the fact that when the Revenue agents called on Biow and Zinneman on August 20, 1952, all the checks prior to August 1, 1948, had been destroyed. So had the account books prior to January 1, 1948. The checks I received from Biow covered a period from 1946 to 1951.

Biow testified that he met me for the first time in March of 1943. He declared that I went to him and demanded three-quarters of 3 percent of the Schenley account in payment for convincing Lewis Rosenstiel to shift his advertising to Biow.

My God, I couldn't believe my ears!

He met me for the first time in March of 1943? Alfred Lyon of Philip Morris testified that he arranged a meeting between Biow and me in Miami in early 1942. I produced letters from Biow to me in 1942, proving we had met before March of 1943.

As to the demand that I receive a percentage of the Schenley account, that was pure fantasy. And even if I had demanded the amount Biow stated, he would have underpaid me $105,000.

I took the stand in my own behalf and told the story as freely and openly as I could. How Al Lyon introduced me to Milton Biow, who wanted me to help swing the Schenley account to his agency. How I suggested to Lewis Rosenstiel that he look into the matter. How Al Lyon said I was a fool not to accept Biow's offer of payment out of gratitude. How I told Biow to make some donations to friends of mine and to political causes if he wanted to. How I wanted him to make out the checks to me but he insisted on using other names.

It was hard for me to take the trial seriously. To me it was just like the grand jury investigation or the Crime Commission hearing or the Kefauver Committee appearance. I thought it was just another show. I couldn't believe that the government had anything on me.

The judge was Oliver Hamlin, a man I had known—I used to give him tips when I ran into him at the racetrack. I guess I should have been more concerned by the fact that both Hamlin and the prosecutor, Lloyd Burge, had been protégés of Earl Warren.

When I heard the verdict, on November 17, 1953, I had to smile. I just couldn't believe it when the foreman of the jury said I was guilty on eight counts of willful attempted evasion of income taxes.

Afterward, some of the jury admitted that they had been confused by the technicalities in the instructions. I didn't blame them. I was confused myself. Anyone who wasn't a tax lawyer would have been. My case should have been tried in a tax court, not a criminal court. And it probably would have been—if my name hadn't been Arthur H. Samish.

Naturally I appealed the verdict. I couldn't imagine that an appeals court would not recognize that I had *not* willfully, intentionally, and knowingly attempted to defraud the government. Nor could I imagine that a higher court would place any faith in the testimony of Milton Biow, in view of the wrongs he had committed.

The United States Court of Appeals, Ninth Circuit, reviewed my case and issued a decision on May 20, 1955. The Court declared, ". . . if Biow's low standard of morality as shown in the record is any excuse for Samish, then Samish ought to go free."

The judges declared that Judge Hamlin had made a mistake in an instruction to the jury that "seemed to pass lightly over the keeping of dishonest books" by Biow.

But in the end the Appellate Court judges decided against me. This was their reasoning:

"One begins with the business background. Samish, without question, had done Biow a huge business favor. Biow offers to pay Samish. Can Samish avoid tax liability by saying, 'You can't pay me. But you can make some gifts to friends of mine (not yours). Give me the checks. Let me present them. And you can also give me some political money.' Someone owned the checks at the moment they were in Samish's hands. That man was Samish."

Again I couldn't believe that I had broken the law. I took

the case to the United States Supreme Court, where Earl Warren was now sitting as chief justice. Warren disqualified himself in my case, but it was denied a hearing.

Finally I realized it wasn't a joke. It was all too true. Yet I wasn't bitter. It had been a very enlightening experience. Because of it, I learned who were my friends.

One of the first to desert me was Lewis Rosenstiel. The same Rosenstiel who had written to me in 1946: "Dear Pops, First and foremost, there is nobody in the world that I love better than you. . . ." We were the greatest of pals in the years when I was running 10 High whiskey out of California for him and performing other chores that added to his millions. But when I got in trouble and needed him, he got lost.

But for all those who turned tail when trouble started, there were just as many who stuck by me.

Many friends wrote to Judge Hamlin to ask for probation for me. I quote just a few excerpts from the letters:

Herbert Bayard Swope—". . . in the twenty years or so of our friendship, I have never known him to behave in other manner than one reflecting credit upon him. He has shown loyalty to his friends; generosity, courage and a sense of social obligation . . ."

Louis B. Mayer—"I have known Arthur Samish for some twenty years. During that time I have always found his two outstanding characteristics to be loyalty and truthfulness. . . ."

Gene Fowler—". . . will you allow me to say that this man has in the past done many acts of great charity; and in his personal life—away from the hurly-burly of politics—has been both honorable and kind. . . ."

One of my great friends who remained steadfast in my time of trouble was Judge Timothy Fitzpatrick. He was one of the great, dedicated public servants of San Francisco, an early supporter of the reforms of Hiram Johnson and later the dean of superior court judges.

Judge Fitzpatrick wrote to Judge Hamlin in support of my

application for probation. Judge Fitzpatrick began by quoting from Shakespeare:

> "The evil that men do lives after them,
> The good is oft interred with their bones."
>
> The events of the past few months, the atmosphere surrounding the trial, the highly colored and prejudicial accounts carried by the newspapers, which I feel must have greatly influenced the attitude of the jury, and the general tendency to ignore facts and aspects which might be favorable to the accused, testify eloquently to the truth of this quotation. I think in simple fairness it behooves those who have known Mr. Samish through all the years to speak up courageously and bring into consideration the many good and noble things that this man has done."

I won't bore the reader with Judge Fitzpatrick's recital of my virtues. But he did say that for thirty years he had represented the superior court in all legislative matters affecting the judiciary of the state—"in all matters affecting the well-being of our courts and our judges he [Samish] has not only cooperated wholeheartedly, but has gone out of his way and spent his own money." He added:

> While it is true that Mr. Samish has wielded great power in our legislative bodies in Sacramento, I know of no instance in which he applied that influence to the detriment of any person, or in a manner contrary to civic and governmental interest.

Referring to my conviction, Judge Fitzpatrick said,

> I think emphasis must be laid on the fact that the crime was not one of moral turpitude, but one of the economic derelictions unknown to the Common Law and

> originating in the recent past. From a study of the facts and circumstances known to me, I firmly believe that Mr. Samish did not willfully and intentionally violate the law; and I feel that the fact that in his entire life this is the first time that a criminal accusation of any nature has been leveled against him is entitled to great weight in arriving at a decision.

This fine judge's plea fell on deaf ears and I was sentenced to three years in federal prison and fined $40,000. In addition, the Internal Revenue Service decreed that I owed income taxes on the moneys I received in connection with the Brewers' Fund. I settled that for $919,374.

I didn't give a damn about the money. I didn't even fret about going to prison—hell, I was willing to take the bad with the good, and I'd had it good for a long, long time. My only concern was the grief and sorrow that the whole affair caused my dear wife and my two daughters. But they were so brave and wonderful that I was able to go off on my next adventure in good spirits.

CHAPTER 27

The Isle of Magic—and Afterward

AS I FLEW FROM SAN FRANCISCO TO THE STATE OF WASHINGTON with a deputy marshal as my traveling companion, I couldn't believe it was happening to me. But it was, and I was going to make the most of it. I had managed to pull myself through a lot of sticky situations. I could do it again.

McNeil Island wasn't so bad. As a matter of fact, I was prepared for it. All those Christmas parties I gave at San Quentin, those visits to Folsom and other prisons—they had made me ready for my life on the Isle of Magic.

As you might expect, Artie took over.

I decided that the prison was unsanitary. Absolutely unsanitary. I went around the place, inspecting the nooks and crannies and pointing out conditions that were dangerous to the health of the inmates.

I was appointed Chief of Safety and Sanitation.

Naturally I had to have an assistant for such an important post, and I chose a buddy of mine named Smokey. He was a nice little fellow who had been in the stir a couple of times or more, and he was willing to go along with anything I suggested. Why not? Smokey and I had free run of the Isle of Dreams.

We got ourselves some spray cans and we went all over the place. We'd go into the woodshop and I'd run my finger along the windowsill.

"Hmmmm, terribly dirty. Unsanitary. Smokey—spray it."

We'd walk along the cellblock and I'd peek into a corner.

"Smokey—spray it."

We went all over the damn prison spraying here and spraying there. And you know what was in the spray can? Not a goddam thing but water!

Except once. That was the day I found out that my fine of $40,000 was being paid in San Francisco. That day I pissed into the spray can. I had the distinct pleasure of being able to piss all over McNeil Island prison on that memorable day.

The warden didn't bother me and I didn't bother him. We had sort of a hands-off policy. I was always saying, "I love everybody in this place—except one." The warden never knew if he was the one, and I never told him.

I made some good friends at the Isle of Dreams. One of them was a lieutenant who was tolerant of my funmaking ways. One night Smokey and I were caught in the kitchen by a guard I called Moustache Pete.

Moustache Pete got all excited and rushed to report to the lieutenant: "I found Samish and Smokey in the kitchen and they were eating steaks—a dozen of them!"

"Yeah?" said the lieutenant. "Tell 'em to save one for me."

I had the Isle of Dreams so well organized that I didn't give a damn whether I stayed in or got out. But I did get out in March of 1958 after twenty-six months as a guest of the place. And I went out in style. I had one of the boys in the woodshop make me up a plaque on which was written the notice that I had "graduated from the Isle of Dreams."

When they checked me out, I asked for the oldest, most disreputable suit they had. Then I got a beat-up old cap and turned it to one side. When the reporters greeted me as I stepped off the ferry, I looked like a real character.

And so—back to San Francisco to pick up my life once more.

I was through with politics. I had been at the heart of the California political scene for forty years, and I had no desire to go back to it. A few organizations indicated they would like to have me represent them, but I told them I wasn't interested.

Fortunately I didn't need the money. The income tax suit and penalties had cost me over a million dollars, but I had some investments left. A few oil wells here and there. I built a couple of hotels in Palm Springs. And I had been retired with a comfortable pension by the Brewers Institute.

I kept my office in the Kohl Building, and I engaged in some import-export enterprises. I had fun opening up a classy hotel for dogs called Pets Inn. But my main interest became my wife Merced, my two daughters, and seven grandchildren. I had neglected them too long. Now I was determined to make up for it.

During the past decade I've steered clear of politics. But I had fun one day in 1969 when I accepted an invitation from the Sacramento Press Club to address their membership. And guess where the meeting was held—the Senator Hotel. Yes, the same hostelry that once housed the famous Samish Alley, where I once conducted a circus in the lobby to celebrate the defeat of that fellow who wrote "Mexicali Rose." I forget his name.

It had been fifteen years since I had been on the Sacramento scene, and there were a lot of new faces among the members of the Press Club. Many of them hadn't been born when I was pulling off my stunts in the legislature. But they had heard of Artie Samish.

"This'll sound like I'm biting the hand that used to feed me—and feed me well," I smiled. "But I'm going to say it anyway. The fact is that my former clients aren't paying enough in taxes."

Liquor and cigarettes, especially. As long as I represented

the liquor industry, there was no increase in taxes on liquor. I saved the beer industry $10,000,000 a year by keeping taxes at the same level as 1935. Not until 1959 was the beer tax increased. The distilled spirits tax went up in 1955. In 1959 the state started to tax cigarettes for the first time.

Today's taxes on liquor and cigarettes are still not enough, I told the Press Clubbers.

"The tax on beer was two cents a gallon all those years I represented the brewers," I said. "Now it's four cents. I think it ought to be eight cents."

Thanks to my work in the past, liquor wholesalers have the state working for them by enforcing prices. Yet those wholesalers pay only an annual license fee of $328. Chickenfeed.

"As far as I'm concerned," I told my audience, "the state could tax cigarettes out of existence. At any rate, cigarettes aren't taxed enough. There should be a twenty-five-dollar tax on all cigarette machines. And the dealers should be forced to prohibit sales to minors. There's no enforcement at all; children can buy cigarettes anywhere."

Then I turned my attention to other former employers of mine, the lovin' racetracks. They get away with highway robbery. The state keeps giving them longer racing seasons—822 days in 1971—and the tracks get richer. They should give up a bigger part of their take. And the state should get a share of the admissions, concessions, and parking, too.

Those oil companies have a soft touch, too. There should be a severance tax of fifteen cents a barrel on the oil taken from under California. With production at a million barrels a day, that kind of taxation would ease the burden on the property owner. Potash, gypsum, and other minerals should be subject to a severance tax.

"Unless there is a change in the taxation structure," I said, "some day all of us will need a poor people's lobbyist in Sacramento. Not me. I'm retired from the lobbying business."

CHAPTER 28

A Surprise Visit from a Bearded Stranger Affords a Summing-up of a Well-spent Life

THE OTHER DAY I WAS GOING THROUGH SOME OLD LETTERS IN MY office in the Kohl Building when I heard a knock at the door. I opened the door and saw a husky young man, bearded, wearing an old shirt, blue jeans, and sandals. I thought maybe he was a hippie from Haight-Ashbury looking for a handout.

He introduced himself and said, "Mr. Samish, I'm a political science major at the University of California across the bay, and I'd like to talk to you."

Well, he sounded like a nice fellow even if he did look like a bum. So I invited him in and we sat down in my office. He came right to the point.

"Mr. Samish, I'm writing a paper for my upper-division poli sci course on your activities as a lobbyist in California," he said.

"My, my!" I said. "I feel very complimented."

"Maybe you won't be when you see what I write about you," he said bluntly.

"Oh?"

"Yes, sir. You see, I've been doing some research in the library. You are mentioned in an incredible number of books, in every history of California, in fact."

"And those books say I was a son of a bitch?"

"Not in those words. Let me cite some references." He opened up his notebook and started riffling through the pages. Then he began reading: "For instance, in *The Politics of California* by Farrelly and Hinderaker, it says that there were good lobbyists and bad lobbyists in Sacramento."

"And I was one of the bad lobbyists?"

"Yes, sir. That book quotes from the Philbrick Report."

"Oh, yes. Philbrick the Bug."

"Sir?"

"Nothing—go ahead."

"Here's this from the Philbrick Report: 'This "fourth branch" of government represented by the Samish type of lobbying is responsible not to the public but only to individuals or interests able to pay high fees. It operates in great secrecy—secrecy so great that neither the public nor the regularly constituted agencies of the government, nor, on occasion, the fee-paying clients know what the lobbyist is doing.' End of quote."

"Very interesting. What else have you discovered in your research?"

"This from *Big Wayward Girl* by Herbert L. Phillips: 'He'—meaning you—'was a fascinating, almost incredible figure who worked his little miracles in California politics for a very long time and left an indelible mark on numerous phases of legislation in which he was hired to interest himself.' "

"Yes, I have Herb's book," I said, taking it from a shelf. "Here's what Herb also wrote: 'Samish unquestionably exerted great pressure leverage. Oddly enough, though, he was not necessarily the most potent lobbyist in Sacramento in terms of effective, restrained operations or from the standpoint of huge and powerful interests represented. . . . The legislative interests of the major utilities, the insurance companies, the oil corporations and other important financial institutions have seldom been poorly served by their lobby spokesmen . . .' "

"Yes, sir, I realize that. But to continue. In *California: An Interpretive History,* Walton Bean says that the song 'Mexicali Rose' struck your fancy and you got the composer elected to the assembly."

"I got to plead guilty to that," I admitted.

"And later Jack Tenney got angry with you and said you were a Communist."

The young man seemed surprised when I burst out laughing. "Is that amusing?" he asked.

"I think so," I replied, wiping my eyes. "You would too, if you knew that bum."

"This," he continued, "is from the Kefauver Committee Report: 'The strange tale of the part played by an almost unbelievable character, Arthur H. Samish, in the California picture nearly defies description. Mr. Samish can safely be called "Mr. Big" in California.' "

"He was a fine gentleman, Senator Kefauver. And a good judge of character."

"I could quote many other references to you from books and magazine articles. For instance, the *Collier's* articles, 'The Secret Boss of California.' "

"Yes, I've heard of them," I said.

"Instead of going over all this old stuff, I'd like to ask you a few questions."

"Go ahead."

"How would you define a lobbyist?"

"A lobbyist is one who ably and properly qualifies to represent industry or any other organization before a legislative body. He is a short-cut man."

" 'A guy who gets things done'?"

"That's right. That's what they called me."

"But how could you defend the way you 'got things done'?"

"Defend my methods? I never felt compelled to. I wasn't

one of those guys who wined and dined a senator and then expected a favor in return. I never did any of that. The guys who did made me sick. And I had nothing but contempt for any legislator who could be influenced by a few drinks and a steak dinner."

"But you obviously wielded great power. How did you manage it?"

"Very simple, young man. I selected and I elected."

"What do you mean?"

"Just that. I selected the candidates that I thought would be agreeable to my clients, and I saw that they got elected. And if they didn't behave, I saw that they got unelected."

The young man with the beard shook his head. "That's not right, Mr. Samish," he said. "It's undemocratic."

"I make no excuses," I said. "I was doing a job for my clients, and I did it damn well. I was the highest-priced lobbyist in the business, and I delivered. And I operated within the law. I don't think I did anything wrong."

"But I still say it was undemocratic," he insisted.

"I can't argue on that score. But maybe I did accomplish something."

"What was that?"

"You remember what I told Velie at the end of his articles?"

"You mean about how the people of California could get rid of people like Artie Samish?"

"Yeah. I told him the people would have to pay more attention to their elected representatives. Maybe they're doing that now. At least the legislature can attract a better kind of lawmaker. When I was in Sacramento, the senators and assemblymen were getting $1,200 a year. Now they're paid $19,200, and they have fancy offices, cars to drive, paid staffs, and all the frills."

"Then perhaps a man like Art Samish could not operate today in Sacramento the way he used to."

"Probably not. But I wouldn't want to."

"Why not?"

"No fun. Goddammit, I had fun when I was up there in Sacramento. I whooped it up. I had a helluva time."

The young man from Berkeley couldn't understand that. Like so many in his generation, he didn't know what it was like to whoop it up just for the hell of it. They're all so dead serious about everything. I feel sorry for them.

He folded up his notebook and put away his pen and went back to the university. God knows what he wrote about me.

After he had gone, I sat at my desk and gazed out on that wonderful view of San Francisco. The late afternoon fog was starting to swoop in through the Golden Gate and the tops of the bridge had disappeared. The talk with the bearded young man had started me thinking about some of the great old times. The reason for this book is to share them with you, the reader.

Why did I tell my story, after all the years of keeping it to myself? As I told you before, it was time to raise hell and have fun. After all, every man in politics is entitled to his last hurrah.

Hurrah.

INDEX

DATE DUE

APR	1976		
JUL	1976		
GAYLORD 234			PRINTED IN U.S.A.

D-76
A-77
M-3-77

The Black Eagle

The Black Eagle

JOHN PEER NUGENT

SD

STEIN AND DAY/*Publishers*/New York

First published in 1971

Library of Congress Catalog Card No. 73-149808

Published simultaneously in Canada by Saunders of Toronto, Ltd.
Designed by David Miller
Manufactured in the United States of America
Stein and Day/*Publishers*/7 East 48 Street, New York, N.Y. 10017
ISBN 0-8128-1370-7

Asante sana

To one who really cares for all people and is gifted with the warmth to bring out only the goodness in even the worst of us: my bride, Phyllis.

Contents

The Black Eagle

Prologue

Attempt at Dissection

WHAT'S AHEAD is not fiction.

Hubert Fauntleroy Julian, who gives chase to adventure under the *nom de guerre* of The Black Eagle, is as real as Timbuktu. By measures long and short he stands as one of the true swashbucklers of any century.

This is an accounting of his life, a picaresque one, and the howl of twentieth-century events he has been heard in. It details the deeds, and misdeeds, of a bold Promethean who has soldiered for his fortune along most of the world's trouble fronts since World War I.

The episodes are marinated in adventure and spiced with humor. They all feature Julian as *chef d'affaires* because it happens that way wherever and whenever he appears. Most of them take place in the eye of the historical storms of reckless, frantic, often cruel times—the Roaring Twenties, the Depression years, World War II, Latin America exploding, Africa awakening.

Tracing Julian's madcap odyssey means circling the globe —from Ethiopia, where he ran an Imperial Air Force, to Guatemala, where he ran guns. Participants, willing or not, range from Ché to Goering to Truman, from the CIA to the UN and through the White House.

Even today this lone adventurer is still in quest of his grail. It is not necessarily a holy one, but it is surely an honorable one. For in Julian's world, making it is based more on spirit than on accomplishment.

In Edmond Rostand's drama *Cyrano de Bergerac,* the long-suffering romantic warrior exits life saying: "One does not fight just to succeed. Oh no, it is much more beautiful when it is in vain." When—if—Julian goes, he'll probably say it that way—approximately, and provided there's time.

Once encountered—and if you travel often and far enough, there is always that chance—The Black Eagle is not easily forgotten.

An Irish soldier of fortune (nameless because he's safer that way) who has commanded men in battle for governments in the Congo and Biafra and is now looking over the Cambodian scene, recalls Julian this way: "He is a fantastic character, larger than life, born two hundred years too late. What a buccaneer he would have made!"

To a keen United Nations troubleshooter like Brian Urquhart, Julian is "one of the more engaging rogues of our time."

He moves today much as he did when he was a young eagle stalking fame, fortune, and action. He is cut of warrior cloth: six feet two inches tall and two hundred pounds of coordinated muscle trained to go the full distance, alone. He neither drinks nor smokes. His smile is infectious. His sharp, clear, mocha-brown eyes are constantly in action, sparkling with a verve at all they behold. His voice is deep, rich as mahogany. When maddened, it pounds with the fury of a storm; for a child, or a woman of beauty, it is a calming whisper. His head is always at full mast. His chin seems to be searching for something the rest of us can't see—or dare not seek.

Hubert Fauntleroy Julian is now seventy-three. But don't be fooled by that figure. The voice and manner are still commanding, the mind as quick as a skid. Dreams still come true, if more briefly than before; he still commutes to arenas of action on international jetstreams as if they were crosstown cab rides. It will be that way to the end. There's always more ahead than behind for Julian; no other way is possible.

When wanted, he may usually be found at the luxe hotel in whatever capital is embroiled in some international incident. Recently, in London, it was Claridge's, where he was discussing the location of 100,000 ex-NATO bulletproof vests he had a client for in the Middle East; the Federal

Palace in Lagos during the Nigerian crisis; the Ritz in Madrid, raising ransom money for the release from an Algerian prison of the late Congolese Premier Moise Tshombe (until a heart attack claimed the client).

Considering he is a solo operation, Julian has been the subject of an uncommon number of written reports. Few editors of major newspapers and magazines, here or abroad, can't recall his appearance on their pages. He's been profiled by *The New Yorker* and *Esquire*. A. J. Liebling covered him in numerous columns; so did Evelyn Waugh in his book *When the Going Was Good*. The late Drew Pearson was hard on him, but the very much alive H. Allen Smith was understanding in his *Low Man on a Totem Pole*. No one has ever described him in middle-ground terms; he doesn't work that way.

Julian seeks out stages to perform on not so much because of the money—although, to be sure, he won't turn it down—but because of the demands his unique quest makes on him. He has, above all else, mastered that illusive art of weaving himself into the fabric of history.

Some of his faults are inexcusable. He plays dicey games with the law, domestic and international, because he engages in ventures that sometimes violate covenants like the UN charter. Many of his enterprises have been as legal as larceny. Throughout all sorts of rascally capers, however, he has remained the complete gentleman—always gallant, ever chivalrous, and never deliberately cruel in word or action. He aims his lance at institutions, not people.

Julian has lost more than a few skirmishes. Some critics claim it's his own doing. That's partly true; he does push luck. It goes much deeper than that, however—back to his young manhood in the 1920s. His style, perhaps his whole way of life, sprang from the cold indifference of an excluding society obsessed with grabbing off all the prizes. Julian decided early on that he was not about to abide by rules that were decreed to make these arenas of challenge the special preserve of a few.

Hubert Fauntleroy Julian, by the way, is black—a fact that has both hurt and helped him. He has utilized his color only as he has his strapping size, tireless energy, sense of timing, and flair for language. He worked perfecting all of them. Why not; who doesn't? He asks no favors because he's black. He blames no flops on it, either. God-given abilities and self-honed talents, not slogans and excuses, have been his clout.

In past ages he would have been hailed a romantic. In this cynical century, when people are suspicious even of themselves, he has often been rendered to ridicule. The ones most guilty of ridiculing have been those bred to disbelieve that a man born black would dare to make dreams come true—to walk with royalty, to sleep in a corner suite, to order in French, to race about in a chauffeur-driven Rolls.

Some of this thinking was even tattooed on his own people. Half a century ago, when he first mounted his charger, most blacks did not dare to dream as Julian did. They were allowed little more challenge than a pick and shovel. But such limitations did not imprint on Julian. From the beginning, life for this Quixote has been a champagne rite to be tasted when bubbly and rejected when flat.

He has been labeled a self-promoter. So was Henry Morton Stanley; so is Doctor Christiaan Barnard. For him, and an elite few like him, there were only two choices: stay downed or rise up. He realized the need for publicity to make a move, and the press clipping became the hard currency of his world. With victory aforethought, he pushed himself into the ring where, usually alone, he challenged the racial pecking order decreed by social dermatology.

I must admit that in writing this book I have often been tempted to change the ending of the odd episode in order to hand Julian a big win. It hurt to see him lose when so much was involved. But after thinking about it for five years, visiting many of his battlegrounds, and discussing it with veterans of his many campaigns, I now know that when his story is presented as it happened, Hubert Julian comes out more human than most of his fellow beings. He has, in the most profound sense, won the big ones. He walks where he wants to, as he wants to.

And now, *Allons!*—as Julian delights in roaring when charging off to a new adventure. On with the story!

JOHN PEER NUGENT

Santa Monica, California
December, 1970

1

Jumping the Gun

Have you seen the President's limousine,
my good man?

THE BLACK EAGLE
Congo, Winter, 1961

IT IS MIDMORNING in mortar-shattered Elisabethville, the once-splendid Congolese city of broad boulevards named for Astrid and Stanley that are shaded by fragrant jacaranda trees. The season is winter 1961, and a savage little war is exploding all around: President Moise Tshombe and his secessionist province of Katanga versus a distraught United Nations that, just weeks before, had lost its beloved leader, Dag Hammarskjöld, to Africa's fating. It is filthy duty for all concerned. The Gurkha troops insist the local Baluba tribesmen are eating their dead; the Katangans insist UN fighter-bombers are napalming black innocents. Worse, both sides are thirsty. The Simba brewery, knocked out of action two days ago, is still unrepaired. No spare parts will be available until Sunday.

From out of a boarded-up boutique on Avenue President Youlou steps an ebony giant. A handful of foreign correspondents watch him course smoothly toward their place of shelter, around smoldering mounds of rubble, in pin-striped and spatted splendor—lemon-colored gloves, umbrella furled tight, homburg at a devilish angle. It must be an apparition.

As the rage of firefights throughout the city takes a brief break from its sporadic crackling, this swart Titan loudly addresses no one in particular.

"Have you seen the President's limousine, my good

man?" He looks up, then down, the street, which is empty because snipers have been sighting in on it all morning from atop the Hotel de Ville. "I told the driver I'd only be a short while. I heard *madame* had some fine Dior ties in here, but now I must rush to luncheon—with *Monsieur le Président,* of course."

Suddenly a royal blue Lincoln Continental appears at the safer end of the shooting gallery, where it stops but with motor still running.

Julian roars with laughter at the driver's nervousness to come closer. Tipping his hat and shouting *"Au revoir,"* he sets off with his package at a jaunty clip down the avenue to the limousine. He makes it. No shots are fired. The limousine rips off, leaving a lot of rubber on the red brick road that's been hit not a few times by shot and shell.

Immediately members of the press begin chattering like wire machines about him. Those who've heard of The Black Eagle before are delighted at his presence. He always thickens plots.

Not too long after this incident *Monsieur le Président* announced to the world press that henceforth The Black Eagle, accoutered with an intriguing kit of portfolios, would be his roving ambassador.

For those who had never before encountered him, awe replaced disbelief. They've been Eagle watchers ever since.

It all began in another century, long before Lincoln produced Continentals, Dior made ties, Dow turned out napalm, Gurkhas heard of Africa, and a black man knew how to angle a homburg and twirl an umbrella. It was inside a white frame house at 21 Charlotte Street in Port of Spain, Trinidad. The birth of Hubert Fauntleroy Julian was duly recorded by J. Wilkinson, the British registrar of the colony, as the island's 525th official birth of the year 1897 in the reign of Queen Victoria.

The only child and pride of Henry and Silvira Julian, a handsome and respected couple in the community, grew quickly under the Caribbean sun. His mind drank heavily of the traditional fireside stories about heroes, sometimes warriors and sometimes knights, whose quests were never finished, and of the driving, life-asserting force of calypso lyrics, which gave a message of pursuit to all children of the West Indies.

Hubert Julian's young manhood contained experiences that broadened the horizons of an ambitious lad by giant steps. His father, who managed a cocoa plantation, could afford to send him to the best private school on the island, the Eastern Boys' School on Nelson Street. His speed and coordination allowed him to star in cricket and rugby; the prettiest of the local girls were always along the grassy sidelines cheering the talented buster on. He already walked with the cocksurety of a hailed hero. He grew tall, his muscles long and lithe in scoring action.

At fourteen, he witnessed the arrival of a flying machine on a lumpy savannah outside the city. He was especially impressed with the pilot's panache—the proud gait, the elegant jodhpurs and brown boots, the plaid cap, and the dashing twist of the silk scarf around his neck. Even though he also witnessed the plane's crashing on September 7, 1911, and the pilot's death, the initial impression created within him a determination to one day and somehow become a member of the elite and adventurous profession that in those days numbered no more than eight hundred members.

His parents and teachers spotted the hunger in his eyes for challenges beyond what Trinidad offered, and he was sent to London to live with a relative working there.

Three years and several impressionable trips to the continent later, he sailed off to Canada to further his education in less dangerous climes than now covered most of Europe. It was August of 1914.

West Indian friends living in Montreal arranged for him to attend a Jesuit-run high school. There he received his first shot of school French—and it took.

To fly was still his goal, however. When he heard that Montreal's aerodrome was named St. Hubert, he interpreted it as a good sign. The airfield was a major training base for the Royal Canadian Flying Corps. On weekends Julian began studying the takeoff and landing procedures of cadets in de Havilland biplanes and Sopwith Tabloids. And he listened intently to the snatches of conversation he could pick up through the fence during outdoor briefings.

A black face wasn't rare in Canada. There were about twenty thousand Negroes, many of them descendants of American slaves who had fled north on the Underground Railroad. But a black face on a rugby player's frame, speaking lyrical English with polish, attracted the eye of several of the flight cadets and instructors. Their main concern, however, was getting to Europe and into the air war as quickly as possible, and there was little time left for anything else. Julian's wait was long and lonely as he came out time and again to watch and wish.

One afternoon in late 1918, he was summoned over the fence by an instructor. William A. Bishop, the Canadian ace who had just come home with seventy-two confirmed enemy kills and a Victoria Cross, was impressed by the patient vigil he had noticed over three months.

The year 1919 was an eventful one in aviation. With the war over and the victors busy sorting out the spoils at the long table in Versailles, anxious young flyers got on with advancing the daring new science in altitude and distance. It was a time for writing history in the sky. A defeated Germany was first to establish a regular passenger-carrying airline service; an American naval pilot became the first to make a transoceanic flight. And another first took place, noticed by only a handful of men. On a chilly November Sunday Hubert Julian climbed down from a ten-minute solo flight in "Billy" Bishop's Sopwith Camel. He had just become the first Negro aviator in history.

Nearly a thousand miles away in central Minnesota Charles Lindbergh, then seventeen, was busy convincing farmers that the milking of cows by machine was a great scientific breakthrough. He was three years away from a flying lesson.

2

Harlem Nocturne

I will endeavor to live by my wits,
gentlemen.
THE BLACK EAGLE *to skeptics in the Elite Barber Shop Harlem, July, 1921*

ON MARCH 9, 1921, Hubert Julian took on America with, among other things, a pair of new gray spats and briefcase containing a *parachuttagravepreresista.* It was a flight-safety invention, Da Vincian in name and design, which he had been working on for two years. Shortly after soloing he realized that if you didn't wear a parachute—and many pilots didn't—there were two choices when your engine failed in flight: jump out for the quick death or attempt to ride the plane down and chance a fiery end.

Theoretically, Julian's contraption went into action when a plane developed trouble. The pilot flipped a switch that engaged a helicopter-like horizontal blade. Its spinning blew open an enormous ribbed umbrella capable of letting the plane down at twenty feet a second—certainly a more gentle descent than without a *parachuttagravepreresista.* (A New York engineering firm, Aircraft Safety Release Corporation, conducted successful small-plane-saving experiments using the same basic concept in 1968. The chief test pilot for the program was Tommy Walker, who flew for the Congo in the early 1960s when Julian was a diplomat and arms dealer for a parade of Congolese strongmen.)

Using a crude model made from balsa wood, Julian experimented for months, dropping a cradle of eggs hooked up to his *parachuttagravepreresista* from the rooftop of a Montreal apartment house. He used up quite a few eggs, and splattered not a few pedestrians, in his pursuit of science. But by late 1920 he was successful in landing eggs with shells cracked but yolks intact. That was good enough for him. He hired a lawyer and obtained a Canadian patent. Then he set out for Washington to obtain a United States patent.

"Be it known that I, Hubert Julian, a subject of the King of Great Britain," his written application proclaimed, "hereby do declare that the following is a full, clear, and exact description of the invention such as will enable others skilled in the art to which it appertains to make and use the same . . ."

The trip was cut short by a long-distance call from Montreal. Julian's attorney, William Linton, said he had received three offers from Canadian aircraft firms for rights to the invention. Returning home immediately, he sold the *parachuttagravepreresista* to the Gerney Aircraft Corporation for a combination of stock and $3,000 in cash.

On May 25, 1921, Julian received a special-delivery letter informing him that he had been issued U.S. Patent No. 1,379,264. The patent people, an unimaginative breed, had changed the name to an "airplane-safety appliance."

Julian's quick trip to America had left him with good impressions. The pulse of the place seemed livelier than Canada's. The buildings were bigger, the cars seemed faster, and he noticed that there were many more black faces. A little reading told him the country was in an economic boom and that the flying bug was catching across the nation. It smacked of adventure and profit.

He prepared to make the move in an extravagant manner. Since his childhood he had always approached competitive situations that way. He usually came out of them—an exam or sports match or debate—leading. For him the aura of self-confidence not only counted, but also worked.

He had a good bank account now, and at twenty-three, he was 190 restless pounds on a six-foot-two frame built for action. His jaw was trim, his face a rich mahogany, his eyes full of the sparkle of anticipation of challenge. He moved with ease and an air of pride wherever he went. Negro friends in Canada advised him to head for New York first, and gave him a number of written introductions to people and directions to places. They assured him he'd make it big there—with both sexes. Julian's ego was already in flight; he could hardly wait.

First he purchased a handsome tan McFarlan automobile (the Buick of Canada) with wheel spokes of lacquered wood, and hired a white chauffeur (there weren't any Negroes available who knew how to drive). Then he acquired a new wardrobe—an impressive assemblage of hand-stitched shoes, tailored suits, silk shirts, pearl-gray gloves, enough ties for a regiment, and a black homburg.

Hubert Fauntleroy Julian, gentleman flyer and inventor, formally joined America at Rouses Point by Lake Champlain on the Canada-New York border on July 10, 1921. He seemed to be a suave plenipotentiary from a misty Shangri-la who came across the international line.

"Why d'you wanna live in the US of Aye?" asked the immigration officer as he fingered through Julian's British passport.

From a comfortable position between orderly stacks of leather luggage, Julian announced, "It's the challenge, my good man."

"Don't think you'll like it here," answered the officer with a scowl on his face. "Now whose car is this?"

From under his rented brown cap, the driver piped up. "It belongs to the boss," he said, pointing a gloved finger to the back seat and producing the registration.

Julian proceeded to snap open a briefcase that revealed orderly bundles of new American bills.

The officer's jaw dropped and he looked embarrassed. "Er—welcome," he finally said. "I wish we'd get more niggers like you over here."

"Motor on, driver," Julian commanded, pretending not to hear.

Once rolling through the piney countryside, Julian leaned back to take in the scenery while salting an egg from the picnic lunch. By the time they passed through Albany, he was well into planning his Harlem arrival.

Across the restless nation a post-war generation was seriously engaged in losing itself in a frenetic blare of marathon dancing, wife switching, pole sitting, bootlegging, Mah Jongg playing, and Freud reading, as if the cuckoo in life's clock had gone berserk. Lovemaking in the rumble seat, swigging from a metal flask, cheering wildly for old school colors at the football oval, and strumming out tinny saccharine sounds on the ukulele—all orchestrated a cacophony that people labeled "fun!" Writers called it the Roaring Twenties.

The sensitive Negro writer Langston Hughes said of Harlem during this period, "Jazz filled the night air and people came from all around after dark to look upon the city within a city."

Reaching Harlem, Julian headed for the Elite Barber Shop. Negro VIPs like Bill "Bojangles" Robinson had their hair trimmed and fingernails manicured in this neat storefront at 2311 Seventh Avenue.

The adventure-seeker entered, nodded hellos around, and handed a letter of introduction from a Montreal friend to the man pointed out as Jimmy Garrett, the most famous Negro barber of them all.

The graying barber agreed to store Julian's luggage and briefcase for a small fee until he learned "the lay of the land," as the cocky youngblood put it.

"I will endeavor to live by my wits, gentlemen," the newcomer announced. It brought a howl from all present. Even Julian chuckled, although he was quite serious.

Within forty-eight hours a new-found friend introduced Julian to a famous madam. She was an older woman, but wore well despite an extravagant application of lipstick. She was pleasant, and Julian was at his suave best at the meeting. She fell full force for the tall, lean islander with polished manners and elegant accent. Julian instantly picked up on the situation. It seemed to him to offer a great potential for a minimum investment. He confided to her a suddenly concocted saga of coming to America to work his way through medical school while supporting his poor old parents living in steamy poverty back in the Caribbean.

The madam bought the story. She insisted he come live in her salon on the top floor of the five-story brownstone pleasure palace she ruled. As soon as he arrived, she outfitted him in a silk dressing gown, monogrammed pajamas (that had belonged to a former live-in client who had left in a hurry), and Spanish leather slippers.

Julian refers to this period as his "buffet flat days." He had the run of the place. The only house rule: Hands off the labor line—with the exception of the madam, that is.

Even Julian, by now a firm believer in the power of positive thinking, was overwhelmed by this chance success. The house rule, though tempting to break, was kept. He did his sporting outside the premises, when supposedly rapt in study in the stacks at Columbia University's medical library—the location of which he only had a vague notion about. The madam felt all the more sorry that the poor lad had to spend so many nights in lonely labor as he crammed for exams right through to sunrise. When he finally trudged up the stairs exhausted, she was always there eagerly waiting to comfort and bed him. After a few weeks, even the fit rake began to weaken under the demands of double sessions.

One day the madam met Jimmy Garrett on the street. She confided to the barber, a longtime friend, the story of her magnificent treasure trove.

Her description of the young buck matched that of someone Garrett had been looking for. After Julian left his luggage in the barbershop, Garrett had peeked in the briefcase. The bundles of cash he spotted had made him nervous.

The money was either stolen or soon would be, he told the madam in confidence. Either way, he wanted nothing to do with its coming or going.

That evening she entered her salon to find Julian already dressed and ready for his night sessions.

"Where you going?" she asked.

"To the library," Julian answered in his best overworked student's voice. "Would you be so kind as to let me borrow five dollars for the purchase of a textbook on anatomy?"

"Liar, you owe me one hundred dollars!" she screeched. "Now get the hell out of here!" She caught him on the forehead with the leather heel of her right shoe, and the affair was ended.

Minus dressing gown, pajamas, and slippers, Julian hastily retreated and took refuge for the night in a broiling walk-up single at the Hotel Olga.

The next day he brought his car out of storage and picked up his luggage and briefcase at the barbershop. He had guessed what had happened, and when he confronted Garrett with his suspicions, the barber confessed. Julian left, handing Garrett a sealed envelope containing $100, addressed to the madam.

He settled down in the Olga. Due to the eased schedule caused by the abrupt break in his sporting life, he immediately started putting weight back on. The fling of living by his wits was out of his system, temporarily at least. He got down to the serious business that had really attracted him to the U.S.—launching his flying career.

His timing was right. Aerial circuses were flourishing and daredevils were making headlines. Businessmen were increasingly turning into patrons of the sky gypsies—the barnstormers, the wing-walkers, the stunters, and the parachute jumpers. Bankrolling an outfit meant profit. On weekends tens of thousands of Americans everywhere—in wheatbelt towns and industrial cities—were jamming parks and fields, carnivals and county fairs, to pay a dollar for the show and half a buck a minute for a short hop.

It was all there. How to get a piece of it was Julian's next project.

For openers, he concentrated on building an image that would attract attention. Recognition as a Harlem playboy would gain him the social entrees to potential sponsors. Initially, he reckoned, they would have to be Negro business leaders with the funds and the faith to back one of their own on a glory mission.

He began frequenting the clubs where Harlem's elite unwound—the Savoy Ballroom, Small's, Baron's, the Cotton Club, and the Capitol Club. At the big Negro musical reviews like *Put 'n Take* and *The Brownskin Models* he became Mr. First Nighter complete with velvet-collared black cape.

A spartan for conditioning who neither smoked nor drank, Julian possessed the stamina to Charleston all night and the automobile to squire dates home in style. His knack was uncanny for arriving at affairs as the belles warmed up and their beaux passed out. It made him successful in various pursuits that he offered up for the cause which he only occasionally forgot was flying.

By the end of 1922 he was well enough known in what he considered the right circles to declare a moratorium on social climbing. The decision came none too soon. He was about out of breath and money; he was also losing weight again. He now set out to create an aerial act.

Since parachuting seemed the specialty of the daredevils who attracted the largest crowds, he decided to begin there. Back in Canada Billy Bishop had given him a letter of introduction to Charles "Casey" Jones, a pilot at the Curtiss Aircraft Company on Long Island.

Julian located Jones at the Mineola field, introduced himself, and handed him Bishop's letter.

The lanky ex-mail pilot read it. "Well, I'm broad-minded," he said, folding it and putting it back in the envelope. "But we do have some tough Southerners here. It doesn't look too good for you."

After giving it some thought, though, he came up with an idea. "Next Sunday there's a benefit for a 'flying parson' who crashed recently," he said. Perhaps if Julian were to perform as a parachutist—"but for free, of course"—something might come of it.

Julian leapt at the opportunity. That he had never jumped before didn't bother him.

The next Sunday he arrived early at Curtiss Field and rented a parachute, packing it himself into the canvas bag, as he had learned from endless reading of flight manuals.

Jones brought him over to a pilot named Slim Hennicke, who gave him a five-minute briefing on the subject of jumping. The nervous but determined student then tied the bag to the plane's undercarriage, strapped himself into the harness, and braced himself between the rickety wheels. Hennicke checked his procedure and gave him a thumbs-up. If there had been time to think, Julian would have been frightened; but Hennicke took right off.

From what he reckoned was an altitude of about four thousand feet, Julian grew excited as he spotted growing clusters of dots—people, paid viewers, hundreds of them. They stared up, waiting.

The wind tore at his hair, lips, limbs. His half-closed eyes were full of tears. He hadn't felt this good since his solo.

The plane hit an air pocket, and the sudden drop of one hundred feet tossed the unprepared birdman off his perch. He frantically grabbed for the nearest thing, which was the red-hot exhaust pipe. It snapped off. Out into space he tumbled in considerable pain, and doubt.

The chute opened, jolting his whole body, and after about three minutes the world's first Negro parachutist landed on a Nassau County chicken farm.

As Julian wrestled with his runaway chute, a furious

farmer charged out of a shed, shotgun at the ready. Julian did some fast talking in an effort to convince him his was not a new approach to chicken stealing. A phone call to Jones at the field cleared up the matter. To pay for the call, Julian had to leave his brand-new Sam Browne leather belt with the farmer.

As he walked the dusty mile back to the field, his badly folded chute draped around his aching neck and his hand a growing, throbbing blister, his strongest sensation was exhilaration at having made it. Jumping, he decided, was not a bad way to break in—at least not until he could afford his own plane.

Jones greeted him with a warm smile and a pat on the back and told him he had an idea. He wrote down the name of a barnstorming pilot in New Jersey who was interested in helping young men ambitious for a flying career.

Clarence Chamberlin was soon to become one of the greats of American aviation's pioneering era. In April 1927 he was to set the world's record for an endurance flight: fifty-one hours, eleven minutes, twenty-five seconds. Just two weeks after Lindbergh's historic May 21 solo of the same year, Chamberlin was to fly a man across the Atlantic to Eisleben, Germany, in forty-two hours, thirty-one minutes, becoming the first man to make a nonstop transatlantic passenger flight.

Chamberlin was especially good with parachutists, Jones said. He assured Julian that he was the right man to train under in order to become a regular on the circuit.

The twenty-five-year-old apprentice daredevil drove home to Harlem with his mind wildly spinning off all sorts of possibilities. Now he was even more certain of achieving fame and fortune. The obstacles he knew; he lacked the backing and color. But the obstacles only served as added incentives.

3

Mission Impossible

In ancient days, I would be put on a charger and led to the king, who would take a sword from the sheath and touch my shoulders, announcing, 'Arise, Sir Hubert, well done.'
THE BLACK EAGLE *to the Judge*
New York City, April, 1923

THE CRESTED parachutist reached the pilot's ramshackle little hangar on a chilly March afternoon in 1923. Clarence Chamberlin conducted his flying business from a few not-so-very-level acres of the remote flats behind New Jersey's palisades. Entering the hangar, Julian found half a dozen surplus World War I planes in varying stages of repair. Walking around, he saw only one man, lying under the wing of a plane, apparently taking a nap.

Julian straightened out the tunic of his sky-blue uniform and firmly pulled down the kepi of the same color, putting it at a tilt that could be called rakish. He then cleared his throat in such a way that it woke Chamberlin up.

"Good afternoon, Major," he said. "I'm Lieutenant Hubert Julian just down from Canada looking for an opportunity to pursue my profession. I follow the parachute-jumping business. Maybe you've heard of some of my jumps up around Montreal."

Chamberlin, totally unprepared for the unexpected arrival of a black man dressed like the chief of an air force, explained that he hadn't heard and that he wasn't a major. Neither comment, however, seemed to land with any visible impact on Julian.

"Well, Major," Julian continued, "they told me out at Curtiss that you had some ships here, and I thought maybe I'd ride with you and practice a few jumps. It don't do to get rusty in my business."

After several minutes of conversation, Julian produced Casey Jones' letter. Reading it, Chamberlin agreed to take him up in an old Avro that was gassed and ready. A slight delay was caused by Julian's not having a parachute with him. It was customary for the jumper to bring his own gear.

"The truth is," he explained, "I left all my chutes in Montreal. You know how it is traveling around."

Just before taking off, Chamberlin asked Julian how he preferred to jump—out of the cockpit or off the wing.

"Lord," said Julian, "I quit doing pull-offs more than a year ago. I go bang right out of the cockpit."

At three thousand feet, a good jumping height, Chamberlin leveled into position and signaled the jumper out. Nothing happened. He tried four more times without luck and then landed the plane in a fury.

"What happened?" he demanded.

"I just couldn't seem to hit it right," Julian explained slowly. "Just couldn't seem to get organized. To tell the truth, I don't much like that cockpit of yours. Too narrow for my kind of work. Maybe I'd better try it off the wing till I get sort of used to the ship."

They took off again. This time up Julian performed magnificently. His first pull-off from the wing was clean. They went up a second time, and the jump was even better. Chamberlin began to feel that perhaps he had come across a real daredevil.

Julian was so exuberant that he asked to go up a third time with a new type of chute: one with a ripcord that demanded a chancy leap into space based on faith that a hard yank would release the canopy. It didn't always.

In the air, Julian froze again. He held onto the fragile right wing strut tighter than ever.

Chamberlin, who was beginning to grow bored, pulled

the ship into a sudden turn that catapulted Julian off the wing tip—still holding the strut. With the wings flapping dangerously, Chamberlin had a most difficult time landing the plane.

When he finally landed, he walked over to where the jumper was tangled in shroud lines, still holding the strut.

"That certainly was my most remarkable jump," Julian said. "Yes sir, my most remarkable."

And with that performance, according to *The New Yorker*, "Julian emerged from the anonymous millions to open his career as the bright star of Afro-American aviation."

In the early 1920s, if you made a couple of jumps and survived, you were a veteran. Julian, convinced his apprenticeship was over, decided he was now accomplished enough to take a dive for pay. He announced plans to record another aeronautical first: parachuting over Manhattan.

Within a week he had lined up as sponsors a prominent Harlem optician and the New York distributor for a St. Louis hair-straightener manufacturer.

With contracts signed (but no money until the performance was completed), Julian returned to New Jersey to discuss procedure with Chamberlin. The first thing, the pilot explained, was to pay in advance for the flight. Julian tried to bypass that with a wing shot at the former Signal Corps pilot's patriotism.

"Just think of it," he said. "We can revolutionize military tactics by showing that troops with equipment can land safely anywhere. Why, I'm going to invite the Army to be guest observers at our operation!"

Chamberlin's patriotism failed Julian. He still demanded cash—or some of it, anyway. Julian reluctantly parted with a $25 deposit.

The jump was set for Sunday, April 23. The target: a vacant lot between Seventh and Eighth Avenues and 139th and 140th Streets.

WATCH THE CLOUDS THIS SUNDAY—JULIAN IS ARRIVING

FROM THE SKY HERE, read big black-and-white signs nailed up on the posts around the lot that Julian rented. Admission: $1.00 was in small print.

Newspapers and citizens alike displayed considerable interest in the venture. The plan was rather daring; the jump area was not an obstacle course in needle-nosed skyscrapers, but it was not in a prairie state, either.

Shortly after the announcement, a number of morticians phoned Julian requesting display rights to his body. Only when one of them agreed to reimburse him for Chamberlin's full fee—$100—was the parachutist's pride soothed enough to make the ghoulish deal.

The winner of the stiff bidding, undertaker Adolph Howell, announced, "It will be worth a fortune displaying the brave fool's body."

The event started on schedule, which was two days after the Army Air Service announced that three out of every hundred flying enthusiasts were killed annually because of the occupation's special hazards, including parachuting.

Chamberlin cruised along smoothly at about 3,500 feet, occasionally nodding encouragement to the windblown star, who hunched over in ready position on the right wing. Julian looked splendid. He was in a skin-tight scarlet outfit, brown sneakers, a leather bandolier looped tightly across his chest.

Over 141st Street and Riverside Drive, Chamberlin slowed almost to a stall. He banked abruptly and Julian spilled off and away, waving good-bye.

The chute opened fine, right on time in a westerly wind. In swaying descent Julian unpacked his bandolier, and the wind unfurled the large banner: HOENIG OPTICAL IS OPEN TODAY. At 2,500 feet he noticed he was going to be short of his mark. Below him were the tracks of the Ninth Avenue El. His eyes riveted on the electrified third rail. Instant death came closer and closer.

He rocked frantically, attempting to alter the chute's angle of descent. He'd about given up when a gust of wind socked into the canopy. Just in time he cleared the tracks to land hard on the tar-topped roof of the U.S. Post Office building on 140th Street near Seventh Avenue.

He gathered in his chute and looked down. Pandemonium raged over in the lot and out into the streets. Under the pressure of the surging crowd, many nearby store windows were shattered inward. Traffic was snarled in all directions with happy, laughing people.

Julian slipped out of the harness, packed up the chute, pinned on the sash announcing the St. Louis hair straightener, and skipped down the fire escape. He jumped the last ten feet into the welcoming arms of the crowd and was immediately hoisted onto strong shoulders that bore him in triumph to Liberty Hall, headquarters of a return-to-Africa movement. The meeting was no longer in progress due to the circumstances outside.

He was carried inside to the stage. At the podium, almost breathless, he finally managed to coax the throng into silence. He then began the paid announcements which were greeted with cheers that made all the clients happy—except perhaps Howell the mortician.

While Julian was explaining that one reason for the jump was to warn that a certain Negro department store was in danger of falling into white hands if not better patronized, a policeman elbowed his way to the front of the stage. He caught Julian's eye by waving a manila envelope.

"Please take this," he shouted over the jubilant din.

Certain it was a donation or an invitation to a speaking engagement, Julian did. He ripped it open with a great flourish. It was a summons for inciting a riot.

The next day, Julian walked into court sharply turned out in dark suit, spats, bowler, and pink boutonniere.

The judge, a short, black-robed Irishman of considerable years, was musing over the press clippings on the jump. Julian saw him as kindly. He had an inspiration and tried it.

"Your Honor," the aerialist began in a deep, clear voice,

"am I not to be knighted for proving the worth of parachute troopers? Now, it seems, I am here as a common criminal. In ancient days I would be put on a charger and led to the king, who would take a sword from the sheath and touch my shoulders, announcing, 'Arise, Sir Hubert, well done.'"

With that he stepped up to the bench and handed the judge a calling card: HUBERT JULIAN, M.D., WORLD'S CHAMPION DAREDEVIL PARACHUTIST. (The M.D. meant Mechanical Designer, he later explained.)

"Well, there was a lot of damage, young man," said the judge, staring at both card and bearer.

"But I did apply for a permit, Your Honor," answered Julian.

A police sergeant who held the case file confirmed it was true, that he had applied on April 16 of the same year. The problem was there was no ordinance to cover a parachute jump over the city.

The judge decided to dismiss the case. He prohibited Julian from jumping over Manhattan for six months, though, noting that by then he would hope a city ordinance would be drawn up covering the matter.

Julian now strolled along Lenox Avenue, Harlem's *Champs-Elysées,* to the waves and shouts of all he met. His picture appeared in many newspapers, and his daring caper was on most news broadcasts. He was the crown prince of adventure for many of the ten million black Americans. In the weeks following, at paid lectures in places like Atlantic City, Philadelphia, and Detroit, he proclaimed his mission.

"I want to prove," he said, "that science and good will can go hand in hand and make the world a more fundamental place in which to live."

Outside, aides sold his eight-by-ten likeness for a dollar, and his autograph went for fifty cents. Airman Julian was fast learning entrepreneurial ways.

Having been catapulted into the Negro hierarchy by the

jump, he became a prime recruitment target for Marcus Garvey, a fellow West Indian who, along with George Padmore and Dr. W. E. B. DuBois, was an advocate of Pan-Africanism. Garvey was one of the first black leaders to preach the gospel "Black is beautiful."

The fiery Jamaican's ambition was to lead American Negroes back to Africa. In preparation for the exodus he had already declared himself the provisional president of the Empire of Africa under the banner of the Universal Negro Improvement Association. It claimed nine million faithful leaguers, or about ninety percent of the Negro population in the nation. More realistic figures placed his support at anywhere from four million to about ten thousand.

The UNIA was an elaborate operation. There was the Universal African Legion, the Universal Black Cross Nurses, the Universal African Motor Corps. Officers received the sash of the Knight Commander of the Distinguished Order of the Nile, and close advisers were named dukes of the Niger and Uganda.

Garvey was just about ready to announce the starting date to the land he promised when he realized he had an image problem. He was short and stout, hardly the dimensions of the Moses he believed himself to be or of one Negroes would venture far from home to follow. What he needed up front to make them follow was a man with the heroic proportions of a noble warrior or knight.

So he asked Julian to help. Julian agreed, and was soon rallying people to the black-is-beautiful banner. When he said it, they believed. They believed because they could see it there in front of them—tall and eloquent, their own black adventurer who bowed to no obstacle. Garvey's movement boomed, and Julian received a handsome fee for his services.

Six months and one day after the first Manhattan jump, Julian suited up, ready to do it again into another rented lot. The Martin Saxophone Company, in conjunction with the Wurlitzer people, had contracted with him to play a new gold-plated saxophone as he came in for this landing. A free instrument was part of the fee. Julian took ten fast lessons, mastering "Runnin' Wild."

As he descended with an easy sway from four thousand feet, he unhooked the saxophone and fingered the keys.

At about two thousand feet he started playing. Suddenly a wind picked him up. The next thing he knew he had hit the roof of a building on 123rd Street—six blocks south of the target area where the paying customers, full of peanuts, soda pop, and other good things, waited anxiously.

The strong wind scooted the chute's canopy across the rooftop. Julian fought and tugged, but was dragged along. He was slammed against the ledge. Although he was almost able to reach at the canopy, it was too late. Over the ledge he went. He grabbed the flagpole.

Hanging from a flagpole three floors up, he felt the pole bending dangerously under his weight. Frantically he kicked in a window. Two policemen with service revolvers drawn rushed into the room—Julian had landed on a police station.

He was only released by the desk sergeant after promising to pay for the window and put on a show for the next fall's policemen's picnic.

When he stepped outside the 123rd Street precinct building, he was greeted by an angry crowd demanding a refund: they hadn't seen much of the landing and felt cheated. He turned quickly into the police station and ducked out the rear door.

Before entering the 135th Street subway station to go home, he did speak to a few of his more faithful but somewhat shaken followers. He confided to them that what he was really doing this time—and thus the reason for the bad landing—was testing a new and very secret invention.

Its name? they asked. "Why, the *saxaphonaparachutta-*

gravepreresista," he answered. As the group heatedly debated the merits of his excuse, Julian borrowed a nickel and disappeared through a turnstile.

On Monday morning life perked up considerably as he read the *New York Telegram.* Until now, many newspapers thought they were doing him a favor describing him as "the Ace of Spades." But in describing his most recent aerial feat, the *Telegram* christened him "The Black Eagle."

4

A Most Historic Non-Crossing

Now folks out there, just chip in a quarter or a dollar apiece, and then I can fly like you want me to.

THE BLACK EAGLE, *at his Harlem river launch site for Africa Noon, July 4, 1924*

Now see what you've done! You've kept me waiting here and the tide's gone out.

THE BLACK EAGLE, *same place, two hours later*

BILLED AS "The Black Eagle," Julian jumped his way across the country for the next two months. Sometimes he barnstormed with Chamberlin. On long-distance engagements he hired plane and pilot for a parachuting performance, then rented a Jenny and stunted it himself.

The demand was not only for him as a daredevil at air shows, but also as a lecturer. At Negro colleges he gave pep talks on making it in spite of obstacles.

"You can do anything anyone else can do," he exhorted students. "Just get up, brother, and try. If you fail the first time, don't quit. Try again. You'll make it eventually." He illustrated his philosophy with case studies out of the ever-expanding Julian file.

Still, he was restless. He yearned for more far-reaching excitement. Marcus Garvey had interested him in books on African history. Time and again he came upon stories about Ethiopia, the three-thousand-year-old African empire begun by Solomon and Sheba. He was fascinated by the saga of a black land that had been in business longer than most white nations. One morning during the Christmas holidays of 1923 he decided: The Black Eagle would become the first man to attempt a solo flight to Africa.

He made the project public on January 10, 1924. To date six men, flying in pairs, had crossed the Atlantic. But no one had yet considered attempting the longer, more hazardous route, and alone, to what was still a dark continent known mostly to Explorers Club members.

He consulted Chamberlin on routing, type of aircraft best suited for the safari, and last but far from least, the financing of an airship for such a project. His instructor, who had recently gone into partnership with several hard-nosed businessmen, told him he could no longer afford to ignore bills and their collection. Julian told him not to worry; he'd raise the cash.

Chamberlin recommended Julian purchase a hydroplane, which would give him added safety on such an untried voyage. The proposed flight plan was to city-hop down the Eastern Seaboard to Florida, then island-hop through the Caribbean to South America. The southern crossing of the ocean would start from Recife, Brazil, and end at Liberia's capital of Monrovia after a mid-ocean refueling stop at a speck of an island called St. Paul's Rock. Once in Africa, the course would take him along the Gold Coast, across the North African deserts, down the Nile, and finally up the plateau to Ethiopia.

"The plane will be named the *Ethiopia I*," Julian announced at a New York press conference in early February. He set the takeoff date at July 4 as a symbol of what the flight would mean.

"Funds," he stated, "will be raised among the patrons of flying and fans of The Black Eagle."

Almost overnight the flight became a conversation piece. But not a fund raiser. The donations amounted to a scattering of dimes, quarters, dollar bills, and a small pile of stamps, most of which were canceled. Another funding tack was needed.

Since the project could result in an impressive first for his race, Julian approached the National Association for the Advancement of Colored People for backing. (The NAACP had been established fifteen years before, on February 12, 1909, the centennial of Abraham Lincoln's birth.)

Julian arranged a meeting at national headquarters in New York with James Weldon Johnson, the first Negro executive secretary of the NAACP. Johnson was the author of the novel *Autobiography of an Ex-Colored Man,* and writer of "Lift Ev'ry Voice and Sing," which had become the Negro national anthem.

"I propose to fly to Africa to stimulate Negro interest in the aviation age," Julian told Johnson. "You're the organization for this. We have blackbirds and white doves. I want to see black pilots as well as white pilots flying. It's coming, Mr. Johnson. We must be ready for it."

He showed Johnson his projected budget. It stated that Julian had pledged $7,500 of his own money and that $5,000 more was needed to fund the project completely. Julian emphasized that he would be doing the flying and taking the chances.

"The trouble is, we're only incorporated to help Negroes in court," Johnson explained, handing Julian back his presentation.

The rejection was bad enough. Almost immediately, however, rumors started about the validity of the whole project: that Julian was not qualified for the flight; that the flight was for personal glory. One Negro newspaper insisted that on takeoff day, the plane "would suddenly disappear into the hands of the white men who really own it." This caused other Negro organizations to have second thoughts about backing the project.

At one point Julian remarked sardonically, "My biggest support comes not from Negro groups, but from the Chinese. They know nothing about the flight and, more important, say nothing."

Finally he saw no other way but to go directly to the people. He launched a public subscription campaign by advertising the cause in the nation's Negro newspapers like the *Amsterdam News* and the *Pittsburgh Courier.*

The advertisements brought more complaints than funds. Cranks and skeptics phoned, wired, and wrote the FBI and U.S. postal authorities about Julian's soliciting through the mails.

One wintry day when he was in a conference with Chamberlin in his new quarters at New Jersey's Teterboro Airport, a Negro agent from the U.S. Post Office Department arrived to inform him of the trouble he was in. The Federal government, the agent explained, had evidence that in Julian's advertisements he was urging every black American to contribute one dollar for what was called a "scientific undertaking."

The agent politely told Julian, "On behalf of the United States government I beg to inform you that you either make that said airplane flight or else."

Julian asked him about the "or else."

"Friend," the agent said, "there is a law against collecting funds through the mail with intent to defraud. You better go ahead with your flight to Africa." He bowed and left.

Julian turned glum. He told Chamberlin he had about $3,000. And that was mostly in pledges.

The rest of the winter and spring proved a nervous, tough stretch for Julian. In May he put a deposit of $1,000 on a $4,000 World War I third-hand plane that Chamberlin had hammered, wired, patched, and glued together for him. It was the best he could afford. Chamberlin assured him it could at least get airborne.

He also rented a vacant lot at 135th Street and Seventh Avenue, where an enormous sign now announced:

COME IN—FOR THE DOUBTING THOMASES, BEHOLD THE MIGHTY *ETHIOPIA I* THAT I AM GOING TO ATTEMPT TO FLY TO AFRICA,

LAND OF OUR FATHERS. WHEN YOU GET INSIDE, TOUCH THE PLANE AS THAT DOUBTING THOMAS WANTED TO THE HANDS OF THE LORD.

Admission was one dollar.

On June 10 the Boeing hydroplane passed Chamberlin's flying tests and was trucked from New Jersey to the lot. Two weeks later nearly one thousand of the curious paid to watch the breaking of a precious magnum of upstate New York bubbly on the plane's nose.

In flying togs, Julian held up selected newspaper clippings to the audience and read them out loud through a megaphone. The *New York American* had just hailed him as "The Booker T. Washington of flying—calm and smiling at 26."

Hopping into the cockpit, Julian revved up the engine to create excitement as well as to signal his aides it was time to work over the crowd. Their hats produced $500 more. It was slow going. But it was fly or else.

By the end of June he was about $1,000 short. And he had yet to purchase thermos jugs, blankets, pills, a compass, life preservers, and a pilot's uniform, which he insisted had to be elaborate for formal arrivals in foreign lands and meetings with rulers.

All through the night of July 3, Julian kept waking up, trying to think of reasons to cancel the flight. He hoped for rain; but the morning of July 4 dawned clear.

At breakfast, the front page of the *New York World* caught his eye:

NEGRO AVIATOR EXPECTS TO LAUNCH WORLD FLIGHT FROM HARLEM TODAY

Lieutenant Hubert Julian, M.D., of No. 106 West 139th Street, a West Indian, who has been making

Harlem gasp for months by his parachute leaps . . . says he will start at 1:30 o'clock on a one-man airplane tour of four continents and expects to arrive at his starting point, 139th Street and the Harlem River, just thirty-one days hence.

He winced, dressed, and left for the launch site.

The Harlem River's banks and bridges, the surrounding rooftops and fire escapes, and a nearby lumberyard were already filling with holiday spectators. They brought box lunches, crying babies, and yelping pets.

By 9:00 AM the police estimated the crowd at thirty thousand. Straw-hatted and white-aproned vendors couldn't keep up with the rush of orders for franks, hot pig's feet, watermelon, ices, and soda pop. Authorized and unauthorized agents sold photos of the day's hero and colorful but often inaccurate flags labeled Ethiopia. Nearly everyone was given an orange balloon with instructions to release it to the skies the instant The Black Eagle soared.

Wearing a blue uniform, black leather cavalry boots, and a cynical scowl on his face, Julian stood in the riverbank's mud by the right pontoon. He stared at the people as they arrived and shouted angry warnings to those who kept pushing to get close to the plane to touch it or pull off a souvenir piece.

An aide finally loaded Julian's luggage aboard the plane. Bags were marked with such stenciled notations as: "Tropical," "Arctic," and "Stormy Weather." The nearby grandstand was now packed with dignitaries, including many uniformed members of Garvey's various military forces.

At noon Chamberlin's partners arrived and a heated argument over money erupted. They refused to let Julian take off until he came up with another $500. In desperation he went again to the people, informing them through a megaphone that he himself had already sold his car and pawned not only his suits but "even sixteen of my seventeen shirts."

"Now folks out there," he implored, "just chip in a

quarter or a dollar apiece, and then I can fly like you want me to."

Aides quickly spread out with baskets. Some came back with very little, mostly because they had first extracted what they thought was a last salary.

Shortly after 2:00 PM, his uniform soaked through with perspiration and his patience worn out from anxiety, Julian yelled, "Now see what you've done! You've kept me waiting here and the tide's gone out."

The pontoons stayed stuck in the river's bottom mud for about an hour. Then the tide slowly flowed in again and the plane floated. It was getting late, well past flight time. Chamberlin's partners still refused to allow the takeoff.

Julian again appealed for funds. But the crowd, already highly entertained by the ground-level antics of the pilot, was not very anxious to pay money to cut the show short. Or so it seemed to Julian as he fingered the thin receipts.

As the sun began its descent over New Jersey and patches of people started drifting homeward to get ready for the evening's display of fireworks, a man pushed through the ring of aides around Julian.

"I want to wish you good luck, Mister Julian," he said. Julian knew without looking who it was.

"I thought I'd stop by to make sure the schedule was still in order," the postal agent said.

Julian closed his eyes and shook his head slowly as if in pain.

Just then Lt. William Wellington Grant, one of Marcus Garvey's bright young officers, stepped forward. He knew all about the fraud sword hanging over his friend and fellow officer. He took immediate control, snapping orders at his men, who had been standing at parade rest behind the VIP platform. They quickly spread out to raise the money in the name of Marcus Garvey. Julian gave Grant a weary smile of thanks. Within minutes more than $500 was raised.

Chamberlin's partners, by now also exhausted, finally okayed the flight. They reminded Julian, however, that he still owed them about $1,000, payable upon his return from wherever he ended up.

He said good-bye to Chamberlin, then stepped into a small boat and was rowed out to the *Ethiopia I*, now resting in shallow water about thirty feet from the west bank.

Shortly before 5:00 PM the hydroplane's engine roared to life. The *Ethiopia I*'s tail dipped back as the plane bolted forward along the calm waters of the lazy river. It skipped and hopped, then lifted. A marching band struck up loudly amid excited cheers and whoops. And thousands of orange balloons floated slowly up in the hot air.

For the first time in weeks Julian felt free. He was up with the wind, away from the fickle crowd—alone. No more creditors, no more money counting, no more begging. He was flying.

Before starting for Africa he made a pass over the launch site, dumping out a sack of pamphlets that filled the air like ticker tape. The Rev. Theophilus Martin, who had earlier led the benediction and blessing of the plane, had asked Julian if he wouldn't mind seeding the crowd with pamphlets in payment for the spiritual services. They announced the Rev. Martin's next revival hour.

Climbing to two thousand feet, Julian suddenly felt something wrong. He couldn't get the plane to level. It kept tilting heavily to starboard, refusing a turn toward New Jersey and dead-heading on a curve toward Queens. Suddenly there was a ripping sound, then a loud snap as the right pontoon broke off.

The plane now limped at a sharp port angle westward and began to lose altitude rapidly. Julian could do nothing to get the nose up. He was headed for a crash landing. There was no time to bail out—too low, too late.

The *Ethiopia I* slammed into Flushing Bay in a foaming, spraying cartwheel. The solo African flight time: just under five minutes to splashdown.

Frederick Hess of nearby College Point was caulking

boats when he saw the plane go down about fifteen hundred feet from shore. He raced to the crash site in his launch and pulled the half-drowned pilot out of the water.

The next morning Julian woke up in Flushing Hospital. Few areas of his body were not bruised. Both shoulders were dislocated. His right leg was in traction. It hurt to breathe.

A visitor quietly entered his room. "Mr. Julian," said the postal agent, "on behalf of the United States government I wish to inform you everything is all right. You did your best; and if luck was against you, that isn't listed among the crimes in the postal laws and regulations. We're satisfied."

He left a bouquet of tea roses and exited.

The injured pilot wasn't soothed by the morning papers the nurse brought, either. HARLEM'S ACE FLOPS INTO FLUSHING BAY AT START OF GLOBE CIRCLING TRIP, announced the *New York Sun.* NEGRO AVIATOR, STARTING FOR AFRICA, FALLS IN FLUSHING BAY, said the *New York Herald Tribune. The New York Times* noted that his landing spot, "while more or less on his course, had not been a scheduled stop."

This first attempt to reach Africa cost him one month in the hospital. But, as the story in the *Sun* pointed out, "Julian's head is bloody but unbowed."

5

Flying Kites

> I got a physical examination this morning from Dr. Louis R. Burnett, the official doctor of New Jersey. He said I had the lowest blood pressure on record and was phenomenally perfect.
>
> THE BLACK EAGLE *to a reporter*
> *New York City, May, 1929*

ON MAY 27, 1927, while Charles Lindbergh was taking the applause of the world, Julian was taking a honeymoon with his bride, Essie Gittens, a shy West Indian beauty he had first met as a child in Port of Spain.

The new team of Eagle and wife decided that what was needed to raise funds in a proper fashion for a successful international flight was respected credentials. First Julian obtained membership (No. 6206) in the *Fédération Aeronautique Internationale;* his certificate was signed by Orville Wright. Next he joined the 369th Colored Infantry, an all-Negro National Guard unit that had distinguished itself in combat in France during World War I. And finally he established the Julian Aeroplane Fund. State Assemblyman A. Spencer Field, considered a patron of flying in New York circles, volunteered to act as custodian of *all* contributions.

On March 17, 1928, a feature story on Julian finally appeared in a popular tabloid, the *Evening Graphic.* It stated:

> Has the destiny which guided white flyers to so many heroic deeds decreed that a Negro shall also inscribe one of the most illustrious chapters in American avia-

tion? This question will be answered sometime in June when the Black Eagle takes off on a transatlantic flight to Paris—*and return.* He will go alone, this only black bird ever to cleave the azure on man-made wings, and he will be financed for the most part by members of his own race . . . eager for a Negro to attain greatness in flying commensurate with that of his brethren in other branches of the arts and sciences.

Though it read like advertising copy, it set the right tone for the new image.

Assemblyman Field arranged a press conference for Julian at Long Island's Curtiss Field, the airport from which Charles Lindbergh often flew and Julian first jumped. The pilot attended, not in his usual flying outfit, but in businessman's attire. Essie was also present as dialogue coach and silent prayer leader.

Julian picked his words carefully. "I hope to bring to the 369th regiment," he stated, "the same kind of prestige Colonel Lindbergh gave his National Guard unit. I shall remain abroad but a short time and then attempt to fly back to this country. This is a non-commercial proposition. There is no prize to be gained. And I have no desire for personal aggrandizement, whether it be material or honorary. The sole purpose of my proposed flight is to stimulate a greater interest in aviation among my own people. Too much stress cannot be laid on the fact that this flight is not being attempted for commercial purposes but solely in the interests of the flying game and to help Negroes anxious to take up the science. . . . It is certain that if another war comes, it must be fought in the air."

He handled questions with direct answers. Asked by one reporter why he planned a solo flight, he explained, "If anything happens, I shall be the only sufferer. That's why I want to be alone. While I am sure the outcome will be satisfactory, I have no desire to place the life of another human being in jeopardy."

He left the press conference with Essie, quietly. There were no waves or raves, no raised arms and no calling cards. It was straight low-profile.

Julian's *noblesse oblige* impressed Giuseppe M. Bellanca, one of the nation's leading plane designers. (It was to Bellanca that Lindbergh first went for a plane capable of crossing the Atlantic. The Italian's price of $15,000 had proved too high for the flyer's backers, however.) Bellanca pledged $3,000 to the Julian Fund and commenced manufacturing a handmade diesel-driven plane capable of speeds from 100 to 135 mph and reportedly worth $25,000.

Once again Julian was in the news, this time in a most determined role. Now a plane was actually being built at Bellanca's Staten Island plant, and Julian had a photograph to prove it. Clipped to it was a note from Bellanca himself that read, "With compliments to Lieutenant Julian—this shows the type of plane we have under construction for you." Julian read it aloud and often.

On June 20 he announced a flight schedule. "If no one takes off before July first," he told a reporter from the *New York Herald Tribune,* "I will be the next man to attempt crossing the Atlantic.

"On second thought," he added, "I would prefer July fourth, if that isn't already taken." Of his training routine he said, "I am staying awake four nights every two weeks. I don't anticipate the trip will take more than sixty-eight hours. But still, I believe in order to carry a fifty-pound weight, one should train with a hundred. Do you follow?"

Unfortunately the flight did not. The problem was caused mostly by Julian's inability to settle on a firm takeoff date. Between the time he announced his intention to fly the Atlantic and picked the date, four other pilots had beaten him across. Even a woman, Amelia Earhart, had made it.

Reaction to Julian's forced ditching of his latest attempt was captured by the *New York Sun.* "Our faith has not been the same since," said an editorial, "although our interest has never lagged."

Describing Julian as "one of our favorite truth-is-stranger-than-fiction characters," the *Sun* said, "For a long while he raised money until it almost seemed as if he preferred raising money to flying. During this period he was more elusive than a political figure, but in an exclusive with us he revealed that he was on the very verge of waking up some morning and saying to his wife, 'My dear, I think I'll fly to Arabia today.'"

In May 1929 brochures announcing the formation of the NAAAACR—National Association for the Advancement of Aviation Amongst Colored Races, Inc.—began circulating around New York. Julian was listed as a sponsor. The firm took offices in Manhattan and opened several branches throughout the city. The proclaimed aim of NAAAACR was to raise $500,000 for flying scholarships for Negroes.

Just as the publicity got started, however, the NAAAACR's organizer, a man named S. Fenimore Hoffman, declared that Julian was no longer a sponsor and recalled all literature on the project.

"He is not sufficiently outstanding in Harlem aviation circles," charged Hoffman, whose credentials included having been a publicity agent and circus cashier.

"Not sufficiently outstanding in Harlem aviation circles!" roared Julian to members of the press who told him the bad news. "I am the most outstanding and only Negro pilot there is anywhere. Harlem aviation circles? I *am* those circles. I am the only colored pilot licensed at all—that is, I am practically licensed. All I need is a few formalities. I got a physical examination this morning from Dr. Louis R. Burnett, the official doctor of New Jersey. He said I had the lowest blood pressure on record and was phenomenally perfect.

"Mr. Fenimore Hoffman is not disassociating me from the NAAAACR, by the way," Julian announced. "I am disassociating myself from it. That association is attempting to raise $500,000. . . . I disassociate myself from that idea. I don't say that anybody is trying to defraud anybody. All I say is that in the last paragraph in the contract Mr. Hoffman got me to sign it stipulates that he can take out life insurance on me in his own favor. I don't say there's anything wrong with that. All I say is that it's kind of funny in a contract where I stipulate to do all the flying. That's a curious kind of insurance."

The legal fight dragged on for months and only faded away, unsettled, when the Wall Street crash of October chased the principals off in a dozen desperate directions.

6

Shangri-la Trip

Yes sir—er, *oui, roi!*
THE BLACK EAGLE *to the King of Kings*
Addis Ababa, June, 1930

FOR MOST of the nation the Depression offered little opportunity and even less luck. Not so for Julian. In the spring of 1930, when 10 percent of the population was unemployed, he suddenly found himself well employed—and by an emperor-elect.

On the afternoon of April 19, as he sat listening to gloomy forecasts on his Atwater-Kent radio, he had a caller.

Opening the door of his walk-up apartment, now at 24 Lenox Avenue, he saw a slight man, young, of *café-au-lait* complexion, who stood straight as a lance. The man asked for The Black Eagle. Julian identified himself, already intrigued by the caller's accent. It was neither English nor American.

Once inside the apartment, the man stated his mission. "I am Ras Malaku Bayan," he said. "I am studying medicine at Howard University. My cousin is Ras Tafari, soon to be crowned Emperor of Ethiopia."

Julian grew excited as Bayan quickly got to the point. For his November coronation the Emperor-elect wanted to put on a spectacular affair for the invited dignitaries. Word had reached him in his far-away capital of Addis Ababa about the black pilot's historic jumps and attempt to solo to his African empire. It so impressed Tafari that he wished to commission Julian to perform at the coronation. Many foreigners from all over the world would be attending,

Bayan explained. Thus, for reasons of racial pride, the coronation had to be the most spectacular ever.

Before Bayan could go further, Julian accepted. For the price Bayan offered—$1,000 per month plus all expenses, starting immediately and continuing through the coronation—he was willing to do more than perform.

They shook on the deal, and Bayan promised that the travel tickets would be in Julian's hands within a week.

When Essie arrived home that evening from an unsuccessful job hunt for anything, including housekeeping, she was overwhelmed. But during the night she became nervous about it all and decided Julian should go over alone first. As far as she was concerned, anything African was not only a long way from civilization but also an invitation to sudden death.

The tickets along with a $1,000 advance arrived on time, and Julian sailed aboard the *S.S. Europa* on April 25, in a first-class stateroom. Bayan accompanied him.

For the next six weeks they made their way across seven thousand miles of the world—to Paris, Marseilles, across the Mediterranean, through the Suez Canal, down the Red Sea, between the straits of Bab al Mandab, and into the Gulf of Aden.

They landed in Djibouti, the harbor capital of French Somaliland, and boarded the wood-burning Franco-Ethiopian *chemin de fer* for the final leg of an exhausting journey: the 486-mile, short-gauge, wood-burning train trip to Addis Ababa, which was only slightly more comfortable than a mule ride.

Julian's senses feasted on the exotic scenes of the ancient and mysterious land. What he saw and heard was as rich and rare as a pageant.

Hundreds of camel caravans trudged endlessly in and out through Addis Ababa's ancient walls, bearing panniers of spice, incense, and hashish from distant provinces. Their shuffling movement coated everything with thick brown dust. The buildings were of sun-baked mud and wattle, their slanted roofs covered with rusted, odd pieces of metal sheeting. Black-robed priests, wearing tall, brimless *kamel-aukions* and carrying decorated staffs and silken purses, moved by on mules, followed by trotting servants who held wide umbrellas over their sinister-looking countenances. The tan-skinned women in their flowing white *shamas* were reedy, nubile beauties, shy at a man's look. Their eyes were enormous almonds ripened to a sensuality that excited, yet cautioned, the beholder, as Andalusian eyes do. It was indeed at Shangri-la—high in the clouds and far removed from the twentieth century.

Julian was suddenly certain that this mission was going to be more exciting than he had planned.

When they reached the Hotel de France, he and Bayan parted. The young prince told him that he would hear from the palace shortly about the time for his audience with the Emperor-elect—the highly polished little thirty-eight-year-old ruler who was, according to the royal books, the 255th descendant of Solomon and Sheba as well as the one charged with awakening his slumbering empire.

On the fifth day after his arrival in Addis Ababa Julian was summoned to the palace, located at the sacred Gebbi Grounds. Barefoot, puttee-wearing sentries saluted him as he passed through the black wrought-iron gates at the main entrance. He was led by a sword-carrying guard past the two chained royal lions, both asleep in the morning sun. At the steps of the palace he was greeted by the Royal Chamberlain, who wore a blue cape.

Inside, guards swung open the large carved doors of the throne room. As the Chamberlain had instructed, Julian bowed the traditional three times. Then he looked up. Sitting on a red-velvet-covered chair of antiqued gold at the far end of the long, chandeliered room, sat the Emperor-elect. His feet barely touched the parquet floor's enormous Oriental carpet. The face, though bearded, radiated warmth and appreciation.

The monarch clapped for his interpreter, and the Chamberlain departed with a bow.

"*Excusez-moi, votre altesse,*" said Julian in his best Canadian-learned French, "*mais, je parle français.*"

Tafari smiled at the pilot's eagerness, but still ordered the translator.

During the audience they discussed Lindbergh's historic flight, the dangers of stunt flying, the future of aviation for transporting and even dropping troops, and the enormous problems of making ocean-crossing solos.

The Emperor-elect congratulated Julian for his earlier attempt to fly to the empire, a recollection that so embarrassed the pilot that he hastily turned the conversation to the flying he hoped to do for the Emperor. As Julian talked about stunts and jumps, Tafari summoned his Chamberlain. After a brief whispered discussion with the Emperor-elect, the Chamberlain asked Julian in English if he was up to putting on a private flying exhibit in two days.

"Yes sir—er, *oui, roi,*" said Julian, delighted.

"*Bon,*" said the Emperor-elect. With another handshake and three retreating bows, the audience was over. It had lasted one hour.

Julian returned to the hotel elated. He wondered what the Imperial Air Force looked like. Even the Chamberlain didn't know exactly. But it didn't really matter. As far as The Black Eagle was concerned, a Shangri-la should be full of surprises. He was glad he had come.

7

Bull's-Eye in Africa

Here I am sitting next to the Emperor-elect like he was my brother.
THE BLACK EAGLE *to himself while riding in the royal Rolls*
Addis Ababa, June, 1930

THE IMPERIAL Air Force consisted of three aircraft: two German-made Junkers monoplanes and one British-made Gypsy Moth. The all-white Moth was a gift to the Emperor-elect from the owners of Selfridge's, the London department store that handled much of the royal mail-order business. It had arrived only the week before, and was already the air-minded monarch's most cherished mechanical possession. A sleek little biplane, the two-seater racer cruised at sixty knots. Tafari planned its inaugural flight for the coronation, when he would be its first passenger.

Two French pilots ran the air force. They were assigned and salaried by the French government, which was most interested in maintaining a strong presence in the empire. The French Foreign Office was convinced the mysterious hills and mountains of the empire were rich in mineral treasures never touched.

News, like rumors, whipped around Addis Ababa fast. The French pilots soon heard about Julian's arrival and mission. He represented a direct threat to their positions as well as to France's presence. One black pilot would no doubt lead to more. Eventually the French would be thanked for their help and asked to leave. It was an unsettling thought for them.

The midday flight time at the rocky pasture that served as an airstrip came with a heavy rainstorm. Still, more than five thousand Ethiopians had turned out because of word of mouth about a black pilot from a faraway land that was a mysterious planet to them. Guard rails of rope were hastily put up to keep the people at a safe distance from the airplanes—especially the treasured Gypsy Moth that the French pilots had just finished assembling.

Shortly after 2:00 PM the rainstorm moved south toward Kenya and the field began to drain. Palace workers quickly unrolled a great length of carpet up to the large tent, where other workers were rushing about, tying down the blue canopy to wooden poles. With a bugle fanfare a troop of colorful lancers charged up the road, signaling the Emperor-elect's approach. Finally the crimson Rolls-Royce arrived. Tafari stepped out, walked quickly to the tent, and took his seat, which faced out to the runway.

A few minutes later Julian arrived in a limousine in front of the airplanes. He was dressed in dark brown jodhpurs and brown suede jacket. With parachute slung over his shoulder and carrying flying gear in a canvas tote bag, the black pilot walked with big, determined steps. He carefully inspected the ground he would soon be rolling over on takeoff.

Ahead stood the two French pilots. Captain André Maillet was the senior man, chunky and graying at the temples. The other was a much younger, taciturn-looking man with a moustache. They were talking.

"*Bonjour, messieurs,*" said Julian with a friendly wave. "*Je suis Monsieur Julian, l'Aigle Noir.*"

Ignoring his greeting, the Frenchmen turned abruptly and, in animated conversation, walked directly toward one of the Junkers. Only when they reached the plane and leaned against the fuselage did they face Julian, but in stony silence.

The move had the stiffness of a badly rehearsed scene. To Julian's eye, something was wrong; he moved to find out what. Instead of climbing aboard the other Junkers left to him by the French act, on a hunch he walked straight over to the Junkers they seemed to be claiming. Strapping on his parachute, he climbed up on the wing and slipped neatly into the open cockpit.

The Frenchmen immediately broke for the other Junkers, gesturing excitedly at an Ethiopian ground-crew member and pointing to a rather shaky-looking stepladder. When the Ethiopian had rushed it into place, Maillet climbed up, shouting for his toolbox, and pulled the cowling off.

Julian made a fast cockpit check, hung his compass on a knob by its cord, and strapped in.

At the throwing of the ignition switch the engine coughed to life. A good breeze came up. Julian eased the throttle in, and the engine roared with refreshing strength. He checked the flaps, released the brake, and said a short prayer.

A cloud passed the sun as he firewalled the throttle, slamming it all the way in. The plane leapt forward like a quarter horse and lifted easily almost in front of the Emperor-elect's canopy.

At fourteen thousand feet Julian commenced his aerial curvets—looping, spinning, sliding, and tight eights. He possessed the clearing skies for half an hour. On the ground the natives were spellbound. It was a miracle—white man's magic in a black man's hands.

Observing the maneuvers through binoculars, the Emperor-elect radiated pride and considerable relief, for controversial reports about the Black Eagle's flying prowess had recently reached even Ethiopia. Now, though, he felt sure he had made the right choice for the coronation.

Julian brought the ship down smartly onto the strip as the crowd cheered wildly. As soon as he cut the engine, he hopped off the wing and trotted over to the other Junkers. The cowling was clamped back on and the engine was idling. The two Frenchmen were having a heated argument.

"*Allons!*" Julian called to Maillet as he slapped his hand over his shoulder onto the parachute pack and crouched in a springing position. He then climbed aboard the second Junkers.

When Maillet didn't move, Julian pierced him with a steely look. With an arm stretched taut with impatient annoyance, he ordered him to the plane.

"*Toi, viens ici!*" he shouted. "*You*, come here!"

The crowd roared all the louder at the obvious drama. They thirsted for an encore. Maillet shrugged, slipped his leather flying helmet off his belt and on his head, and climbed into the cockpit. He didn't look very well as he took the controls, saying nothing to Julian. It was rather apparent that if he refused the flight he would have to answer to the Emperor-elect, who couldn't help seeing the incident. To Julian, of course, refusal would have meant that the French had indeed sabotaged the plane.

Julian instructed Maillet to go to five thousand feet and level off there.

As the plane climbed in big lazy circles to the assigned altitude, the crowd watched in silence, hands visoring their straining eyes against the sun.

The plane suddenly pulled up sharply and roared away, and a human body tumbled earthward, over and over, in wild rolls.

The crowd screamed its worst fears.

Julian struggled to stabilize. Finally he got into spread-eagle form and jerked the D-ring.

He counted slowly. "One—two—three—four—five—six—"

The canopy whipped out of the pack and raced away. Then it bit into the air, blooming fully, beautifully, as its silky whiteness glistened in the sun. The black pilot descended with the sure swing of a pendulum. When he landed fifty feet from the royal tent, it caused an explosion of noise that for any other reason would have been frightening. Men chanted and danced as if readying for battle; women howled eerie stygian-sounding ululations.

Astounded at the bull's-eye feat, the Emperor-elect sprang as if catapulted from his portable throne. Waving away his aides' protests, he pushed through the pandemoniacal circle to meet the hero, now busy disengaging himself from the chute's shroud lines. Tafari commanded his people to help, then led Julian by the arm back to his tent. As they walked together, the Ethiopian crowd boomed even louder approval.

Inside, a beaming servant rushed a cup of tea to Julian, who was covered with dust and soaked with sweat. Tafari pointed to a canvas-backed chair and urged him to sit.

"You shall receive a handsome reward for this historic performance," the Emperor-elect told him through his translator. "I am commissioning you a colonel in my air force. I am also going to present you with the Order of Menelik."

Even though he didn't know the award was the empire's highest for gallantry, it was Julian's turn to be overwhelmed. Pulling off the silk scarf from around his neck, he wiped the grime from his face. His grin was wide.

"It shall be arranged for you to receive citizenship immediately," added Tafari. "It is important for your future here."

As the Emperor-elect turned and snapped orders to the Chamberlain, Julian made a fast decision. Maybe he would lose his British passport for taking the Ethiopian one; he might even jeopardize his position in the United States. At the moment, with the juice of success still bubbling, both seemed trifles.

His mind was made up: He would go Ethiopian.

Exhausted but exultant, he traveled back to Addis Ababa with the Emperor-elect. As he passed, the two French pilots, busy tying down the planes with sisal ropes fastened to wooden pegs, turned toward him slowly. He read their stares, but dismissed the clear message.

Ethiopian peasants in shaggy wraps herded goats and cattle along the rich green sides of the dirt road that wound through rolling pasturelands into the city. At the first sound of the Rolls's approach they fell to their knees, for they dared not set eyes on the one soon to be crowned the King of Kings. Traditionally, to look was to die.

"Here I am sitting next to the Emperor-elect like he was my brother," Julian said to himself with a chuckle.

Tafari grinned too, seemingly privy to Julian's thoughts. Even the palace guard in the front seat, ready hands on his loaded Thompson submachine gun covered by a dark shawl, smiled. He didn't turn around, though.

The next night Julian was the guest of honor at a grand fete held at the palace with more than a hundred royal and high official guests attending. There were elaborate silver servings of fish from Lake Tana and *poulet chasseur,* magnums of the best French chablis and burgundy offered by an endless processional of white-robed servants, and afterward, cognac and Burma cheroots along with demitasses of rich *Arabica* coffee.

When the brassy strains of *"Ityopia Hoy Dass Yiballish!"* —"Let Ethiopia Be Joyous!"—began under the direction of the bandmaster, Julian swiftly picked up the national anthem's melody and hummed along. Not knowing the words was no deterrent to him. The faces of Ethiopia's aristocracy glowed with admiration. The performance was a touch of diplomatic genius.

Thus, overnight, Col. Hubert Fauntleroy Julian emerged the reigning court favorite of Ethiopia. Reliable word around Addis Ababa's *tej* houses, those smoky pubs where the throat-burning local brew was consumed over heated discussions about the affairs of the empire, was that The Black Eagle would be named to a dukedom.

Within a week, it was announced that Colonel Julian was henceforth the Emperor-elect's private pilot.

He quickly became part of the palace inner circle, attending most conferences and joining in the courtly procedures. He was one of the very few the Emperor-elect ever received in his private quarters in pajamas. He soon found himself actually giving advice on how to run an empire: Holders of the royal purse strings thought him a wizard for coming up with the concept of an Ethiopian shipping line and a commercial airline. He also showed a good flair for international affairs and business.

The Chamberlain accoutered him in a magnificent uniform of white jodhpurs, blue tunic, tan pith helmet with the royal crest, and high leather boots with spurs. The ensemble arrived from the tailor with a long aiguillette and a brace of epaulettes.

Wherever he traveled, he was accompanied by aides-de-camp assigned him from the officers' mess of the palace guard.

His salary of $1,000 was raised $250 per month, and he was given the use of a fine villa with staff on a good slope of Mount Entoto. The high life he had so often dreamed of had at last come true.

At night he was the playboy of the dusky world, hosting elegant soirees that even the Emperor-elect occasionally dropped in on. More than one young lady of the court became enamored of him, with Princess Tsahai, daughter of the Emperor-elect, leading the rumor list (although she was estimated to be about ten years old at the time). Always the gallant, Julian opted not to hurt feelings by mentioning anything about a girl named Essie.

There was little doubt that Julian wallowed in all the social high jinks and palace drama. After a while, though, he began to experience the roving urge that drives swagmen and adventurers alike. Having achieved fame and fortune in his adopted land, he began to feel that he should let the people at home know the good news. He felt a responsibility to his American public, too. In the last few years they had not heard much about the Black Eagle—at least not much that he wanted to clip and save.

With the coronation still four months away, Julian devised a plan of action for an American safari and went to the palace to sell it.

8

Hometowns Are Not for Heroes

> The Emperor-elect is a fine man with a beard, who looks something like I do.
> THE BLACK EAGLE *when asked to describe Haile Selassie New York visit, July, 1930*

NUDGED ALONG by three stout Moran tugs, the liner *Île de France* moved slowly into New York harbor. Seagulls lofted by the ship's fantail and sailors in baggy blue denims made lines ready for the docking.

It was a cool and clear twilight on Wednesday, July 30, 1930, the day on which *The New York Times* carried the headline MAN OF FUTURE PICTURED AS BLIND AND DEAF UNDER STRAIN OF LIGHTS, MOVIES AND NOISES.

In his portside cabin Julian suited up with the ritualistic care of a matador. Once his boots were on, he reviewed himself in the mirror. Elegant was the conclusion. He had come a long way from cricket-green days in Port of Spain, he reflected. And now he was arriving triumphant, a true black hero personally assigned by an emperor-elect to carry out missions fit for a prime minister. No longer was he a mere daredevil; he was now a personage of government, a diplomat, a decision-maker. Even he had never dreamed it could be *this* good.

The arrival date was an auspicious one for the aerial adventurer. The big news for much of the world was the crossing of the Atlantic by Britain's giant dirigible, the R-100. Right now, according to the latest ship's report, the craft was somewhere over Newfoundland. Its final destination made Julian particularly proud—St. Hubert's aerodrome in Montreal, where he had first soloed eleven years before.

Jauntily he adjusted the blue ribbon of his Order of Menelik medal and put on a high-crowned tan pith helmet. Walking to the mirror for one final check, he took out of his pocket the *pièce de résistance* of his new image. Once the monocle was in place, he couldn't resist snapping a salute to himself.

He felt confident that he was now ready to seriously rival another flamboyant flyer, Roscoe Turner. Currently a movie star because of his aerial daring in the popular film *Hell's Angels,* Turner, accompanied by his pet lion, Gilmore, was overwhelming city after city across the nation in a scarlet helmet, cobalt-blue tunic, and fawn cavalry boots. The press couldn't get enough of him. Julian hoped for the same.

"The members of the press have just come aboard from the cutter, *monsieur,*" interrupted the cabin boy with a shout from outside Julian's door. "They would like to meet with you in the lounge on the promenade deck."

Dozens of reporters and photographers jammed the ornate, chandeliered lounge. They represented *The New York Times, Daily News, Herald Tribune, World Telegram,* and *American,* and the wire services. Pathé News cameras were set up, and phosphorous lights flashed as press cameras clicked. It was a time when most Americans hadn't been to the Grand Canyon yet, let alone overseas. Fewer still were the number who had ever stepped on Africa's shores. Only Henry Morton Stanley and Teddy Roosevelt came to mind. Many a citizen only vaguely remembered Eugene O'Neill's 1921 drama, *Emperor Jones,* that told of an American black's building, then losing, an African empire.

Julian walked up to the dais with a Sandhurstian snap, broad back straight and determined chin leading the way.

Before taking questions, he made an announcement.

"I wish to state that Ethiopia, or Abyssinia, as you might prefer, is now very much advanced in aviation. My good friend the Emperor-elect has asked me to return to America to recruit the type of people who will advance the empire even further in all fields.

"Next, I am proud to announce that the Emperor-elect has ordered me to make preparations for a flight from his capital to New York next winter. It will be done for the greater glory and advancement of Ethiopian aviation."

The skeptical looks were anticipated by the speaker. Among the reporters—Julian had already spotted A. J. Liebling and H. Allen Smith—were many who had often made light of his previous Atlantic non-crossing. It was different this time, though; the skeptical looks didn't bother him.

"His Imperial Majesty will stand all expenses, of course," he continued. "This flight will be made about the first of the year, after the November coronation. I shall land at Roosevelt Field, where Mr. Lindbergh started on an historic flight."

When he finished, the questions began. The first reporter addressed him as "Lieutenant Julian."

"It's Colonel," Julian corrected, dismissing the man and his question with a hard look.

Another asked how he became involved with Ethiopia in the first place.

"The Emperor-elect," Julian explained, "had heard of my parachuting and flying for years. Once I got to his capital, though, it was a case of willpower and personality—the alpha and axis."

When asked where his accent had originated, he advised, "Be yourself, brother, and talk as you were born, not as you were educated. I was born partially in the West Indies and partially in England. I know that sounds complicated. I've been trying for a week to think of the word that fits the situation, but I can't. I keep thinking of 'ambidextrous,' but I know that's not the word. But whatever the word is, that's what I am. Look it up for yourself."

As the reporters pondered that and the loudspeaker announced they had finally docked at the North River's Pier 88, Julian said, "That's all, gentlemen. Thank you."

He left the promenade deck, skipped down the forward gangplank as more cameras captured him, and waved away a mob of tardy reporters who had missed the cutter.

Cheered by various Ethiopians who were waiting to greet him—the Honorary Consul and his staff plus a group of students—he stepped into a chauffeured limousine and was driven to a reception at the Consulate.

Then, after an absence of three and one-half months, Col. Hubert Fauntleroy Julian returned to Harlem and Essie.

Before taking the first sip of breakfast coffee, Julian, in silk pajamas and embroidered slippers, opened his morning copy of the *New York Herald Tribune*. On the second page he read:

> Hubert Julian, Negro aviator, who left this country eighteen months ago on a freighter after a career in the air which had been only partly successful and not at all remunerative, returned to Harlem yesterday. He arrived on the French liner *Île de France* . . . with many and impressive habiliments of grandeur including a middle name—Fauntleroy. He is now, he says, Colonel Hubert Fauntleroy Julian, chief of aviation of the Abyssinian army, and in this the officers of the ship bore him out. Colonel Julian, they said, was an honest-to-goodness colonel in the Abyssinian army.

Describing his outfit as an "undress uniform," the story detailed a "pith helmet, a monocle, a pink polo shirt, white breeches with green stripes, and spurred riding boots size 12½, especially made for him in Paris of deer skin."

As he read what he considered egregious errors, his fury rose. The story had toyed with his rank, mission, and adopted homeland. He had, in effect and in print, been smeared in minstrel-show grease.

The Ethiopian Consul phoned, equally furious. He read

Julian the *New York Telegram*'s headline: HE'LL FLY A SEA OR TWO FOR DEAH OLD ABYSSINIA. "Incidentally, Julian's middle name was acquired with his monocle, uniform, expense account, English accent, and boots while in 'Abssinia' (*sic*)," the story read.

After they had commiserated with each other, they detailed a counterattack: the Consul should ring up the various city editors involved. Using stern diplomatic language, he should explain the great international embarrassment the story was already creating. He should also note the U.S. State Department's distress over the matter—but without giving specifics, for, unfortunately, there were none. Finally, he should demand corrections.

"Suggest a press conference, an official one at your place," said Julian. "That way we can clear up the misunderstanding."

Within an hour it appeared the plan was having some effect. Most city editors took the indignant Ethiopian diplomat's phone call seriously. A few even admitted that perhaps their reporters had been in too frisky a mood with the always colorful flyer. It was sometimes difficult, of course, for them to cover Julian any other way, some noted. It was also rather traditional to write about all blacks in a light vein. To most reporters they were after all a carefree race who did most things for laughs. And besides, with a depression on, humorous copy to brighten bleak days was hard to come by.

By late afternoon half a dozen reporters had gathered in a large room at the Consul's residence where they chatted and joked until Julian entered. His head was high and unturning; his face was hard and his lips pursed. He was in a dark business suit, not a uniform.

"Hey, the Eagle's really mad," one of them said in a loud whisper. The reporters were obviously taken aback.

For ten minutes Julian ticked off the inaccuracies and corrected them. He particularly labored over the report of his upcoming solo. Several papers had claimed it was to be from Paris to New York. He detailed again the Addis Ababa-New York routing as well as the specific types of people he was recruiting to return to Ethiopia with him. He also mentioned the possible recourse of settling the errors "through international channels if this conference does not produce clarifying results."

"How dare you call a size nine a size twelve and a half," he said at one point, displaying his foot in thin-soled black brogues. Even he smiled at that.

At the end of the statement one of the reporters asked the conference's only question: What was the distant monarch really like?

Julian gave it serious thought. "The Emperor-elect is a fine man with a beard," he finally said, "who looks something like I do."

He left the press conference and headed for the one major newspaper that hadn't sent a representative to the press conference. At the *Herald Tribune* he met with reporter Beverly Smith and set another record straight. "I'm no Rhodes scholar, that's a libel," he told the Oxford-educated Smith. "I never went to Rhodes College in my life.

"It is also an understatement that I am going to fly from Paris to New York. I am going to fly from Ethiopia to New York."

"Don't do that, Colonel," reporter Smith cautioned. "You are sitting pretty in Abyssinia now. Why tempt fortune?"

The Black Eagle looked down implacably. "Nothing ventured, nothing gained," he said.

The follow-up stories made recourse to international channels unnecessary.

His arrival now properly noted in the press, Julian got busy boosting the empire in lectures throughout New York City.

"His Majesty is very much a Christian," he told an audience at the Abyssinian Baptist Church, where the pastor was Adam Clayton Powell, Sr., father of the Harlem congressman-to-be. "He spends three days a week, at least, implanting the Christian religion into the hearts of his subjects. When the men dig stones to build churches, he will look on for hours, inspiring them by his mere presence to increase their production. Now that's a real emperor-elect."

Though politely applauded, the talks didn't produce recruits. Something appeared to be lacking.

James Cannon, then a reporter for the *New York Telegram* (and later one of the nation's more perceptive sports writers), asked Julian after a lecture, "Why doesn't Harlem take you to its bosom—for aren't you the Lindbergh of your race?"

The man Cannon described as "a hero of the air, chum of a king, a Senegambian Lindbergh," answered, "No great man is honored by his own people. The pioneer is never acclaimed by his own hometown."

It seemed he was not about to be acclaimed outside of his hometown, either. In Washington, D. C., he suffered setback after setback in attempts to meet with State Department officials on the recruiting project. He never once got beyond minor bureaucrats of the cubicle-king variety. Although it was not detailed in so many words, the inference was clear that involvement in foreign affairs was not the concern of a Negro—and an alien named The Black Eagle at that.

Confidential memos between State's Division of Near Eastern Affairs, which then handled Ethiopia, and the Addis Ababa legation's head, Addison E. Southard, had discussed Julian's assignment. (The Emperor-elect had announced it with some pride at a state banquet right after Julian's departure.) Southard's position was that a colony of American Negroes in Ethiopia would impair what he described as "American prestige."

After the Washington rebuff, Julian's trip completely collapsed. Attendance at his lectures fell off. It was a scorching summer, and no one wanted to spend time sitting in a hot hall. There was a deeper, more painful reason that slowly surfaced, however. To a people oppressed for so long, Julian's message—a free, all-black empire making it without white strings—seemed suspect. Rumors about his real intent began to circulate, which, based on his record, were understandable even if not now true. Hustling, like jiving, was a household word in Negro communities. No one had ever done anything for nothing for them before. Why now?

Attempts to change these doubts weren't helped by the bickering among militant black leaders themselves. They were a house divided, given to expending precious energy on internecine squabbling. Marcus Garvey, for example, often referred to Dr. W. E. B. DuBois as "that mulatto," and the fiery doctor publicly returned the shot by labeling Garvey's African scheme as an exercise in "spiritual bankruptcy and futility." Most Negroes backed away from both of them. The same strategy was used on Julian.

After a month of taking the worst beating of his mercurial career, Julian wanted out of the United States. He was badly shaken and felt defeated—a vilified figure who couldn't even convince Essie to journey with him to his new homeland. She, like many, was basically afraid of a place called Africa, even though it had been home to her ancestors.

On the evening of August 31, 1930, Hubert Julian prepared to sail back to Africa. At the foot of the forward gangplank of the German liner S. S. *Europa,* he told the skimpy circle of reporters and friends how he felt about the short and not-so-sweet visit.

"The papers, even of my own race," he said, "have harassed and maligned me. They have treated me with absolute *partiality*. They have claimed I was soliciting funds for an air force, that I was buying bombs, that I will never make an ocean-crossing flight. They are all canards."

The *New York Herald Tribune* in an *au revoir* story said: "And so the Black Eagle of the air sailed away for the glamour and danger and mystery of the Dark Continent. May all good luck attend him . . ."

Julian didn't waste much time anguishing over the America-revisited affair, however.

By the time the ship reached the high seas, he was deeply committed at the winning end of a ping-pong table.

9

Crash Landing

I wanted to give the Emperor a thrill. After all, even an emperor needs a thrill now and then.

THE BLACK EAGLE *in New York harbor December, 1930*

ONCE BACK in Addis Ababa, Julian went directly to the palace to detail the cheerless results of his mission to America.

After listening solemnly to the recounting, Tafari stated that the coronation was crucial to the empire's future—and emphasized Julian's aerial role in it. Foreign guests had to witness something so outstanding that they couldn't help but return to their countries proclaiming utter enchantment with a new Ethiopia under a forward-looking young emperor.

He ordered Julian immediately to take over full command of a recently started and Julian-inspired cadet training program. He said that the French had been keeping it up, but barely. It now needed the thrust of the Negro pilot to produce flying Ethiopians by coronation time.

Julian's return apparently caught the French pilots off guard. Despite reports from America about his zest for the place, they had privately told many Ethiopian officials he would never return. They had reasoned it all out: Julian was strictly a headline-seeking soldier of (minor) fortune not up to handling the intrigues that seethed in the Ethiopian league.

What they had overlooked, however, was that regardless of consequences, Julian couldn't afford *not* to return.

The French also missed the variation on the same theme

that played for the Emperor-elect: he needed an Ethiopian-run air force as a rallying symbol of African ability. Imperial pride demanded it.

The hardest blow to Gallic pride, and logic, landed within the week. A palace proclamation named Julian "Air Marshal in charge of all planes and pilots." Tafari apparently felt it was the least he could do for Julian after what the pilot told him he had been through for the cause in the United States. And besides, he wanted an air marshal for his Imperial Air Force and could hardly name a Frenchman to the post—not if he wanted visitors to believe Ethiopia a truly independent operation.

Sensing more turbulence to come because of Julian, the French pilots stepped up their activities to dispose of the new Air Marshal. Maillet, courtesy of his Foreign Office's research department, possessed a dossier on Julian. He fast-fed the most appetizing pieces, like the NAAAACR fiasco, to court contacts who knew for a price how to bring them to Tafari's attention.

However, the Emperor-elect had long ago been briefed not only on his chief pilot's background but also on his flamboyance and propensity for the preposterous. What counted was the service he was providing; as long as he did that, his position was secure. Tafari was a complete pragmatist. His concern was the coronation less than a month away.

Julian immediately got busy with the cadets, pushing them from dawn to dusk, weekends included. He even curtailed his night life and palace promenading.

Several days before the coronation he received a personal note from the Emperor-elect. He was anxious to see the cadets perform at a private dress rehearsal, he wrote, and asked Julian to make the arrangements.

The new Air Marshal organized it with misgivings. He wasn't happy with the part of the note requesting he be at the Emperor-elect's side for consultation and program planning during the entire showing. He was anxious to be on the flying stage himself for such a command performance.

On the breezy morning of October 31, 1930, the Emperor-elect stepped out of his Rolls-Royce at the far end of the airstrip, where Julian had calculated the planes would become airborne.

At the other end of the strip, near a recently completed wooden hangar, the planes were being warmed up. Julian gave last-minute instructions to his young pilots, double-checked their flight plans, and pep-talked them into forgetting their inadequacies by reminding them that the mission to be accomplished in forty-eight hours was for the glory of the empire.

Satisfied they were ready, he waved them to the planes and ordered the French pilots to help strap them in and check their controls out. The Frenchmen did as they were told.

At the sight of the first Ethiopian-piloted plane lifting off the ground, Tafari came to his feet in a spontaneous salute. A dream had come true: Ethiopians *could* fly. The Emperor-elect stood proudly as his entourage applauded him and excitement bubbled everywhere around the royal tent. While accepting the congratulations, he motioned the Chamberlain to his side to inquire after his private Gypsy Moth. He couldn't see it at the end of the strip where it usually was positioned for his viewing.

The Chamberlain explained it was inside the new hangar having a few last-minute adjustments made at the Air Marshal's request.

Tafari returned to enjoying the air show. At about five thousand feet up, the Ethiopian pilots performed several respectable turns and dives.

Away from the crowd and inside the quiet hangar, Julian hurriedly pulled on a suede jacket over his blue tunic and buckled his leather flying helmet under his chin. He hopped into the cockpit, started up the engine, taxied out to the runway, and ran the engine up for takeoff—in the Emperor-elect's Gypsy Moth.

Ever since the previous June when he had first gazed at

the sporty Moth and been informed it was being saved for the coronation, a craving to fly it had been gnawing. It had reached almost uncontrollable proportions during the last week when he had taxied the plane around the field in preparation for the ceremony.

Now he had surrendered to it.

As surprised aides nervously pointed out the fast-approaching plane roaring down the runway for takeoff, Tafari snapped forward in his throne chair. When his plane left the ground and nosed up quickly for altitude, the Emperor-elect's eyes closed and his mouth opened. Julian was flying it himself, contrary to orders. No one had ever dared disobey him so brazenly before. That someone had defied him now, on the very eve of his becoming the most powerful leader on the continent, caused his fury to rage almost beyond control.

Directly over the strip, Julian made two sharp turns. Banking tightly, he fluttered the plane downward. It was obvious that although the plane was new to him, he was in complete control. Below, hundreds of onlookers quickly lined both sides of the strip. They shouted their delight; word had spread fast that their Black Eagle was performing once again. Tafari, still angry, also looked up.

Julian gazed down and sensed the crowd was with him. Gliding closer to the ground, he pulled back easy on the stick to level out. Nothing happened. He pulled again. Still nothing. The engine began to sputter. The plane nosed over further. Suddenly it was out of control and deadheaded for the ground at an angle that ruled out the chance of a soft landing.

People scattered in all directions. Only the Emperor-elect kept his place, seated in frozen disbelief as he followed the plane's wobbly progress into the branches of a stunted eucalyptus tree. With a loud, crunching sound the wings crumbled and the undercarriage collapsed; there was no explosion or fire—just a deathly quiet everywhere.

Once it seemed fairly sure the plane wasn't going to fall

from its precarious perch, royal aides climbed the tree and pulled Julian out. The Emperor-elect had just observed his Imperial Air Force reduced by one-third.

The story was flashed around the world on the wires of the Associated Press. *The New York Times* placed it on page three, under the headline ETHIOPIA BANISHES HARLEM "COLONEL." The report read:

> Addis Abeba (*sic*) Abyssinia, Oct. 31 (AP)—The Emperor of Ethiopia, Haile Selassie I, has clipped the wings of his "Black Eagle"—"Colonel" Herbert (*sic*) Julian, formerly of Harlem—and ordered him out of the country in disgrace.

The Emperor-elect's decision to expel Julian came only after a lengthy night conference with his foreign minister. The advisability of putting Julian in jail was given earnest consideration until Tafari decided it would be too expensive for the government to feed him.

Julian left the next morning quietly, on a nearly empty train. The two French pilots were not invited to see him off, but they were there anyway. When the train finally disappeared down the plateau, headed for Djibouti, they returned to the airstrip to refine their own version of a coronation air show. They had worked it all out long ago—just in case.

AN ABYSSINIAN TRAGEDY was the heading of a story in the *New York Herald Tribune:*

> Sometimes we have treated his adventures lightly but we have never questioned his persistence or courage. The great success of last Spring, the glory, the high hopes, the assured future, the promised dukedom—and then, at the last moment, the crash, is high tragedy. The least we can do is withhold judgment until the Black Eagle returns to New York and gives his own version of the case. I feel sure the colonel will have an explanation. In any case, the

Black Eagle is uninjured and Harlem will have him back. Abyssinia's loss is New York's gain.

Two days after the crash, on November 2, 1930, Ras Tafari was crowned Emperor—the King of Kings, the Elect of Zion, and the Conquering Lion of the Tribe of Judah. It was a magnificent $4-million fete. *Rases* carrying great medieval swords and broad shields of wild animal skins rode into the city swathed in golden capes and followed by barefoot serfs bearing exotic gifts. The Royal Marine Band from the British frigate HMS *Effingham* came up from Djibouti and played resounding martial music while dozens of Ethiopian bands marched in procession through the streets blaring battle hymns of the empire. Their cymbals crashed, their sistrums rattled, and their zebra-skin drums boomed. The whole city seemed to shake with thundering sounds: bands, guns, galloping horses, roaring crowds.

Accompanied by his wife, the Empress-elect Menon, Tafari rode to the coronation cathedral in a chariot once owned by Kaiser Wilhelm II, drawn by eight white stallions. The lengthy Coptic ceremony was conducted in Ge'ez, a practically extinct ecclesiastical tongue only spoken in Ethiopia when monarchs come, and go.

Even as the bearded patriarch proclaimed him Emperor, Haile Selassie I remained somber. The crash was not a particularly auspicious way to start a reign, and he knew it.

As the *Île de France* moved slowly up New York's North River in a cold December-morning fog, the press piled aboard in search of the ex-Air Marshal and his tale of woe. He was intercepted strolling the promenade deck. The Parisian buying spree in which he had just indulged was in splendid evidence. He sported homburg, cutaway, striped trousers, wing collar, gray gloves, and, as one reporter noted, a carved cane "as big as Babe Ruth's bat."

Julian wanted to be alone, however. He said he had received cabled instructions from his "American advisers to keep quiet." He refused the microphones and waved off the cameras.

"But the world wants to know the truth," one newsman shouted. Then they all started in on him—cajoling, begging, promising. And eventually he succumbed to his favorite sweet.

"Gentlemen," he said, calling for silence, "it is a canard that I am *persona non grata* since the contretemps. I can state categorically that the Emperor and I were the best of pals when I left. You can prove the logicability of this statement by sending him a cable at my personal expense. I resigned for the sake of my own safety and health. I am not afraid to die, but I want to go with my boots on, fighting. Somebody crooked that British Moth I crashed in. There was a plot perpetrated by foreign influences which made it necessary for me to leave the empire. The Ethiopians loved me like a son—if only the foreigners had left me alone."

Then he began to detail the intrigue according to Julian: "When I first got there, I was instructed to revise the Air Force. The first thing I did was to condemn some foreign equipment. I took the position that only the best make of American planes was worthy of the Emperor's birdmen. That began the trouble. They tried to bump me off. I supplanted the French aviators and that did not set well, either. Those French pilots are absolutely not gentlemen.

"The day of the flight in which the plane crashed was in the nature of an air demonstration." He paused for a moment, deep in thought, then his head nodded as if agreeing with a suggestion.

"It is true that I didn't exactly have his permission to fly the plane. I wanted to give the Emperor a thrill. After all, even an emperor needs a thrill now and then."

Two nights later, in white-tie splendor, Julian appeared as guest of honor and head speaker at the Benefit Promenade and Grand Carnival of All Nations, sponsored by the Brotherhood of Sleeping Car Porters.

Though he had just been publicly grounded as an international adventurer, he told the more than eight hundred guests, "From the streets of New York to a brotherhood with kings is a career that can be pursued with success by all who are within the sound of my voice."

Not just a few eyes became misty when he touched on the Ethiopian affair. "I will never return to that country," he said, "even if they offered me the crownship. Harlem is my home. It was good enough for me when I was an unknown, and it is good enough for me now."

The applause was deafening. However, few in the audience believed that the Black Eagle was going to stay grounded long.

10

Between Acts

Greetings. I bring thee blessings from his Imperial Majesty, the African Emperor who is my ruler.

THE BLACK EAGLE *to a gas station proprietor* *Amarillo, Texas, 1931*

THE YEAR 1931 was not what one would call particularly auspicious for an ex-Air Marshal, or anyone else in America, for that matter. Bread lines and shanty towns were the only indices expanding. The best job Julian could find was flying bootleg whiskey down from Canada to the Eastern states for a Mafia syndicate headed by Owney Madden of Jersey City. It ended abruptly, however, when the syndicate started including satchels of narcotics in the cargo. That was going too far for the abstemious flyer. He decided to go straight and get a legitimate flying license. On July 30, 1931, he successfully passed the Bureau of Aeronautics test in a plane borrowed from designer Giuseppe Bellanca at a field in New Castle, Delaware.

Julian decided to buck the trend of business, which was witnessing twenty-five hundred bankruptcies a month. He organized an all-Negro flying circus and hired an unemployed musician named Tom Moore to be his public relations man.

"I find that this boy is chargeable with almost every fault, but not a single crime," Moore told the press. "His greatest liability is his overwhelming egoism. If anybody gave him a parachute and asked him if he could jump off the Empire State Building, not only would he say he could, but he'd do it. His career, particularly in the newspapers, has been most extraordinary. Well, you can laugh that off, but you can't laugh off a license from the Department of Commerce."

Traveling with Negro aerial performers Marie Dickenson and William Powell and renting planes along the circuit, Julian's troupe, "The Blackbirds," performed for audiences in Pittsburgh, Cleveland, and Detroit. He handled most of the flying; the others wing-walked and dangled about on rope ladders hanging from landing carriages.

At a Chicago reception a reporter for the *Times* asked him if he had any more record flights planned. Julian, in an expansive mood, announced a hop to Bombay.

"I'll hit straight for Gibraltar," he said, "and if I have enough gas, I'll just keep going. This flight will be a continuation of my earlier attempt to cross the Atlantic."

Although solo ocean crossings were by now not too newsworthy, Julian could never pass up a chance to take a trip—at least with words.

The troupe finally made enough to buy an old but presentable Cadillac. After performing in St. Louis for a weekend, Julian decided to head for Los Angeles, where, he was told, there were about fifty thousand Negroes and racial barriers were not as evident as in many Eastern cities. There Negroes and Mexicans were allowed into public swimming pools on Thursdays—the day before the water was changed.

The routing, especially through Texas, where necks were particularly red, made his colleagues nervous. Julian told them to relax; he had a plan worked out.

When they reached the Texas border, he changed into his old Ethiopian uniform with the gold epaulettes and instructed his colleagues to leave the talking to him.

Hungry, thirsty, and seat-sore after an all-night drive from Oklahoma City, they pulled into a gas station and roadhouse just west of Amarillo's city limits.

Julian braked to a stop under the wooden portico and close to the single gas pump. He turned the motor off, and they all got out, stretching, sucking in the fresh morning air, and eyeing the faded red sign on the building's weathered wall: EATS.

An unshaven face appeared at the screen door and stared for a long time.

"What you damned niggers want here?" The man growled.

"Greetings," Julian said expansively. He clasped his hands in prayer and bowed reverently with the grace of belted royalty. "I bring thee blessings from his Imperial Majesty, the African Emperor who is my ruler."

The proprietor scratched his head, slowly shifting a toothpick from one side of his mouth to the other with his tongue. Then he pushed open the screen door as he shouted back into the house, "Hey, these ain't no field niggers. They're African princes."

His wife and three children rushed to the doorway. A scrawny, long-eared dog came out cautiously to sniff the strangers with a low growl.

Elaborately, Julian produced an envelope from the inside pocket of his tunic and pulled from it photographs of life in the empire featuring him as Air Marshal in full regalia. As he shuffled through them with the smoothness of a faro dealer, he communicated to the proprietor that they were royalty with empty stomachs. The man quickly ordered his wife to the kitchen.

Whenever the roadside host looked at Julian's two partners, they bowed their heads and said "Hooblama goosh." It sounded regal enough.

While the threesome devoured a meal of eggs, hamsteaks, and hominy grits, the proprietor explained the problems he had with local Negroes. "But you royalty folks is fine," he added.

Fed, washed, and watered, Julian paid the bill and bowed his way to the car, which was gassed and ready.

Then with a wave he took off down Route 66 headed

for New Mexico's border, the accelerator to the floor in case his hosts had second thoughts.

There was tremendous excitement throughout low-slung, sprawling Los Angeles about The Blackbirds, the upcoming aerial show, which starred Ethel Waters. Sports-minded Angelenos were already warming up for their host role at the next summer's Olympics. The Blackbirds' local sponsor arranged motorcycle parades through the downtown business area, and Mayor John C. Porter made a speech about The Black Eagle's heroic accomplishments. "It was the first time a Negro had been received by the Mayor on the steps of City Hall," *Esquire* claimed.

After a winter in the sun and sky of Southern California, where The Blackbirds found themselves celebrities forbidden to touch a bill, Julian returned to New York in the spring of 1932 with enough of a roll to do some playing while plotting how to get himself back overseas on someone else's money. He was a regular at parties thrown in Greenwich Village by Luke Theodore Upshure.

A janitor by day, at night the self-educated Upshure was a patron of Negro arts and letters. He invited Julian to his affairs because the pilot-adventurer was not only the most traveled man in Negro society but also a splendid figure and eloquent *raconteur.*

Humorist H. Allen Smith described Julian at an Upshure affair: ". . . a tall, prepossessing Negro in elegant dinner clothes . . . stood in one corner and bowed stiffly from the waist when anyone approached him. . . ."

Also present was a buxom Negro poetess and, beneath the spell of Luke Theodore Upshure's punch bowl, she consented, after much urging, to recite her masterpiece. It was the longest poem ever composed in any language, encompassing the history of the Negro race, but she was a woman of great staying power and ample lung spread. She went on and on and on and at last reached the signing of the agreements of 1885, under which the boundaries of Liberia were established. At this point she bogged down, forgot a line. She stumbled and stammered and then looked wildly about the room.

"I've forgot that darn line," she said. "I just can't think of it to save my life."

Colonel Hubert Fauntleroy Julian stepped forward smiling. "Perhaps," he said, "if Madame would start all over again from the beginning she would remember when she got to it."

Apparently she did start up again, but Smith didn't wait to see if she made it over the hump the second time.

On July 24, 1934, Julian crossed the Atlantic on the S.S. *Europa.* His assignment: personal escort of Mrs. Amy Jacques-Garvey, the wife of the deported West Indian crusader en route to England. She had hired him because she felt his credentials in African affairs would be invaluable to her mission, which was to recruit support for her husband's back-to-Africa movement among African intellectuals and leaders studying and visiting in Britain.

Once in London, Mrs. Garvey asked Julian to arrange what she called "an intimate air show" at Heston Aerodrome. She invited a select collection of African dignitaries, mostly from the Gold Coast (now Ghana) and Nigeria, Britain's two most sophisticated African colonies. After successfully taking a British flying exam and renting an airplane from Wrightson and Pearse, Julian was ready.

The guest of honor at the affair was Sir Nana Aforetta, the paramount chief of the Gold Coast. Sir Nana, an enormous, jolly man in a colorful gown of *kente* cloth, energetically applauded Julian's aerial performance. When the pilot landed and was presented to him, the powerful Ashanti tribal leader asked if he might take a hop.

"Of course, milord," said Julian. He led the chief to his plane, strapped him in, climbed into the cockpit, and prepared for takeoff. But a royal bearer insisted on staying by the plane with an umbrella over his master, despite Julian's attempts to urge him away. In fact, the fiercely dedicated servant started to climb into Sir Nana's cockpit with the umbrella still open. The chief chuckled, waiting to see how Julian would handle the awkward situation.

He did it the fast way. He gunned the engine, sending an unexpected rush of propeller wash lashing back along the fuselage. The immense umbrella became a ground-running parachute and the servant was whipped away like a shot.

As they cruised in the clear summer sky over the green English countryside, Sir Nana roared with laughter.

When they landed, Julian tried to convince the chief to contribute to Garvey's cause. Although the cocoa-rich ruler was impressed that Julian was the first Negro pilot to obtain a British flying license, the best he could offer was a plot of land outside his capital of Accra upon which to build a Black Eagle flying school. Julian passed on that; he had had it with flying schools.

One of Mrs. Garvey's guests at the aerial show was the American singer Paul Robeson, who was in London to star in the movie *Saunders of the River.* Despite his all-American background (in football, at least), Robeson was rather hostile about most things American. When Julian confided to him that he was actually either Ethiopian or British, depending on the advantages to be gained, they laughed together and rapport was established. They met socially several times after that and Robeson once suggested that the pilot consider representing the black race in the upcoming London-to-Melbourne plane race. It was shaping up as a spirited contest over an eleven-thousand-mile course for the best pilots in the British Empire, which at that time was black, white, brown, yellow, and Australian.

Julian was interested—providing someone put up the plane, for he was also finished with trying to raise funds himself.

Robeson arranged for him to make contact with Lord Wakefield, the wealthy Englishman who developed Castorol, an engine lubricant still a favorite with pilots around the world. Julian called Wakefield, who was on an extended business trip to Paris, and set a September date to discuss the project with him there.

At the same time he was negotiating with Wakefield, a Negro musical troupe arrived in London from New York for a series of performances. Julian spent his leisure hours with the members of the chorus line. He was especially attracted to one rather young dancer who was long of leg and bold of kick. When a surprise birthday party was planned for her backstage at the Palladium on the evening he was to return from his Paris meeting, he decided his contribution would be roses and French perfume picked up on the trip.

Early on the morning of the party, Julian flew to Le Bourget Airport for his meeting with Lord Wakefield.

When he landed, he felt like Lindbergh. Dozens of airport workers rushed to get a look at the first Negro pilot ever to land on French soil. Julian ordered his plane gassed for 3:00 PM, met Lord Wakefield at the Hotel George V for a working lunch, then purchased roses and perfume along the Rue de Rivoli.

Returning to the airport, he found it shut down and all planes grounded. Bad weather was moving in, and a dangerous electrical storm was reported banging around over the English Channel.

Julian was undaunted by the weather; he had an engagement in London and he planned to keep it. Despite pleas even from the airport officials, he ordered his plane untied. He took off into a lowering sky, the wind already running against him at forty miles per hour.

Fighting up through thick clouds to eight thousand feet, he leveled off and pointed north-northeast for the cliffs of Dover. The betting on the ground was fifty to one against his making it.

Midway across, the storm tagged him with furious bolts

of lightning and claps of thunder. The rain poured down with the intensity of a tropical cloudburst. His tiny plane bounced around and the dangerous sighs of wing stress grew louder by the minute. He was barraged by a storm of hailstones as big as pigeon eggs. Only when he caught a glimpse of Big Ben's tower through a break in the clouds did he think he might have a chance. The sky over Heston was clear, but it was also dark.

Suddenly the lights of a dozen automobiles flashed on down below him. The French had telephoned ahead, alerting the aerodrome just in case he did make it.

According to *Newsweek,* the evening landing was so dramatic that "field attendants' eyes bulged." Airport officials trotted out to inspect the plane. Much of the doped canvas was in shreds. The fuselage was as waterlogged as the pilot.

"I had a most trying time," Julian commented, peeling off his wet gloves. "I would have felt ashamed to admit defeat, however." He confided that for a good part of the voyage he actually flew upside-down "to avoid getting drowned in the cockpit."

The roses were bruised, the perfume box was stained, and the pilot was sneezing. But all eyes were on The Black Eagle at the backstage party. And his derring-do was well rewarded by the birthday girl.

The publicity stirred up by the flight made Julian a serious contender, in the newspapers at least, for entry in the London-to-Melbourne race. He started training immediately.

"This consists," he told the London press, "of drinking plenty of milk and having the hotel switchboard wake me up at all odd hours." He announced he was also training a popular British heavyweight boxer, Larry Gaines, as his co-pilot.

He called the Ethiopian Embassy in Paris to inform the ambassador that he would name his plane, as yet unsupplied, *Haile Selassie I.* A cable came in from the Minister of State at Addis Ababa a week later: DO AS YOU LIKE CONGRATULATIONS SIGNED TECLEMARCOS.

However, when Julian examined the best offer of a plane from Lord Wakefield, he decided it would have a hard time making it off the ground, much less over the Alps. He wasn't about to risk another Flushing Bay incident. Also, since he was the only black pilot considering the race, he didn't want to leave himself open to further ridicule if his equipment wasn't the best. The odds were too great. Other pilots were nervous about making it even with such expensive and brand-new twin-engine planes as the DC-2, the Boeing 247, and the de Havilland Comet—crafts in the $60,000 range for which the race would be a major test. (A British crew flying a Comet eventually won it, covering the last 2½ hours on one engine.)

So after partying and talking himself into near exhaustion, Julian returned home to New York aboard the *Berengaria* on December 6, 1934.

"His belted polo coat, morning jacket, striped trousers and spats easily entitle him to the nomination of best-dressed male for the crossing," wrote John McClain in the *New York Sun.*

When the ship had docked, reporters cornered him to check the ominous reports from increasingly uneasy European capitals that Italy was planning to invade Ethiopia. Had the Emperor contacted him on the matter? they asked.

Assuming a grave expression, Julian thumbed through a smart leather portfolio, slowly passing numerous official-looking documents bearing waxed and ribboned seals.

"Ah, here," he said finally, his thoughts now collected. "Read this cablegram. It will tell you just where I stand with the King of Kings on the matter."

DO AS YOU LIKE CONGRATULATIONS SIGNED TECLEMARCOS, it read.

"Teclemarcos," he explained, "is the Ethiopian Minister of State. The cable came as a reply to one I had sent the

Emperor. I told him about some plans I had. Thank you, gentlemen."

Julian had successfully winged it through the press conference. Now he headed for Harlem to catch up on the news of the world and plan his own part in making that news. Exciting things were happening, and he had no intention of sitting on the sidelines.

11

Back in Action

I shall perhaps use some of the funds contributed to me by a lady in London—no, no names, please—for a flight to her beloved India. After all, India is always there. It can wait until I get back from the war.

THE BLACK EAGLE *announcing his marching orders New York, February, 1935*

BENITO MUSSOLINI and his Black Shirts were obsessed with resurrecting the Roman Empire, though not necessarily in its holy state.

Centuries earlier Roman legions had sought Ethiopia's fabled cities of gold without success. In 1896, at the battle of Adowa, the rifle-bearing troops of Italy's King Humbert I made another try, only to be driven out of Africa by spear-chucking warriors who charged on muleback. Italians had not forgotten the disgrace of that battle.

Now, in late 1934, with all Europe jittery about Adolf Hitler's intentions, the chancellor of bombast decided to grab the empire, and take his revenge under the guise of "a civilizing mission."

By the end of January 1935, nearly one million Italians were in uniform and children were ordered to search World War I battlegrounds for old shell cases. The infantry was training with *yperite,* a mustard gas, and the air force was practicing mass-bombing tactics. In Turino, Italian scientists labored on a secret weapon—powder that when spread on the ground would blister the feet of the shoeless Ethiopian troops.

All these published reports brought Julian's fighting

blood to a fast boil. Despite problems with the empire, it was still his adopted homeland, and he cherished his Ethiopian passport. Also, things were not exactly booming on the work front at home. He was doing odd charter jobs for various black leaders like Father Divine, but nothing steady. So, since he was obsessed with causes (and considered himself a cause worthy of obsession) he easily reached a decision.

"To take off immediately was my initial reaction to news of Italy's aggression towards my friend," Julian told reporter A. J. Liebling of the *New York World Telegram.* Liebling had decided to visit the pilot at his Harlem home on February 18, 1935, when he heard rumors that Julian was the first Harlem freedom-fighter to volunteer for Ethiopian service. "But I restrained my ardor whilst assembling some combat equipment. Italy, of course, is making a terrible mistake. The only disparity between the combatants is in the air. Once that's remedied, Ethiopia should have nothing to fear."

Julian confided that he was busy scouting around for several American-made planes suitable for strafing, which he hoped to sell to the Emperor "at cost, of course."

"I'm going to finance the trip myself," he continued. "I shall perhaps use some of the funds contributed to me by a lady in London—no, no names, please—for a flight to her beloved India. After all, India is always there. It can wait until I get back from the war."

Acting as a self-appointed spokesman for the nation's twelve million Negroes, Julian stated, "We are now organizing a boycott against Italian icemen, fruit stands, and spaghetti houses."

Then he wrapped a white silk muffler around his neck, pulled on a large, woolly overcoat, and announced he was leaving for a meeting with Harlem leaders on even tougher boycotts.

"Remember," he said, "no monkey business with this story. It's very serious and dignified."

On February 22, 1935, the day after Julian left for the front, the *Chicago Times* cautioned: IL DUCE NOTE, BLACK EAGLE SAILS FOR ABYSSINIA.

Eight days later Julian arrived in Southampton, where he told the AP, "I do not mind whether I am a colonel or a private. I came to fight."

Once in London he spent his time on what could best be described as a fishing excursion to find out whether he would be allowed back into Ethiopia at all. His public comments strongly hinted at the role he'd like to play in the impending action.

"Here I am if Ethiopia wants me," he told a collection of Fleet Street reporters who gathered in his Stafford Hotel suite near Buckingham Palace. "I want no finer death than a quick one—in the air. I would like to go down in flames over Ethiopia taking a few of the others with me."

Despite a fusillade of printed reminders of his readiness, Julian didn't receive the sought-after go-ahead signal from Addis Ababa. And beneath all the glamour of this much-heralded journey to danger, the idleness began getting to him.

He finally packed up his kit in late March, headed for Marseilles, and boarded a common freighter for Djibouti. He arrived still uninvited in Addis Ababa on April 12—the day Haile Selassie sent an impassioned warning to the League of Nations about Italy's threatened aggression.

When word reached the palace of Julian's arrival, an official commented, "Ethiopian aviation is headed by competent foreign experts." Nevertheless, he set out to make sure a good part of Addis Ababa knew he was back.

"Colonel Julian walks about with two servants tagging along behind him struggling with two suitcases," reported the AP. "It is a matter of town gossip that he changes his suits three times a day."

After a week of waiting, Julian put on his old uniform, marched by foot directly to the palace, and noisily demanded to see the Chamberlain.

When he came, they shook hands hurriedly and talked quite briefly. Julian had to make his point straightaway; the Chamberlain's weary face told him he had many things on his mind.

"Tell the Emperor I am not here for pleasure," Julian said, "but to fight for him." The Chamberlain explained the heavy pressures the empire's leader was under. But he did assure Julian he'd get word back to him soon on what his military role might be.

Two days later Julian received a handwritten message from the Emperor. It thanked him for coming and informed him that he could indeed be of military assistance to the Army. The Air Force was out, however, "regretfully." The Emperor did not elaborate, but noted he felt Julian would understand. "We only have four planes," he wrote.

Julian's first official appearance in a military capacity came in early July, when he marched through the city followed by a scraggly mob of barefoot recruits. His uniform bore the braid of a colonelcy, and his assignment was to turn one thousand Ministry of Public Works laborers into an effective fighting unit.

Using tactics he claimed to have learned during his National Guard days, the indefatigable bird colonel worked diligently training his men to crawl under barbed wire, dig trenches and fortify them, fight in hand-to-hand combat, and touch their toes without bending their knees. Wherever he marched his men, which usually included passing the palace as well as the more important legations, Julian kept hammering into their fighting spirit the ancient warrior cry, "*Ebalgume!*" or "Mow the enemy down!"

The black pilot seemed content to be grounded—at least temporarily. He had his old rank back, a fine steed, a salary of $100 weekly, and easy credit at the best food supplier in the city, Mohammed Ali's *duka.* Renewed talk of a romance with the Emperor's favorite daughter, Princess Tsahai, rippled through the community. The willowy beauty, rumored to have had a child's crush on Julian during his Air Marshal days, was now one of his staunchest defenders in royal circles.

Few Ethiopians in the palace or the military spoke English, so Julian became the self-appointed briefing officer for the growing squad of American and British correspondents who kept arriving to cover a war that hadn't started. In this capacity he served an important function in propagandizing Ethiopian efforts. From written reports an outsider gained the impression that little happened in the empire without The Black Eagle's being involved.

The New York Times, for example, carried a story on August 1 from Addis Ababa that Julian "rode a white charger down the streets of Addis Ababa during today's military review. That gave rise to reports that the American Negro flier . . . would be put in command of Ethiopia's air force."

Julian's balloon deflated a few days later, however, when he learned of the arrival in the capital of another American freedom-fighter. Chicagoan John Robinson's claim to fight under the *nom de guerre* of The Brown Condor was just too much for him. He could accept, reluctantly to be sure, the arrival of another American Negro. But not one who to him was so patently aiming to steal his style—and next, perhaps, even his stage. For Robinson also happened to be a pilot.

The situation came to bloodied heads on August 8. Julian had just left the American Consulate after an unsatisfactory meeting with Consul William Cramp. He had urged the diplomat to cable President Roosevelt protesting the United States government's lack of sympathy for Ethiopia's dilemma. Cramp told Julian that if he wanted to send such a cable that was his own business, and would be at his own cost, too.

When he arrived back in his hotel lobby, an American reporter told him that several Negro newspapers in America had just carried a story claiming that the Emperor had been finally convinced by a newly arrived American flyer that Julian should never again be allowed to fly for Ethiopia.

The newsman finished the story just as Robinson came down from his room. An argument started over who might have concocted such a story. Tempers flared. Robinson pulled a knife; Julian grabbed a wooden chair. The fight ended in a draw when Robinson, after slashing Julian's arms, was dropped by an overhead slam with a board.

They retreated to their respective rooms to patch themselves up. When the *New York Sun* heard the story, it ran a feature in its "Who's News Today" column headed HARLEM'S BLACK EAGLE GETS THE FIGHTING URGE. The story said:

> A black Don Quixote, flying windmills instead of bucking them, couldn't have more fun and excitement than Col. Julian, the black boy from Trinidad Island. Knocking around the world, but born for deeds of derring-do and finally declaring himself in, in a big way, with innate grace and elegance. . . .

The incident was not taken so lightly by the palace, however. In the last three weeks, five thousand more Italian soldiers had come through Port Said on the way to Italian Somaliland, Ethiopia's neighboring enemy. With a war coming, internal dissension and personal feuds weren't needed.

Also, not a few Ethiopian officials were embarrassed by the brawl between the first two American Negro volunteers for their cause. Both Julian and Robinson were potentially great drawers of black volunteers from around the world. But not if they ended up killing each other.

The War Ministry summarily stripped Julian of his command. Robinson (later killed on a bombing mission) was grounded and told to keep his mouth closed around newsmen.

After a week with no further incidents, Julian was quietly reinstated. However, he was ordered to take up a command at the town of Ambo to the north, three days' ride from Addis Ababa. He was appointed military governor of three thousand badly trained citizen-soldiers. *The New York Times* stated in a September 5 story from the capital, "Despite rumors to the contrary, the Negro airman remains one of the right-hand men of [the] emperor."

Mounted on a handsome, big-chested Arabian stallion, Julian left for Ambo on September 15 followed by a long file of recruit-retainers lugging bedding, tents, rifles, canned food supplies, and ammunition. The column made a detour to a tin-roofed building that served as press headquarters.

Without dismounting, Julian let go with a verbal blast at a group of correspondents who were lounging on wooden benches waiting for the almost daily scoops that now came rolling off the newly acquired mimeograph machine.

"It's a prodigious lie that the Emperor told me he hasn't enough planes for me to crash," Julian roared out, referring to stories that had recently been printed. "I am favored by His Majesty, respected by high officials, and loved by the people. Also, this magnificent assignment is a promotion by the Emperor for my making soldiers in Ethiopia."

He turned and galloped off on the Gulali Road, which led in the general direction of his bush command.

On September 28, with the invasion imminent, Selassie ordered total mobilization. Heralds traveled by donkey and on foot throughout the empire reading aloud the proclamation:

> Everyone will now be mobilized and all boys old enough to carry a spear will be sent to Addis Ababa. Married men will take their wives to carry food and cook. Those without wives will take any woman without a husband. Women with small babies need not go. The blind, those who cannot walk, or for any reason cannot carry a spear are exempted. Anyone found at home after receipt of this order will be hanged. Signed H.I.M. Haile Selassie I.

On October 2 Italian bombers finally attacked Ethiopia at Adowa in the north, just below Italian-ruled Eritrea. Throughout Italy church bells rang triumphantly, jubilant troops marched to cheering crowds of civilians, and fascist rallies were held in the thronged piazzas of towns and villages everywhere. In the late afternoon Mussolini went to his favorite balcony in the Palazzo Venezia.

"With Ethiopia we have been patient for forty years," he shouted out to the Romans, who were ecstatic over the victory. "Now, enough!"

The humility of nearly four decades ago was avenged at last, and at its place of origin.

Seven days later, the Ambo Commander raced into Addis Ababa on a foaming horse. He only stopped when he reached the palace gates where, winded, he explained he'd been riding for thirty hours without rest, making six changes of mounts along the way. His concern was the report he'd heard that the siege had started.

"If the Emperor wishes," he said, tethering his lathered horse to a gum tree, "I will start immediately for Adowa to help recapture the city. I know how to fight the Italians. I knocked a lot of them out in Harlem—with my fists!"

He emerged from the palace an hour later and was mobbed by foreign correspondents anxious to know when they could head for the front.

First, Julian briefed them on his ride, during which he had been attacked by a band of hyenas. He supported the account by displaying a revolver and two cartridges.

"I started with twenty-one bullets," he said. "Smell that barrel!"

As some of them did, he explained he would be leaving for the front in the morning as an aide-de-camp to the Minister of War, Ras Mulugeta. He promised to arrange for them to journey with him and the troops of the Yamahal, or Army of the Middle.

When they all finally reached the battleground, four hundred miles to the north, by forced night marches of twenty-five miles, conditions had become chaotic. There was little mechanized transport. Food, ammunition, and water were in perilously short supply. The badly trained troops were dazed and disorganized. They had never before encountered strafing, bombing, or the sound of heavy artillery. Many had already fled in panic. Others, finding their guns useless, had discarded them.

In one engagement Julian located a supply of ammunition and rushed it to a strategic machine-gun emplacement only to find that the ammunition was the wrong caliber.

"To fight on at the front is no more than an empty gesture that might cost my life," Julian wrote in a diary that evening, within the sound of Italian flea tanks rumbling into position on sand dunes for the next day's battle. "Everyone agrees that, with the lack of ammo and weapons, and the disorganization in the capital, there is no hope of stopping the well-armed and highly trained Italian army. I think, too, of the old proverb 'He that fights and runs away.' "

His feelings didn't keep him from making patriotic statements to the press about the Ethiopian military strength, however. Speaking of the Ambo forces he had trained, he told an AP correspondent, "I put fire and the devil in them. Now under my special training, any one of them can stand up against six Italians."

By the beginning of November it was difficult to locate any organized resistance. The Italians were overrunning practically all Ethiopian positions encountered. They controlled the important northern oasis towns and main roads and railroad line. Addis Ababa was almost isolated from the world—and its own retreating armies.

Within weeks, many of the mercenaries and volunteers who had rushed to Ethiopia's aid from Rhodesia, South Africa, Kenya, Britain, the Scandinavian countries, and

America began packing off. The morale of foreign freedom-fighters worsened when a rumor spread that the Emperor himself had made plans to flee the country.

"All foreigners in the army," *The New York Times* reported, "save the professional Belgian soldiers on long contract, are dissatisfied with . . . the war and appear to want the quickest and most honorable way out."

Mulugeta ordered Julian to return to the capital to help fortify it for what was now the inevitable—a last-ditch battle.

On the night of November 5, a palace guard entered Julian's tent at his military camp near the palace and told him the Emperor wanted to see him immediately. Julian dressed hurriedly by the light of a kerosene lantern. His mind raced with conjectures: a generalship, perhaps, or a special assignment, or even a secret mission.

Inside the palace the Chamberlain handed him a note from the Emperor.

"His Imperial Majesty demands an explanation," the Chamberlain said as Julian ripped the envelope open and began to read.

The note summarized reports from various foreign embassies in Rome that a highly placed American in Ethiopia was in the pay of the Italians. His assignment: assassinate Selassie.

Julian studied it in silence. Then he gesticulated wildly, shook his head madly, and fainted.

"He was revived by the bystanders with water which was hastily brought in petrol cans," the Reuters correspondent reported.

Julian stayed inside his tent in seclusion for two days. On the third day he finally emerged, still visibly upset, to meet with several American correspondents and discuss the charges. It was obvious to him, he said, that he had been fingered as the possible culprit because of his intimacy with the Emperor. Of the dozen men from America fighting in

Ethiopia, he, though not legally an American, was the only one close to the palace officials.

"I surely would not do such a dastardly thing to a sovereign whose talents and wisdom are greater than Solomon's and whose tact and patience surpass those of Job," he told them. "No amount of gold in the world and no title offered me by Mussolini would induce me to perpetrate such a heinous crime."

After twenty-four hours of silence the palace finally issued a statement that cleared Julian of the charges. *The New York Times* on November 8 stated, "Colonel Julian, the stormiest petrel in the Ethiopian Army . . . settled his serious differences with Emperor Haile Selassie." The assassination rumor, it turned out, had come from a story in Rome's leading daily, *La Tribuna.* There was little doubt that the article's aim was to further break Ethiopian morale. It accomplished its divisive purpose. The whole affair not only exhausted Julian; it also discouraged him.

On November 15 he called it quits, this time for good. He spent his last evening in Addis with Linton Wells, the *New York Herald Tribune* correspondent, working on a personal farewell note to the Emperor.

"Your Supreme Illustriousness," it began, "It is with overflowing emotion and bleeding heart that I am resigning as an officer in the great army of the Conquering Lion of Judah, but . . ." The "but" explained such blows to his pride as being grounded, being accused of serving the enemy, and last but not least, being charged by the Royal Accountant with attempting to collect double paychecks.

That done, Julian went out into the night for a last look at the city where wondrous dreams as well as drumming nightmares had come true for him. His chauffeur drove through the streets slowly, but on a narrow turn accidentally ran down an Ethiopian. Suddenly the whole area came alive with angry citizens. They stoned the car and shouted obscenities at Julian.

Before dawn he rose, collected his bags, and was driven

to a small substation outside the city. And thus the Black Eagle departed Ethiopia—after seven months of misadventures in trying to win, if not the war, a place of prominence in it. He was partially successful. After the Emperor he was the single most written-about participant in the action.

The *New York Herald Tribune*'s correspondent, under the headline JULIAN BIDS ETHIOPIA ADIEU FOREVER, wrote the most objective valediction. "The majority of the correspondents here regret seeing the Harlem hero leave," he noted. "In all honesty it should be recorded that he is not leaving under a cloud, but purely voluntarily."

"I'm sorry for the guy," Julian told the *Daily Express* on his way home through London. "I could have won the war for him."

Six months later, on May 5, 1936, Haile Selassie also left his capital—on a donkey—as Italy proclaimed its victory over Ethiopia. World War II was unofficially but irrevocably mounted.

12

In Search of a Perch

I should raise a whole boatload of hell at such an insulting question . . . I am an adventurer. . . . I've spent that much on a short pleasure cruise.
THE BLACK EAGLE *to reporters who questioned his financial ability to bail Father Divine out of a lawsuit* *New York City, 1939*

AS THE SOUNDS of danger tolled louder during the late 1930s, Julian found it increasingly difficult to join in the swirling events. It was not for lack of trying, however. He appeared, for example, on Ripley's *Believe It or Not* radio program over New York's WJZ, where for fifteen minutes he lofted in the glory of numerous dramatic battles fought and historic fights performed. But as he left the stage to the audience's applause, he missed a step. It took twenty minutes of smelling salts to revive him, and he retreated from Rockefeller Plaza with a swollen right thumb.

The mishap, plus the way things in Ethiopia hadn't worked out, convinced him he was star-crossed. His next fall, he thought, might be fatal. In anticipation of this, he deposited $200 with a Harlem undertaker and called a press conference to discuss his fate.

"The purpose of the deposit," he explained "is to insure that I will receive a funeral befitting my station in case of an aeronautical death. I have instructed him to bury me upright. I will be standing at attention, as you might say, in a bronze box."

With a deep sigh he continued to newsmen, "Talk of death is unpleasant but death overtakes us all. Presidents have been assassinated and kings and emperors have been murdered. Why not Julian? I have to think of these things."

A year later, in November 1937, he arrived in New York in an even more funereal mood. As the *Queen Mary* docked in Manhattan, Julian, in top hat and mourning-toned attire, told the press, "As equerry to the late Prince Hadji Ali of Egypt, I have the sad duty to escort my master's body in a special casket, as well as the Prince's daughter, the fair Princess Almeria Ali."

The late prince supposedly possessed two stomachs. Or so he told his salon audiences on the continent and in Great Britain before going into his paid act. This consisted of his daughter in belly-dancer undress making sensual slithers around his sides while he drank a cup of gasoline, ignited it, then extinguished the flames with water brought up from the reserve stomach.

Julian had first encountered the team at a palace function in Ethiopia in 1920. On a recent trip to London he had seen them again. This time the prince had taken him on as a business manager and booking agent.

When the prince died, suddenly and in bed, Julian came up with a scheme to sell the royal cadaver to Johns Hopkins University for scientific purposes.

Two days after their New York arrival, an autopsy proved the anatomical report false. That bit of bad news forced Julian to return the $500 advanced by a publicity-minded New York mortician named Duncan who had read the story and bought the display rights to the two-tummied cousin of Farouk.

In the summer of 1939 Julian was assigned to head for troubled Europe as an accredited foreign correspondent for the *Amsterdam News*, New York's top Negro newspaper. He had gotten the idea the year before when he met Ernest Hemingway during a September crossing of the Atlantic.

The novelist was heading for Europe again, he told Julian, "to be there in the event that a European war breaks out." To Julian it sounded like a good way to get involved with whatever conflict came along.

"You know, I'm always being interviewed," he told reporters as he boarded the *Queen Mary* on August 23. The ship was practically empty; worsening European events had brought about hundreds of cancellations in the last few weeks. Only for adventurers like Julian was it an ideal time to travel.

"It'll be quite an experience for me to do the interviewing," he said. "It's about time that Negroes had an authentic correspondent of their own—somebody who will write the news they want. I can adequately fill the position, and my knowledge of French, Spanish, German, Ethiopian, and Egyptian languages will do me no harm. I understand Mister Hitler doesn't like members of my race. But an aviator must have no fear. I will follow wherever I have to go with the true *esprit* of an aviator. For wherever there's trouble, wherever there's any dangerous situation, it will find me there—on the spot."

When France declared war on Germany on September 3, however, most Americans began packing for home as fast as possible. It was obvious all of Europe would be a battleground. Checking in at the United States Embassy in Paris, Julian was urged to return home immediately. The document he traveled on was a Nansen passport issued by the League of Nations to citizens of the world. The Embassy informed him it guaranteed him about as much protection as the Ethiopian officer's uniform he occasionally displayed.

The former foreign correspondent arrived home just in time to come to the aid of one of the nation's leading "Peace—it's wonderful!" practitioners, who was coming under intensive fire from two fallen angels.

To most of Father Divine's followers he was more almighty than any emperor. His Peace Mission movement, which had started in the 1920s, already had 300,000 devout followers. His churches were called heavens, and at them his faithful, called angels, could receive the biggest catered Holy Communion in Christendom.

Many an early Divine doubter was straightened out when, in the late 1920s, the Father was ordered to appear in a Long Island court for disturbing the peace. The presiding judge, Lewis J. Smith, told the preacher he was a fraud.

"You'll soon die," was Divine's answer.

Three days later the judge did just that, of a stroke.

The Black Eagle had first become involved with Father Divine in the early 1930s, when the squat Georgian decided it would be more efficient to make flying tours of his network of heavens. One of his archangels mentioned Julian, and he was soon hired, not only as Divine's private pilot but also as official flight instructor for all angels wishing to learn how to fly. Julian had enjoyed his work, for there were also female angels in his classes.

Now, five years later, ex-angels Thomas Brown and his wife Verinda were suing Father Divine. They demanded the return of savings and property—$6,500 worth, including household effects—that they had turned over to him upon joining the movement. Disillusionment had come to the Browns when, after several dedicated years as the angels Rebecca Grace and Onward Universe, they happened to inquire about their possessions.

"Everything is in the heavenly treasury where moths, cobwebs, or the rust of corruption cannot enter," they were told, and were refused a look. The lawsuit followed.

The trial took place in Manhattan's downtown Supreme Court building. During the proceedings the Browns exposed such inner-sanctum secrets as the three Long Island Railroad cars labeled The Father, The Son, and The Holy Ghost, hired on weekends to haul the faithful out to the Sayville heaven; and the four-hour feasts, called Holy Communions, consisting of twelve courses of ham, potatoes, rice, corn, cabbage, scalloped tomatoes, hominy, carrots, beets, a cheese two feet long, five different kinds of pie, and six flavors of ice cream.

"It was the most magnificent thing I ever saw in creation," Mrs. Brown admitted to the judge in describing her first Holy Communion experience. "There were two cakes as big as automobile tires." She explained that after the feast Father Divine, who described himself as "driven by cosmic forces and both omnipotent and omnipresent," had invited husband and wife to take their money out of "government banks because they are sure to fall sooner or later."

She said that when she and her husband had agreed, Divine announced, "I am so glad, it's wonderful. I am so tired of staying in spirit and seeing different creatures fleece my children that I take a body and come to feed and clothe them and make them safe under my wings. I am a free gift to humanity."

Father Divine sat silently in the crowded courtroom, surrounded by eager angels with pens poised over shorthand books ready to take down any utterances of his, for his words were as sacred as scripture.

His attorney, Kevie Frankel, sought to convince the court that the Browns were serving as "tools" employed by "unidentifiable people" to destroy the Peace Mission, which he described as "a religious, spiritual movement like the Jewish and Christian movements."

It was a most embarrassing affair that did indeed seem aimed at collapsing an empire. Needless to say, Frankel claimed his client had no money; it was all in the heavens.

Julian followed the front-page action carefully and finally decided to act on Divine's behalf. The religious leader had been generous to him in the past, and right now he wouldn't mind being in the news again.

The *New York World Telegram* reported on The Black Eagle's appearance in the courtroom on December 4, 1939:

"For the first time in legal history, the Supreme Court of New York operated under a master of ceremonies."

Dressed like a diplomat, Julian sashayed about the room, immediately upstaging all others by announcing a peace plan. He had, he said, certain notes, securities, and liens on some twenty-five-year-old whiskey in a warehouse that amounted to $12,000. He would be willing to use these things to settle his friend's suit in a dignified manner.

Judge Benedict D. Dineen took a liking to the plan, and promptly called an adjournment in order to hold conferences in his chambers with both sides plus Julian.

Asked by skeptical reporters if he really did have whiskey receipts of value, the peace mediator bellowed, "I should raise a whole boatload of hell at such an insulting question. I would not permit such a statement to go around if questionable. I am an adventurer. In a few days or a week I could raise much more than that. I've spent that much on a short pleasure cruise."

As the conference continued for a second day in the judge's chambers, the *World Telegram* reported:

> Col. Julian was even more impressive than yesterday despite his impulsive offer. The Black Eagle strode in majesty through the court lurching along with shoulders back, like men are made to march in movies, purposeful and strong under skilled direction and a low camera angle.
>
> Now and again he bent low from the waist and kissed a hand. Once he took a card from his billfold and autographed it with a gallant flourish. He had business all over the house, calling less colorful figures to the conference room where Divine hosts were discussing settlement.

The New York Times said Julian told reporters:

> I am not a follower of Father Divine. But I am a

Negro and I have seen the good things he has done. Any man who can make great numbers of people quit drinking and smoking and even make thieves return the things they have stolen, I am for. I am sick and tired of seeing the Negro race kicked around. Because I am a Negro I want to do my bit to help demonstrate its true dignity.

Two days later he was sorry he ever got involved.

"Since my offer was published," he told newsmen outside the courtroom at a hastily called press conference on December 7, "I and Father Divine have received about twenty phone calls from people who say they have contributed to the heavens and want their money back, too. The sum would run into $50,000 and—"

"I don't want you to say another thing," interrupted his wife, Essie, making a rare public appearance in a black-dyed coat and hat of karakul, the pelt of newborn lambs. "Not a thing."

"But I owe some statements to the press," he said.

"You've said enough already," she snapped. Reporters present could not recall a time in the past when Julian had been so silenced.

Father Divine eventually settled the case out of court and out of his own pocket. He rewarded Julian's efforts by again engaging his flying services on weekends for major Sabbath gatherings around the heavens.

13

A Star Is Born

Paar-don mee-ee! Do I look like a varicose idiot? Do I? Go elsewhere for the ice!

THE BLACK EAGLE *when told there was only frozen custard for chilling the champagne RKO Regent Theater, New York, January, 1940*

THE BLACK EAGLE had now performed as a flyer, stunter, lecturer, Air Marshal, special envoy, foreign correspondent, wheeler-dealer, playboy, promoter, and court mediator. These roles had carried him to numerous stages on a couple of continents. It was apparent to many businessmen that associating Julian's name with a venture represented a trumpeting plus. If the venture didn't make news, Julian invariably did.

It was Julian's nose for timing and eye for news that brought him into show business in 1940. The year before, Hattie McDaniel had won an Oscar for her portrayal of a Negro slave in *Gone With the Wind*. She was voted the best supporting actress in a year that saw a host of masterpieces: *The Wizard of Oz, Stagecoach, Of Mice and Men, Goodbye, Mr. Chips*. Her competition was formidable: Olivia de Havilland, Geraldine Fitzgerald, and Edna May Oliver were also nominated.

To Julian, the win was a sure sign that the time was right for an all-Negro movie. Negroes would go to it for reasons of pride; whites, for laughs. He didn't care about their motives as long as they paid cash for their pleasures.

On January 14, 1940, he announced his theatrical enterprise. He already had completed one film to prove it, he disclosed. It starred Edna Mae Harris and Roberteaerl Jones (the father of James Earl Jones, whose brilliant acting in the Broadway play *The Great White Hope* helped it win a Pulitzer Prize in 1969).

At the press conference proclaiming his debut as a producer and announcing the premiere of his movie *The Notorious Elinor Lee,* Julian explained to a *New York Sun* reporter:

> I have accomplished what I set out to do in aviation. I wanted to show the world that Negroes are capable flyers. There is no more spectacular or transatlantic flying to be done, so at the age of forty-two, I am through with flying. I am now going to devote myself to movie making and improving the place of the Negro in motion pictures. At present the major producing companies give Negroes parts if they are big and black and the clown type, but nothing in the scientific or classical way. Now in our new picture, there are eighteen whites. I am going to practice what I preach. When we need whites in the story, we will have whites. . . . You ask my experience? I know how to tell people to make love and to fight and to hug . . . We have three pictures scheduled for the year. The second is already in production. It is based on the story of Lyin' Lips. That's its title, *Lyin' Lips.* It's about a beautiful girl who is led astray because she wants beautiful things, but her parents are not able to give her a good education. You see, I'm trying to build up the morale of the people.

Asked about the third project, he said, "It will be an aviation picture for which we have had many demands," and proceeded to describe in intimate detail the background of the star.

Then the engraved gold invitations were handed out. They urged all to attend "The world premiere of *The No-*

torious Elinor Lee at the RKO Regent Theatre . . . Nine P.M. . . . January 15, 1940 . . . semiformal."

On the premiere evening Julian arrived in front of the Seventh Avenue theater in a shiny Cadillac at 7:15 in full regalia: a top hat, white gloves, and an Inverness cape, which, according to reporter H. Allen Smith, "he wore as if he had live rabbits concealed in it."

Sweeping into the office of the theater manager, Max Mink, Julian was obviously pleased by what he found.

"Ah, the press! I would have you know that I created this clement weather for this evening, and wagered 50–1 that it would be so. But you looked nulled. Will you not partake? We have even imported port."

He unwrapped a large bundle and produced a quart of rye, a fifth of Scotch, a fifth of cognac, one jug of imported port, and two bottles of champagne.

The elegant host then gave instructions for a microphone to be set up on the sidewalk in front of the theater.

"I will have my man drive me back to my home," he said, "so I can bring the champagne glasses. My police escort will pick me up there and we shall arrive with sirens tooting. Now, about the ice."

Julian looked around Mr. Mink's office for a bucket. Not finding one, he settled for a metal wastepaper basket.

"This will have to do for the champagne," he said, and commanded an usher to go out and find a large chunk of ice. In a little while, the usher returned with the wastepaper basket still empty.

"The man at the candy store told me he couldn't spare us no ice," he said. "So I told him it was for Colonel Julian and that you wanted the ice for champagne. So he says he would stuff it full of frozen custard. He said frozen custard is much better than ice to put champagne in and—."

"Parrr-don mee-ee!" interrupted the colonel. "Do I look like a varicose idiot? Do I? Go elsewhere and get the ice!"

Julian then left to get the champagne glasses and the usher again set out in search of ice. He eventually came back with a big chunk that Mr. Mink chopped up with a Boy Scout axe. The manager then carried the microphone out to the sidewalk and started proclaiming the imminent arrival of Col. Hubert Fauntleroy Julian. Soon there came the wail of a siren. The colonel, unable to get a motorcycle escort, roared up to the theater behind a police radio car. By this time a crowd had collected and Julian stepped from his car like a star. He spoke a few words of greeting into the microphone, bowed, seized and kissed the hand of a woman who happened to be passing, and strode into the theater to get things organized.

"*Allons, messieurs,*" he cried as he reached the lobby. "This is wonderful. Really, there are two things I must learn to do. One is to smoke. The other is to take a little drink now and then."

"Why, Colonel," asked Mr. Mink, obviously not used to premieres. "What are your bad habits?"

Rolling his eyes suggestively, Julian responded, "Tut, tut, tut, *but* tut! One must not, really!"

By 9:00 the theater was filled with those bearing gold invitations and the regular paying audience. Tickets cost from twenty to forty cents.

In the lobby Oscar Micheaux, who had actually written, produced, and directed the film—by investing in it after its completion, Julian became "associate producer" and spokesman—explained that it took ten days to shoot *The Notorious Elinor Lee* at the Biograph studios in the Bronx.

"Sure," he said, "both the boys and the girls get temperamental. They get to reading these movie magazines all about Gable and Garbo, and they start to feel their oats. That's why I make my pictures with all-star casts. Everybody in my pictures is the star. If I made only one person the star, there would be no holding that party with a halter!"

Inside the theater Julian was already on stage throwing out the compliments and naming celebrities who may or may not have been present. He finally announced, "Time is fleeting very fast," and commanded, "Darken the theater and on with the show. Let joy be unconfirmed!"

The lights went out, and the picture started. It was not *The Notorious Elinor Lee,* but Richard Dix in *Reno*—the top half of a double feature.

"We sat through this drama, and at last *The Notorious Elinor Lee* was unfolded before us," Smith reported.

"It was colossal. I remember that there was a man named Stacker Lee who was tried for murder, and the star witness for the prosecution was a parrot. The parrot had been an eyewitness to the crime, and during the trial kept testifying 'Stacker, you done it, Stacker, you stabbed him with a knife.' Stacker Lee was Elinor Lee's papa, and the way Elinor Lee got notorious was in Paducah where she was in the low-down business before she went to St. Louis. It was very gripping and held the interest, and I laughed until I got a pain in my side.

"When it was all over, I left the theater and stopped at the gate long enough to ask the usher when *The Notorious Elinor Lee* would be shown again.

" 'What do you mean, again?' he rejoined. 'It's been showing all day since eleven o'clock this morning. This nine o'clock show was the only one that's the world premiere.' "

After turning in the rented cape, Julian began dressing for a role in World War II.

14

On the Prowl

> Ha! The trouble is there are a lot of people so jealous that they can't stand it. What counts is what I am *going* to do for Finland. Now will you please extricate yourselves from *my* cabin.
>
> THE BLACK EAGLE *returning from the Russo-Finnish theater of war, aboard the steamer* Mathilda Thorden *July, 1940*

RUSSIA WAS in the process of devouring eastern Poland when Stalin convinced himself that Finland had a hunger for Russia. On November 30, 1939, his troops invaded the snowy nation, which appealed to the League of Nations for assistance. The crumbling world organization went through the wasted motion of condemning the invasion. And with that, the Russo-Finnish war was on.

Though outnumbered fifty to one, the Finns put up a fight that cost Russia a million lives. Their mobile ski troops in white battle outfits were well-nigh invisible against the background of the frozen countryside, and they fought with automatic high-velocity rifles. It was a war of ambush; guerrilla tactics were crucial. The little nation's valiant defiance of the Soviet giant made headlines—and stirred adventurous men to come to her aid.

With the war only two months old, Julian volunteered his services in early February by cable to Baron Carl Gustav Mannerheim, the Finnish commander-in-chief. By return cable Mannerheim accepted his offer to fly for the tiny air force. (He also accepted the offers of some five hundred other Americans to fight.) The fighting, however, came to an abrupt halt on March 12, 1940.

Like many other volunteers detained by red tape in Helsinki and Washington, Julian departed for Finland anyway. Cease-fires were fragile arrangements in a world fast being leveled by broken treaties. He felt that by the time he got there, Russia might be at it again. (In fact, the cease-fire lasted only fifteen months; then Finland was really crushed.)

When he finally reached Helsinki on April 16, Julian was immediately assigned to the air force. Finland's Institute of Military History duly records that Julian "served in the Aviation Regiment 2 as a captain up to 20.4.1940. Concerning Julian's short service there is no evidence of any noteworthy influence on the efficiency of the Finnish air defense." After four days of duty, the impatient pilot decided to return home. Now, it seemed, the action had passed.

Before leaving, he asked Mannerheim if there was anything else he could do for the cause. There was. Finland's most urgent problem was to provide lodging for its 600,000 homeless. The government was anxious to send home as many volunteers as possible in order to free living quarters for its own people. Besides, a growing number of these volunteers were running amok—fighting among themselves, drinking heavily, ducking out on bills, and constantly grumbling about their treatment.

Julian offered to escort the first contingent of volunteers home. He said he'd also attempt to raise funds in the United States to buy ten badly needed ambulance planes. To accomplish this, he explained, he would only require one letterhead document verifying his military commission; another addressed to New York Mayor Fiorello La Guardia authorizing him to solicit the funds; a uniform for fund-raising appearances; and $1,000 for expenses.

Mannerheim quickly authorized the requests; he didn't want the volunteers to miss the sailing of a New York-bound freighter on June 10.

It took twelve days for the creaking, 3,641-ton *Mathilda Thorden* to reach New York. She had to plow the longer Arctic Ocean route to avoid submarines.

She docked at the East River's Pier 33 on July 2 with 167 passengers—about 150 more than normally carried. The first Finnish ship to reach the United States since the fighting stopped attracted a considerable crowd.

The returning volunteers, most of them between the ages of twenty-one and thirty-five, looked like unwashed beachcombers. Many were in the same clothing they had worn when they left the States fourteen weeks before. On the crossing they had slept packed like canned pilchards in the aft hold of the ship. Food came from an army field kitchen nicknamed "the soup cannon." Some showed reporters black eyes from food fights; others displayed chipped teeth for which they blamed the hardtack.

"They're all a bunch of no-good bums," the Finnish ship captain, Axel Sjoblom, kept shouting from the bridge. The ship's engineer threatened to throw one Frank Clevenger overboard when the Detroit-born pilot produced a crushed foot he claimed to have suffered "in the battle for the slop we got for food." It was an unpleasant situation, and it was quickly worsening due to delays in getting baggage cleared and passports checked.

Then, through the tense setting of foul air and base words, came the towering soldier of fortune, carrying an attaché case and manning a navy blue uniform. Three gold stripes gleamed on both sleeves, and ornamental gold lions adorned his lapels. Newsmen rushed toward him. His glittering appearance in the midst of his scruffy-looking colleagues almost started a riot.

Clevenger looked at Julian with scorn. "We smoked the butts dropped by the passengers who had better quarters than any of us," he shouted, "and that goes for that fellow Julian. He was louder than a fleet of crows."

An infuriated fellow officer, Captain Albert Ieto, who had served as a volunteer in the Finnish Navy but was now in wrinkled mufti, called out, "You have no right to wear that uniform!"

Wearing any uniform at such a time was in bad taste, Ieto continued, but to wear the wrong one was even worse. Julian's was, he said, the uniform of a military attaché, not a member of the air force.

Looking surprised at the overheard accusation, Julian stepped back from his private press conference.

"You accuse *me!* You accuse *me* of being an *impostor!*" he roared at Ieto.

He then urged all the press—and Captain Ieto—to follow him into the nearest stateroom. There he opened his attaché case, jerking from it a stack of documents in Finnish. Ieto inspected them and reluctantly admitted that they seemed to constitute an authentic commission signed by Baron Mannerheim.

"Now do you doubt me?" Julian said. "Read it! Read these documents! Read them and weep! I am an authorized agent of the Finnish government."

"If you were a gentleman," Ieto insisted, "you would take off that uniform."

"Well," said Julian, "you will never be the gentleman I am. I associate with gentlemen and you don't."

"What have you ever done for Finland?" asked Ieto.

"Ha!" answered Julian. "The trouble is there are a lot of people so jealous that they can't stand it. What counts is what I am *going* to do for Finland. Now will you please extricate yourselves from *my* cabin."

An ample blonde, one of the Polish civilian refugees who had managed to get a cabin on the overcrowded freighter, entered and pushed forward through the perspiring throng.

"You're in my room," she growled.

"Pardon me, madam," Julian said, "but I was just explaining my status to these gentlemen."

"Out—all of you!" she demanded.

"After a bit more shouting," the *New York Herald Tribune* reported, "the colonel won the day by clicking his heels and marching through the group of volunteers who had threatened to tear off his uniform. They appeared a bit awed at the glare of scorn from the colonel. Not a hand was raised to sully his uniform."

Julian departed the ship with his reindeerskin coat and two cocker spaniels. "Presents from my good friend the baron," he said.

Julian's attempts to raise funds for Finland were thwarted by the events of 1940's summer. The British retreat at Dunkirk and the Luftwaffe's merciless bombing of Britain had a sobering effect throughout America. Many citizens suddenly realized that the United States might be next. With an ancient navy and only 23,000 mostly obsolete planes, the country was in no better shape than the powers which were quickly being crushed by the Axis juggernaut. American money and manpower were now thrown into its own race for preparedness. Finland's cause quickly dropped off the priority lists of a nervous nation and an antsy adventurer.

15

Looking for a Fight

. . . I THEREFORE CHALLENGE AND DEFY YOU HERMANN GOERING AS HEAD OF THE NAZI AIR FORCE TO MEET ME HUBERT FAUNTLEROY JULIAN AT TEN THOUSAND FEET ABOVE THE ENGLISH CHANNEL TO FIGHT AN AERIAL DUEL TO AVENGE THIS COWARDLY INSULT TO THE HONOR OF MY RACE . . .

THE BLACK EAGLE *in a cable to Berlin*
New York, September, 1940

THE BLACK EAGLE personally took on Nazi Germany during dinner at the Waldorf. It happened on the evening of September 13, 1940, while he was eating with Giuseppe Bellanca. The plane builder mentioned he was reading *Mein Kampf*, and noted he had just finished the section in which Hitler claimed that Negroes were descended directly from baboons.

"Hitler is no pilot or I'd challenge him to a duel," Julian fumed. "But Goering is, and I'm going to challenge him over such an insult."

The next day Julian consulted with friends on the advisability of the action. They agreed that it was quite the patriotic thing to do. Charles Levine, the New York millionaire who had become the world's first transatlantic plane passenger when he crossed the ocean two weeks after Lindbergh's solo flight, said he would help finance the venture. With that, Julian sent Goering a cable:

REICHSMARSHAL HERMANN GOERING AIR MINISTER BERLIN (GERMANY) AS THE PIONEER AVIATOR AND AERONAUTICAL REPRESENTATIVE OF MILLIONS OF INTREPID

AND CULTURED NEGROES OF THE WORLD WE RESENT EMPHATICALLY AND WITHOUT COMPROMISE DASTARDLY INSULT AS EXPRESSED BY THE CHANCELLOR OF THE REICH QUOTE ALL NEGROES OF AMERICAN AND BRITISH EMPIRE ARE HALF APES AND BABOONS AND SHOULD BE INCARCERATED IN A SPECIAL CAMP UNQUOTE TOUSSAINT LOUVERTURE ONE OF THE GREATEST GENERALS OF MODERN TIMES THE CONQUEROR OF NAPOLEON AND A BLACK GENTLEMAN WAS NOT A HALF WIT AND THOUSANDS OF BLACK SCIENTISTS AND INTELLECTUALS GREATLY RESENT THE ABOVE INSULT STOP I THEREFORE CHALLENGE AND DEFY YOU HERMANN GOERING AS HEAD OF THE NAZI AIR FORCE TO MEET ME HUBERT FAUNTLEROY JULIAN AT TEN THOUSAND FEET ABOVE THE ENGLISH CHANNEL TO FIGHT AN AERIAL DUEL TO AVENGE THIS COWARDLY INSULT TO THE HONOR OF MY RACE THIRTY DAYS FROM DATE WITH NEUTRAL CORRESPONDENTS AS REFEREES HUBERT FAUNTLEROY JULIAN NEW YORK CITY.

Julian's timing was, as usual, excellent. At that very moment whole nations were cowering before the Luftwaffe's apparent invincibility. For a $13.64 cable charge, Julian's bold *mano-a-mano* challenge to Nazism's top pilot purchased masses of headlines. It also gave a boost to black patriotism, which couldn't help but be in sagging condition: in the entire armed forces of almost one million men there were but two Negro officers on active duty, and out of forty thousand pilots not a single one was black.

"I will show that lousy nothing divided by nothing," Julian growled at a large New York press conference. "I have but one life to give and I give it gladly. The die was cast with that cable. On Saturday morning I was out with my dogs around 9:30 AM when a phone call came to my home from Washington. My wife answered. She was very frightened indeed. The man spoke to her saying, 'This is the military attaché of the German Embassy. Tell that black swine his challenge has been accepted and to be on the spot as promised.' Never fear. I will be there."

Julian explained that he had already begun negotiations to obtain a Messerschmitt fighter from the British, who had recovered two in workable condition. He said he would use a German plane "so there will be no question of superiority of equipment.

"Goering must be alone in his plane and I alone in mine," he insisted, getting madder as he talked. "I will machine-gun him out of this life, the lousy creature. If he sends a whole fleet of planes to get me instead of coming alone, that will be that. I am ready. It will be a pleasure to die amidst bomb and shell just to show what rats they are. I will not be fighting for any country. I am a man without a country. I am not an American citizen and I am not a British citizen. No government will be involved. I fight and die for my race, to avenge the insult. We will see who is a baboon!

"Secretly," he confided, "the British government is thrilled by this. It will take only ten minutes to acquaint myself with the Messerschmitt. Then to the battle. *Allons!* I speak French like a native."

The German Embassy in Washington quickly denied that Goering had accepted. That didn't deter Julian. The date was fixed: October 15, 1940.

On October 1 Julian arrived in Montreal, where he planned to catch a hop in one of the dozens of Canadian bombers daily being ferried to Britain. Two days later the bad news tagged him. British officials explained they couldn't allow such a duel, however noble, to take place. The English Channel had suddenly become a congested aerial pit of deadly dogfights as the RAF began to rally and finally to challenge the Luftwaffe.

The turndown didn't stop the irrepressible pilot's war dance. The next best thing to do, he decided, was volunteer for the Royal Canadian Air Force. Somehow he was going to have a whack—if not at Goering at least at his equally Aryan pilots.

On December 11 in Ottawa, *The New York Times* reported, "Julian in morning coat and gray tie passed a medical examination at the Royal Canadian Air Force office." He did not, however, pass the flying test that he took the next day in a twin-engine Hudson trainer. An RCAF spokesman said, "Colonel Julian looks better under a fluoroscope than he does in the cockpit of a warplane."

Julian refused to concede, even to himself, that at forty-three he was no longer up to the precision demanded in wartime flying. He insisted that he wasn't in the best of flying shape because of the weather. He was kept waiting for three hours in the freezing cold of the airfield, he said. By that time his hands were numb—along with ears, toes, nose, and all other parts germane to successful flying.

Whatever the reason, the news of his being grounded after trying so hard to become involved brought only admiration from the swelling ranks who followed his war efforts.

The Japanese attack on Pearl Harbor made December 7, 1941, the most sleepless night in the nation's history. Americans greeted the dawn weary but hardened with determination to fight. War signs appeared instantly: air-raid drills, leaves canceled, convoys sailing, and a growing volume of wires being spewed across America from Washington that began "We regret to inform you . . ."

Without waiting for instructions from the War Department, Julian established a military headquarters in Harlem's Theresa Hotel, staffed and ready to accept volunteers for a most dangerous mission.

"If the Japs could use surprise attacks, so can we!" he said as he issued his first official communiqué on December 10. It went on to state:

> In view of the present crisis, I am recruiting a group of young Negroes to be known as "The Suicide

Squadron," and they're going to be examined by Negro physicians here in Harlem without any cost to the government. They are going to be trained in parachute jumping (headed by your humble servant), marksmanship, gunnery, or anything that will be necessary for them to perform in any part of the world. We are offering to the country the first "suicide squadron"—and we mean suicide!

By the time Julian's suicide squadron was turned down by Washington, it had at least let off some of the fury that had boiled up inside him—as it had inside tens of millions of Americans.

The tense days that followed the United States entrance into the war stretched Julian's frustration to a desperate length. Here was the whole world, civilized and uncivilized, caught up in the most devastating struggle for survival in history. Yet where was one of the era's most daring soldiers of fortune? Selling cars, and used cars at that, just to keep busy.

Although it was the only alternative he could see, Julian had to swallow hard when he made the decision to volunteer for the Army as an enlisted man. Even the most cynical scrutiny of his career produced the conclusion that his talents were surely being misused.

The final hurt came when he suddenly realized he was almost too old for any military service.

On July 3, 1942—the same day his friend Baron Mannerheim was wounded on the Russian front—Julian appeared at the Army recruiting office at Governor's Island with honorable discharge documents from two foreign services and his Selective Service personal history blank listing himself as "aviator, lecturer, and parachutist."

There was a snag even about signing on in the lowest rank of the military. As an alien he could only be accepted at Fort Jay in New Jersey. With his usual impetuosity, he immediately took the ferry across the river and boarded the first Army bus headed for the base.

After being sworn in, he waived the normal two-week pre-induction furlough and insisted on being sent straight out to Long Island's Camp Upton for basic training. For a man who had if not earned, at least gained, commissions in both the Ethiopian and Finnish armed forces, Buck Private Hubert F. Julian accepted his first assignment—to police the grounds, with a special emphasis on candy wrappers and cigarette butts—with unusual grace.

Army service was a singularly unspectacular period of his career. He finally became an American citizen on September 28, 1942, in Boston, but nothing else exciting happened. The United States Army just wasn't Julian's league.

On May 17, 1943, he drew his last military check, for $84.75. No. 323999346, private first class, received an honorable discharge because of age, with his specialty marked "guard" and his character marked "excellent."

He returned to selling cars in silence. There was nothing to hold a press conference about. A new roster of heroes was in the nation's minds: fighting men who took part in the bombing of Tokyo, the Battle of the Coral Sea, the landing at Guadalcanal. They wore the stripes of a new breed of adventuring warrior. Their cause was current; their exploits were better known and much better documented. They owned the headlines and hearts of a nation: "Pappy" Boyington, Audie Murphy, George Patton. The only Eagle in the bunch was a bald one—Russia's Marshal Timoshenko.

December 2, 1945, a cold and stormy day three months after the end of the war, found Julian underground at the 125th Street subway station waiting for change.

A young soldier in the change line pushed a quarter in, but not far enough for the changemaker. The agent snapped something about chow lines, which made the lad all the more nervous, and he managed to drop all his change on the floor. With the line stopped, the agent fired off a swarm of insults.

Julian, who had been watching from his place in line, marched forward and demanded that the agent stop harassing the GI.

"I speak as one veteran on behalf of another," he said, shaking his finger at the subway employee.

"I don't see no button on you," said the agent, and told him to mind his own business.

"I, sir, am a veteran of the United States Armed Forces," Julian bellowed with indignation, "a former colonel in the Ethiopian Air Force, and a former captain in the Finnish Air Force."

At that point subway patrolman Edward Jacobson emerged from the change booth where he had been taking a break. He told Julian to "shove off." As Julian began pumping up to full oratory again the cop whacked him on the skull with his nightstick and hauled him away. He spent the night in jail.

The next morning his bail was reduced from $500 to $25 and the *New York World Telegram* told how COP'S ACK-ACK DOWNS JULIAN IN SUBWAY. Before the magistrate Julian peeled a hundred-dollar bill from a fat roll, insisting he had nothing smaller.

As change was hurriedly made, he said indignantly, "And to think that when this happened I was on my way to Washington. And on a big deal, I may say."

Nearing fifty (but looking much younger), Julian finally decided to give up seeking adventure and fortune in soldiering. The world was tired of uniforms—or so it protested.

It was the time to rebuild cities and businesses. Opportunities were everywhere. Practically a whole world was in need of repair. Millions of people waited anxiously to be supplied with the goods they had been deprived of for so long.

One thing Julian had developed in two decades of travel was contacts, in and out of government. It was natural, therefore, for him to announce an enterprising hand that combined his best cards: Black Eagle Airlines, Ltd.

16

Flying High Without Wings

I was going to de-naturalize myself if Truman wasn't re-elected. Now I go to Paris to de-range the arrangements.

THE BLACK EAGLE, *upon boarding the* Queen Elizabeth *for Europe December, 1948*

IN 1948, WHILE President Hubert F. Julian was trying to keep his charter DC-3s flying full loads of freight, President Harry S Truman was trying to keep his Democratic party in post-war power. Improbable as it sounded, the latter's chances appeared less promising. The party was badly weakened by a breakaway movement that formed two new parties, the Progressives and the Dixiecrats. Prices were rising, the "cold war" and the Berlin airlift were causing depressing moments, trains weren't running, and union after union was striking. By spring it looked as if the Republicans, led by Thomas E. Dewey, would win without trying.

Truman was counting heavily on one factor: a huge turnout of Negro voters. FDR had been their hero, and the late President's number-two man now calculated on pulling a great share of their vote if he showed true and immediate concern for their problems.

The price for the loyalty of the nation's fifteen million Negroes was no longer windy words, however, but hard legislation to end discrimination. This was confirmed by reports of growing discontent among Negro GI's coming in from the American Zone of Germany.

They were fed up with being sequestered in service battalions and insulted by the very people they had recently helped defeat. Repercussions were already being heard in the growl the black population at home directed at the Administration. As long as the nation's focus was on Germany and the airlift, the disenchantment kept growing. Truman's campaign advisers, already having trouble finding a willing running mate for their boss, were greatly disturbed by the bleak prospects.

Julian touched down on the darkening political scene in the new guise of merchant prince. Helmut Isenberg, the vice-president of the Frawley-Eastern Corporation, sought him out to run interference for the Manhattan-based export-import firm owned by Patrick J. Frawley, Jr., who is today best known for his genius with Schick, Eversharp, and ultra-conservative causes.

The pilot was delighted to become involved. His air-freight enterprise wasn't breaking any records. More than five hundred former World War II pilots had plunged into the same business in the late 1940s. Only a handful, like Robert Prescott and his Flying Tiger line, made it. Working Venezuelan and Argentinian markets, Julian's planes flew down with decent loads, but it was hard to find freight to haul back up. About all to be brought north at the time were coffee beans and sunflower seeds, both of which were bulky and made little profit.

What Isenberg offered was perfect for Julian's talents. It promised profit, travel, and limelight. Julian, in turn, offered a known black image, smooth talk, and an ability to get around in the right circles. The project involved the Army, Germany, and stale cigarettes.

The Frawley-Eastern executive estimated there were about $11 million worth of overage (three years old and up) cigarettes in military supply depots throughout the American military zone. He proposed providing the United States military with one fresh carton for every two stale cartons received. His company would then repackage the stale cigarettes for sale throughout the Far East.

The profit could be as high as $5 million, Isenberg speculated. Julian was in for five percent.

There were obstacles, of course. It was the type of business venture that could cause problems if read the wrong way. The key to bringing it off was in keeping it quiet and in gaining the backing of influential Washington figures.

Isenberg knew Julian had good relations with Negro politicians like Adam Clayton Powell, Jr., who were carrying increasing weight in White House circles. What Isenberg didn't know—it came to him as a pleasant surprise—was that Julian also knew Maj. Gen. Harry Vaughan, military aide to the President, who had an office in the White House. Julian had met him through his admirer and close friend, Congressman John Dawson of Chicago, the leading black political power in Washington.

When he was the top Negro in Chicago politics in the 1930s, Dawson had introduced Julian to FDR. The meeting had resulted in an invitation to the White House for Julian, who had discussed with the President the frustrations of young blacks who hoped a career in the military would lead them to a better life but found it as segregated as a Southern bus.

In 1946, when Julian was struggling with his airline, Dawson had introduced him to Vaughan. The congressman had felt that the general might help Julian pick up some of the government contracts being let out to veterans in order to assist them in getting started in the vital new air-freight industry.

On April 22, 1948, Julian visited the White House to explain Isenberg's proposition to Vaughan.

The general felt it had merit, but only if the government was allowed to recoup at least some of its loss in owning large stocks of stale cigarettes. He made two recommendations: that Julian's people not sell the old smokes in any American-occupied areas of the Far East, and that the fresh replacement cigarettes come packed bearing a propaganda message rather than a brand name. That way, if there was an oversupply of cigarettes in an area, they might be distributed as gifts to the German population at a time when the weary people needed encouragement to keep going.

Julian agreed with Vaughan. He then sprinkled his sweetener on the project.

"As the leading Negro soldier of fortune," he told Vaughan, "I am willing to donate time while in Germany to give talks to Negro troops about the President's civil rights intentions."

As far as Vaughan was concerned, this offer was a generous publicity contribution to the campaign fund. At that very moment Presidential aides were drafting an Executive Order—to be announced before the election—concerning discrimination in the armed forces. Vaughan volunteered to assist the cigarette project as much as possible. During the next several weeks he sent numerous letters to commanding officers at various military bases explaining the upcoming visits and encouraging cooperation.

Julian flew to Germany in early July. He landed at Berlin's Templehof Airport—with the airlift the strip had suddenly become the world's busiest—and headed for the office of Gen. Lucius Clay. The brilliant engineer, who was both Military Governor and Commander-in-Chief of the European command, had received a letter from Vaughan and was expecting the visit.

After presenting a personal note from Vaughan and two boxes of Churchillian-length cigars, Julian talked with Clay for an hour. The general was in favor of Julian's visiting Negro troops. He wanted time to study the cigarette situation, however. In the meantime, he issued orders that Julian receive VIP treatment, assigning an Army major as his personal aide.

"I would take a reduction in rank to come here and serve," Julian announced at a press conference following the meeting. "The duty is so good," he said, "that I would shovel coal, drop a bomb—do anything to stay in Berlin and be in the United States Army."

The White House was delighted with the press Julian gathered.

General Clay looked carefully into the cigarette situation. The so-called stale cigarettes weren't really stale, his Quartermaster Corps people said. In fact, many of them could still be considered factory fresh. It was a one-sided deal, the general informed Julian in late July, and that, said Clay, meant there would be no deal.

Returning to Washington in haste, Julian contacted Vaughan and pushed for a last-minute save of any sort. Perhaps, he told Vaughan, they could buy at least the ones the government decreed were stale.

The general told him that he'd see what could be done. Neither of them knew it, but other companies were also looking into the situation, and not necessarily with the same intention.

Vaughan phoned Julian in New York on September 18. "It doesn't look good for your project," he said. He told him to read Drew Pearson's column of that morning.

The story reported the cigarette deal in unfavorable light. "Julian toured the American zone of Germany as a guest of the Army, rated a military aide, and spent an hour with General Clay," Pearson wrote. "Generals bowed and scraped." Julian had been given the VIP treatment, Pearson claimed, because he could be instrumental in delivering the Negro vote. The columnist questioned the ethics of it all in an election year.

Though the cigarette deal didn't work, it opened up a profitable door for Julian. Because of his ability to cut through Federal red tape, he became established as a consultant to several other import-export firms. Soon he was arranging for surplus aureomycin to go to Italy, for flour to Brazil. In thanks for the favors received, he worked tirelessly as a member of the Democratic Speakers' Bureau. He talked up black advances under the Democrats at political rallies along the East Coast.

Six weeks after Truman's surprise November victory, Julian boarded the liner *Queen Elizabeth* for Europe. As usual, the press found him in lively spirits. He hadn't felt so exuberant since his first Ethiopian tour.

"I was going to de-naturalize myself if Truman wasn't re-elected," he said. "Now I go to Paris to de-range the arrangements."

Reporters marveled at his health. At fifty-one, he was in mint condition.

"Strictly *entre nous,* gentlemen," he said, "we starve ourselves for oxygen. We must have more deep breathing and fill our blood with oxygen. And lots of exercise and plenty of food for breakfast. What you eat for dinner, I eat for breakfast. I drink only pure water.

"Just to show you my shape," he said, strolling up the gangway, "I'll give $500 to any man here who can duplicate this." Reaching the first deck he proceeded to balance himself on one foot, squatting until his other leg was two inches from the floor. He swung the leg around behind him, then in front of him. Finally he slowly rose, still on the one foot.

"That's easy," a young photographer boasted.

"Yes, but you've got to do it twice," Julian shouted as he headed for his outside cabin while the more daring members of the press corps rushed to copy the act. He heard the first fall.

During the crossing he met the Aga Khan, head priest of the financially powerful Ismaili sect of Muslims. It happened in the lounge after the finely-tailored Julian had finished entertaining fellow travelers by performing card tricks blindfolded. His dealing four grand slams in a row brought the usually sedentary and very enormous Aga to his velvet-slippered feet and over to Julian's table, where they chatted about world affairs. The spiritual leader of two million was impressed enough to invite Julian to visit him at his villa in Deauville.

Julian promptly accepted. "My business empire can survive a few days without me," he said with a roguish laugh.

During the visit to the Norman-style Villa Gorizia Julian met enough royalty to keep him in fresh name-dropping for months. He saw a good deal of the Maharani of Baroda, who impressed him immensely because of her ability to smoke cigars.

Aly Khan, the Aga's swarthy thirty-seven-year-old eldest, was also present. The two pilots spent an evening discussing travel, adventure, and Rita Hayworth, whom the playboy married the next year. The dashing young Indian prince, then Pakistan's ambassador to the UN, was particularly intrigued with how Julian stayed in the eye of so many stormy ventures.

"My strategy is simple," Julian explained as they both played *chemin de fer* in the black-tie intimacy of a private card room. "Volunteer for all wars, never have enough money to become complacent, make headlines, and always leave calling cards."

After two weeks of dallying with fast cars and beautiful people, Julian thanked his host, sent him a case of Louis Roederer champagne, and motored off to Amsterdam on business.

The Dutch were concerned with the fate of their three-hundred-year-old colony in the East Indies. One of the world's most valuable pieces of undeveloped real estate seemed headed for a serious break with the motherland. East Indian freedom-fighters—rebels to the Dutch—were already clashing rather successfully with Dutch troops.

Julian was brought into the situation by an official in the Foreign Affairs ministry who had heard reports of his White House contacts and venturesome habits. Perhaps, the official figured, an outsider, and a non-Caucasian at that, might come up with a few new approaches to the sticky problem. He might even get the United States government to take a biased interest in the Dutch plight.

Following briefings, Julian left Amsterdam for Batavia (now Djakarta) and arrived without incident—except for losing a pigskin bag with some old letters of credit and a pith helmet while changing planes at Dum Dum Airport outside Calcutta.

He immediately headed for the interior. During the ten-day tour he met with Achmed Sukarno. They had a two-hour talk during which Julian explored the worth of uniting with Holland, at least economically.

Sukarno listened sullenly. He finally said, "It is too late and the hurts are too deep for us to ever live and prosper in a side-by-side relationship."

In fact, he told the visitor, if he really wanted to help the cause, the best thing he could do was to get off the Dutch payroll and get on his—by supplying needed arms for him.

Julian returned to Batavia on January 21, 1949, in time to send an appropriate cable.

> WHITE HOUSE, WASHINGTON COLON PLEASE CONVEY TO OUR PRESIDENT MY HEARTIEST CONGRATULATIONS ON HIS INAUGURATION AS PRESIDENT OF THE USA STOP MAY GOD GRANT HIM THE WISDOM OF SOLOMON AND THE STRENGTH OF SAMSON TO CARRY ON HIS DOCTRINE OF WORLD PEACE AND PROSPERITY STOP LONG LIVE OUR PRESIDENT SIGNED HUBERT JULIAN ENDS

Once back in Amsterdam he wrote up his report and collected his fee even though he told the Dutch it was all over—they were about to lose their property to a freedom-fighter who the people believed would bring them a better life. (Ten months later, in November 1949, the Dutch handed over power to Sukarno's newly constituted Republic of Indonesia.)

Julian got more mileage out of the almost-around-the-world safari than even he had anticipated. In Paris on his way home he cabled Vaughan:

DEAR GENERAL VAUGHAN JUST RETURNED FROM JAVA MADE SOME SENSATIONAL AND DAMAGING DISCOVERIES RE INDONESIAN SITUATION STOP ARRIVING NEW YORK QUEEN ELIZABETH FEB 16 LIKE TO PRESENT PERSONAL INFORMATION TO THE CHIEF STOP PLEASE NOTIFY ME HOTEL PALAIS DORSAY PARIS RESPECTFULLY HUBERT JULIAN

The Indonesian experience had tipped Julian off to a ripening market. A growing number of emerging nations were creating a demand for all sorts of hardware. They appeared willing to pay dearly for the service.

When he reached Washington, Julian discussed his observations with government contacts. To his delight, there was enough encouragement to warrant his entering the field. The government was interested in seeing matériel supplied to favored developing nations and courtable leaders in an informal and unofficial way, as long as it knew the names and the volume. So the Black Eagle committed himself to becoming what twenty years later Aristotle Onassis claimed he would be if he had his fortune to remake—an *armateur*. In March 1949 he registered with the State Department as a munitions dealer under the name of Black Eagle Enterprises, Ltd.

Once the stationery engraved "Office of the President—Suite 2424," arrived from the printer, he was off and selling out of his Harlem residence, using an Italian-made briefcase that had already been more places than a diplomatic pouch.

17

Red Hot in Guatemala

> One day I will fly back to Guatemala in a jet plane at six hundred miles per hour. My friends had better paint their roofs black as identification against the bombing and revenge of the Black Eagle.
>
> THE BLACK EAGLE *on losing the Guatemalan account* *New York, October, 1952*

BY THE TIME Julian was in business, idealistic revolutionaries and Machiavellian colonels of a socialist stripe were already warming up for coups throughout the Americas. Fidel Castro's victory in Cuba on January 1, 1959, was the first significant win. But the first big post-war try was by Jacobo Arbenz Guzman in Guatemala ten years earlier.

Throughout the mid-1940s the Central American republic of four million people rumbled louder than her active volcanoes. The peasants were not-so-slowly waking up to a belief that if they shed a little blood, the soil they worked for the likes of the United Fruit Company might become theirs. Labor unions began striking and university protests became commonplace. When a military junta took over in 1945, the ancient land of the Mayas turned into a shooting gallery. The target was whoever was number one at the time number two got the urge. The plottings and killings made Guatemala foam with intrigue and intriguers: agricultural advisers from the CIA, union organizers from the Kremlin, and linen-suited entrepreneurs selling sordid services were everywhere. Peter Lorre may have been missing, but not Hubert Fauntleroy Julian.

The situation was perfect for Black Eagle Enterprises,

Ltd. Having no track record and no recorded trade policy, the president and major stockholder could go either way—with the in or the out-wanting-in group.

Julian arrived at Guatemala City's La Aurora Airport in early July 1949, and checked into the Pan-American Hotel, two blocks from the National Palace. Within a fortnight, all hell broke loose around the rococo seat of power.

General Francisco Javier Arana was then the chief of the military junta nominally under President Juan José Arevalo. His chief deputy, Colonel Jacobo Arbenz Guzman, decided it was his turn to run things. He succeeded on a Wednesday right after the general had been machine-gunned down on his way to lunch. One of the assassins was the personal chauffeur of Arbenz's wife. (Maria Villanova, a well-born, California convent-educated, burning Marxist, was considered the shot-caller in the Arbenz family.)

By late afternoon the immaculately clean city had been dirtied by the smoky rubble that blazing gun battles make out of stucco and timber buildings. Tanks patrolled around the greenstone palace as it came under mortar attack. Sides were hard to identify, as were immediate reasons for the trouble.

The combatants were not exactly marksmen, and the street in front of the hotel came into the line of fire. As storefronts were hastily boarded up, guests were advised to stay inside.

Coming downstairs the first morning of the revolution, Julian sauntered through the crowded lobby; headed for the piano, his new Panama straw hat at a rakish angle; and broke into a balladic boom of French and English to his own accompaniment, and sometimes that of exploding shells. His aplomb brought stares of amazement from the throng of tourists and salesmen caught in a shoot-out situation for which they had not come prepared.

When he had exhausted his repertoire, he left the piano to chat with a group of twitchy old ladies about the New Deal and his "friend" FDR. As he elaborated on the late

President's views of the Latin American situation, his warm manner began to relax the ladies.

"Shut up, big mouth," a balding man in a rumpled seersucker suit shouted out. "You're full of shit!"

"Well, sir," said Julian, maintaining his composure, "if that is not the truth then I shall eat my hat—and it's a fifty-dollar one."

Julian excused himself from the ladies and marched out of the lobby, but only for as long as it took to collect a briefcase from his room. Back down in the lobby he pulled the zipper open, took out a photograph, and handed it to his detractor. The picture showed FDR, Mrs. Roosevelt, and H. F. Julian enjoying a sit on the White House lawn.

The man barely muttered an apology and left the lobby. Julian returned to enlightening, and calming, the ladies.

Several days later, when the shooting subsided, Julian hired a car and made the rounds of government offices, congratulating the winners, explaining his business, and leaving his calling cards. The timing was perfect. After announcing the success of his coup d'état, Arbenz's first order to his officers was to update and expand Guatemala's weaponry.

Satisfied with the initial interest shown in his portfolio, Julian boarded a plane for New York to begin lining up the manufacturers and suppliers of any hardware a military heart desired.

Two weeks later he headed for Europe to sign agent's contracts with half a dozen major firms in Switzerland, Britain, Italy, and Sweden. His presentation on Guatemala's potential as a paying customer was good enough to obtain several retainer fees.

Phase One completed, Julian packed for a leisurely Atlantic crossing while anticipating the orders already stacking up on his Harlem office desk.

Ralph Bunche, the United Nations mediator in the Middle East, had also just completed some important overseas business. His aim was entirely different from Julian's.

He had been flying from Arab nation to Arab nation attempting to coax leaders to sign armistices with Israel, whose establishment as a state the year before had sent infuriated dervishes whirling to arms. Now, with some signs of success evident, he was headed home after grimy weeks in reeking hotels.

As the liner *Île de France* prepared to set sail from Le Havre, there was a sudden commotion at the port rail. A last-minute passenger had just pulled alongside in a private tender. Bunche, taking a deck stroll, looked down to behold an elegant figure surrounded by a mound of luggage. Sailing was delayed to accommodate the salesman and his sample cases.

That afternoon Bunche and Julian met at tea, over which the mediator noted in conversational passing a frustration over shirts. For weeks, he told Julian, they had been subjected to atrocious laundering and never looked really clean. And now, on a big modern liner, he had just been informed the laundry was not working. That meant, he sighed, the wearing of grubby-looking shirts for the crossing. They both laughed.

Early that evening there was a knock at Bunche's cabin. The porter entered bearing a stack of neatly pressed white silk shirts.

"Courtesy of the Black Eagle," he announced. And they were the right size.

Julian traveled to Washington to organize Phase Two. The reading he received from the State Department on Arbenz was an indifferent one. With an army of ten thousand men, he was considered at least strong enough to maintain stability in the country. To Washington that was of immediate importance until they had a chance to evaluate the players and their goals.

Through General Vaughan, Julian made contact with the chief Guatemalan officer attached to the Inter-American

Defense Boards, Col. Oscar Morales Lopez. They met in secret; the subject was arms.

"Our list of needed equipment is even bigger than before," explained Morales, "but there are so many intrigues going on at home that I wish you to go to my country once again in person. I will give you the proper letters of introduction."

Julian agreed, and got to work on a revised and detailed list of the types of equipment he had available for immediate delivery. Morales, in the meantime, requested permission to authorize Julian as Guatemala's official arms procurer.

In the middle of Julian's study of available equipment, North Korea invaded South Korea, and the war began on June 24, 1950. Almost overnight military hardware of any type was in great demand. The shortage was all the better for Julian. Prices automatically doubled on such items as mortars, machine guns, and military vehicles. And since arms dealers in the United States were getting hit with tightening export regulations, his overseas suppliers were now invaluable.

After two weeks of meetings in late July with Guatemalan officials stationed in Washington, Julian picked up the letters of introduction from Morales and headed south —first to New Orleans by Eastern Airlines, then to Guatemala City by Aviateca, the country's national airline.

Again he checked into the Pan-American Hotel, and waited for the prearranged contact. The call came the first night.

At 9:00 the next morning, a young English-speaking junior minister arrived. In a black silk suit with a monocle dangling down his broad chest, Julian was driven to the palace and escorted to the second floor of the west wing. He was introduced to three colonels, who quickly handed him their shopping list: armored cars, jeeps, combat boots, trailers, recoilless 75-mm rifles. Fill this order, they told him, and there would be more, much more. The deal was struck in under ten minutes. Price was up to Julian. He was now Guatemala's official arms procurer.

After the conference one of the officers took Julian off to a corridor corner.

"I am the man who finds the money for these things," he said without embarrassment. "Nothing is done for nothing here in Guatemala. I will want some of the profit, of course, because the pay is very low in the army."

That settled, Julian flew home with a large, lucrative order.

First were the jeeps. He traveled to Toledo, Ohio, to see the Willys-Overland people personally. On one of his transatlantic crossings, he had struck up an acquaintance in the sauna bath with a Willys sales executive and, as always, put the name into his growing book of contacts.

By taking a few jeeps from various non-priority quotas, the executive—like most people, thoroughly impressed with Julian's manner, style, and portfolio—managed to fill the order. Julian met in Washington with Col. Morales to discuss price. They decided to add 50 percent on top as their profit. The jeeps were loaded on the United Fruit Company ship *Inger Skou* on September 22, 1950—destination marked Puerto Barrios, Guatemala's Caribbean seaport.

Next came the trailers, which Julian located in Poughkeepsie, New York, paying $125 for each and charging the Guatemalans $250. He purchased 4,800 pairs of boots from the Arnoff Shoe Company in New York for $2 a pair and sold them for $20,244.

Upon receiving the shoe order, the Guatemalan government cabled that the price was right but many of the sizes were wrong. It wanted all sizes four to eight but had received some larger sizes by mistake. No problem, Julian cabled back. Return the wrong sizes. He placed an advertisement in the *Journal of Commerce* and sold the returned 1,940 pairs to a supplier in the Middle East for $8,000 while replacing them with the correct sizes.

In March 1951 Arbenz was voted in as President in what were described as free elections. At thirty-eight he became the youngest head of state in the hemisphere. Almost immediately he sent Julian to Europe to organize heavy equipment. Twelve armored half-tracks arrived in August 1951 from Switzerland, along with 250,000 rounds of 30- and 50-caliber ammunition. From Italy came a hefty shipment of recoilless rifles.

Julian was soon organizing monthly shipments to Puerto Barrios. Business was so good and he was getting so well known, that dozens of manufacturers began seeking him out in the Harlem office that was also his home, where Essie was always present to answer phones, letters, and cables. He found himself thriving in the sometimes frightening but always fascinating netherworld of munitions trading. No previous venture could compare. Intrigues blossomed daily. Agents took orders for one item and attempted sending another. Everything had to be inspected at dockside. Letters of credit for millions of dollars went winging back and forth across continents and oceans. Prices changed as demands increased, even when orders were already on the high seas. Top government officials demanded and received a cut on almost everything. It was all about as ethical as trafficking in poppy capsules.

Somehow, though, Julian withstood the strain. Being a transatlantic commuter was to his fancy. His bank account, now in the nation's capital at the Riggs National Bank across from the U.S. Treasury Building, had never been so fat. His first year's profit was $100,000—not bad for a maiden voyage. In fact, this seemed to be one of his best winning streaks.

After observing Arbenz in action for over a year, the State Department began having qualms about him. By mid-1952 the climate in Guatemala had turned pointedly anti-American. Workers were told by union leaders that to be anti-Communist was to be anti-government. Arbenz openly encouraged animosity toward the American business interests in his country—Black Eagle Enterprises, Ltd., being the only exception.

In the late summer of 1952 even Guatemala's neighbors grew nervous as agents of Arbenz began to incite their labor unions to strike. The CIA began providing Honduras and San Salvador with military assistance, including aircraft capable of strafing and bombing. Arbenz quickly placed an order with Julian for antiaircraft guns. The one thing he lacked was the capability to handle air strikes.

One early morning in September a State Department agent appeared at Julian's Harlem office. After identifying himself, he noted, very unofficially of course, that purchasing such sophisticated matériel as antiaircraft guns for a country of dubious loyalty to the democratic process was perhaps not in the best interests of current United States foreign policy. He recommended Julian refuse the deal.

The agent's request came too late, however. Julian had just returned from organizing a shipment of twelve Swiss-made Oerlikon antiaircraft guns. He didn't tell the agent about the shipment, but immediately boarded a plane for Europe to discuss the situation with executives at REXIM, his major supplier in Geneva.

The REXIM people were surprised to hear of the agent's visit. The Swiss government itself had cleared the shipment, and the guns were traveling to Guatemala aboard a United Fruit freighter.

"We cannot believe that the United States government could possibly see anything wrong in this shipment, the direct effect of which is only to increase stability in Latin America," a REXIM spokesman said at a news conference.

Julian was willing to chance it. There was a neat profit in this shipment for Black Eagle Enterprises, Ltd. The guns cost $1,500 each and Guatemala was willing to pay $4,000.

It was not too difficult to rationalize the decision. The

United States was in the middle of an era of Communist witch-hunting led by Senator Joseph McCarthy, and the tension often overlapped into foreign affairs. Any ruler's oratory about nationalization or workers' revolts automatically classed him as red on red. Cautious congressional pressures had made the State Department a wreck of nerves.

The Swiss guns, shipped from Antwerp, arrived in Guatemala in late September without incident. The State Department went silent. A few wise heads, it appeared, prevailed. Guatemala's leftward tilt was not yet designated a permanent one. Also, Julian's dossier showed him capable of turning any interference into an embarrassing international incident.

Once Julian received a cable informing him that the guns had arrived safely, he sailed for New York aboard the *Queen Mary*—in a most expansive mood because of his $30,000 profit.

Reporters at the docking were particularly eager to interview him this time. They had heard of his recent acquisition, for which he had not only paid cash but, rumor had it, even finessed a 10 percent discount due to his "diplomatic status."

"Yes," he admitted, "it is true that I just purchased a $28,000 Rolls-Royce." It was being fitted, he explained, with foam-rubber cushions, pull-up steps for easy entrance, a bar, and a special glass partition to allow him to give driving orders by a microphone while maintaining the confidential nature of his backseat negotiations, which, he confided, could be about anything "from boots to an atomic bomb."

"It will be arriving shortly," he said, "after they finish plating the doorknobs with gold."

Under the heavy pressure of the press for details he yielded. He told how it all happened. In the last two years he had purchased for Guatemala forty 30- and 50-caliber machine guns, six half-tracks, millions of rounds of ammunition and tens of thousands of rifles, three thousand pairs of boots, many jeeps, and twelve antiaircraft guns. He estimated his profit at "about $200,000."

In closing he asked the press to keep the Rolls a secret. "The gift is by way of a surprise for my wife," he explained as he left to catch a plane for Guatemala.

When the stories of Julian's affluence appeared, Arbenz was as surprised as Essie, and much more angry. For months he had been trying to keep his whopping military buildup, costing $10 million annually, as quiet as possible. What particularly irked him was Julian's reference to profit at a time when the government's Spartan line was that only the peasants were reaping the harvest of the "glorious revolution."

Julian arrived at the palace expecting *abrazos* for the Oerlikons. Instead he found that he had been fired.

Riffling through a stack of $1,000 bills and smiling as if nothing had happened, the suddenly ex-chief arms procurer was at the airport with bags packed twenty-four hours later. Before boarding a plane for New York, he told the good-sized crowd, "One day I will fly back to Guatemala in a jet plane at six hundred miles per hour. My friends had better paint their roofs black as identification against the bombing and revenge of the Black Eagle."

From the many long faces to be seen on Guatemalan officials at Julian's farewell, it appeared he was going to be missed. There was only one like him in the whole country—a wheeler-dealer who, according to *Time*, "tipped barbers at the Palace Hotel $5 for a 75¢ haircut" and lavished gifts of cars, diamonds, and Italian-made suits on the numerous red-tape-cutters. At his rates he could afford to raise the per capita income.

18

Not So Red Hot in Guatemala

Say, what's this about Germany rearming? Do you know I wouldn't handle that for all the money in the world. No sir, not after what they did to London. But brother, someone is going to pick up a pile of dough on *that* deal.

THE BLACK EAGLE *London, July, 1954*

WITHIN DAYS of dumping Julian, the Guatemalan President was informed by an aide that an exhaustive search in all the arsenals of the land produced horrifying news: They didn't own one shell that fit the new Oerlikons. That was what Julian had been working on when relieved of his duties, Arbenz now realized.

His first urge was to court-martial his entire military staff. However, there wasn't the time or manpower.

He weighed the sticky situation carefully. Dealing directly with a Communist nation for the shells could be dangerous. The tradition of the Monroe Doctrine, which had the biggest navy in the world backing it up, would almost automatically mean a swift United States challenge to ships representing outside and unfriendly involvement in hemisphere affairs. Washington was already putting diplomatic pressure on all friendly European nations not to let their nationals sell the needed shells, or any other war products for that matter, to Guatemala.

Arbenz concluded that only an independent arms dealer could bring in the shells. He checked with a few of them, but could find none that wanted to venture into such a delicate international situation. It was no small matter, and the stakes grew daily. Both the East and West had much to win, or lose. The United States was geared to stop any precedent allowing a hostile door to open in the hemisphere; the Iron Curtain countries were worried about losing a disciple by not backing him.

Arbenz finally resigned himself to his Hobson's choice, and Julian was quietly summoned back to Guatemala. He returned smugly.

At a palace meeting in January 1953, the chief of Artillery, Colonel José Felix Aguillar, informed Julian that he was rehired on two conditions: that he keep silent and that he find the shells. Julian told him he'd come back on one condition: that they would now pay him a monthly fee just for his name.

The colonel knew he was being had, but he agreed.

Julian immediately contacted REXIM and told them to again get busy locating the shells. Four months of fruitless negotiations, however, showed it was going to be more difficult than ever. Besides the United States' increased pressure to stop sale of the shells, the Korean War had worsened and Russian troops were now shooting down rioters in East Berlin. Gloomy forecasts of World War III were being heard everywhere.

When August came with no shells reported on the high seas, Arbenz sent a sharp communiqué to Colonel Morales in Washington: Get them or else. Morales, who was susceptible to panic, cabled Julian in desperation.

COMMUNICATIONS FROM CHIEF IN REFERENCE TO NEW ORDER AND 53 AND 54 APPROPRIATIONS RECEIVED PLEASE GET MATERIAL FROM ITALY AS SOON AS POSSIBLE AND HURRY WITH INFORMATION OF SHIPMENT TO HEADQUARTERS THE BOSS ANXIOUSLY AWAITING THAT NEWS SO WE CAN DISCUSS OUR FUTURE ORDERS REGARDS SUCCESSFUL TRIP OSCAR MORALES

There was cause for Arbenz's concern. He had received reliable information that an archrival, Colonel Carlos Castillo Armas, was training a well-armed guerrilla force of five hundred anti-Arbenz Guatemalans in the jungles of neighboring Honduras. Armas' CIA-supplied planes were flying every day, studying troop activities along the Guatemalan side of the border.

After numerous refusals from various West European suppliers, on August 20 Julian finally located a company that had the shells and convinced it to make a secret deal. GENAR was headquartered on Rome's Via Veneto and was a registered munitions supplier. By the end of August, the shells were crated and sitting in a guarded warehouse on a Naples dock ready for shipping.

Julian flew to the Italian port to handle the risky logistics himself. For if the ammo came into an American port even for transshipment, it would be seized. He instructed the GENAR people to hold the cargo until there was a ship going direct to Puerto Barrios.

He returned to New York to get the billing worked out on this big one. He had put up $40,000 of his own money for the shipment, but planned to charge the Guatemalans $90,000 for all the work, danger and payoffs involved in the dicey deal.

On November 16 the Norwegian freighter *Knut Bakke* steamed into New York harbor scheduled for a two-day stop while off-loading cargo for transshipment to other ports.

U.S. Customs officers boarded the ship in the Narrows for the routine inspection. Coming upon the eight tons of ammo in 170 cases, they inquired about its final destination. Puerto Barrios, Guatemala, the skipper said after checking his shipping orders.

The phone at the Black Eagle Enterprises, Ltd., office was answered by the president. The customs officer's tone was frosty as he explained about a Norwegian ship's arrival. Julian politely inquired as to why he was being called.

The customs officer then explained the problem: he didn't believe that Julian had the proper import-export license, as required by the Neutrality Act of 1939, for the merchandise in his name destined for transshipment to Guatemala.

"No, it can't be!" Julian stammered. "Something's gone wrong!" He hung up the phone in a rage.

The shells were immediately seized and sent to the Naval Ammunition Depot in Earle, New Jersey. The next day Julian announced he was financially ruined. He had, he claimed, mortgaged everything, including his house, to make the payments for the goods. The ammunition, he insisted, was for guns bought with a valid license issued a year before. He claimed he had thought the same license covered the ammo.

Julian's problems were nothing compared to Guatemala's. While the shells were rather insignificant in the big leagues of modern warfare, they were crucial to the future of a Guatemala that had no air force. Regardless of who attacked first, Arbenz or Armas, the CIA planes would be in action swiftly. At the depressing least, the planes panicked Arbenz's people. The pilots were described by many Guatemalans as *Los Sulfatos,* an earthy reference to the sulphuric waters of the land that made Guatemalan bowels very active. A mere buzzing aggravated the condition.

The Guatemalan leader placed the highest priority on locating another batch of the Oerlikon shells—anywhere and at any cost. He dispatched his most trusted aide, Major Alfonso Martinez, to Europe to find them, as well as whatever other arms he could buy. The odds were fast changing against Arbenz's chances of beating Armas. He felt more modern weapons might even the odds. There was no other choice but to buy big and madly.

While Martinez, assisted by Julian, scurried around the world markets looking for the shells, Foreign Minister Guillermo Toriello opened the first session of the Inter-American Conference in Caracas, Venezuela, in March with a fifty-five-minute blast at the United States. He used such phrases as "big stick" and "dollar diplomacy," recalling the days when "it was common to disembark U.S. Marines in Latin American ports to occupy custom houses to guarantee investments or to correct political actions which did not coincide with those interests."

After Toriello's speech, Secretary of State John Foster Dulles quickly organized a strong resolution that cut off the Guatemalan's censure maneuver. Dulles didn't have to hear thunder to forecast a storm. His brother Allen was masterminding the CIA's Honduran operation.

Guatemala became panic-stricken. Officers were summoned from their quarters in the middle of the night to mobilize forces. Several American correspondents, including the *New York Times* and Copley News Service men, were deported. Moderates disappeared from the streets. The jails were filling quickly. Torture was used to get information; those who remained silent were roasted alive in ovens, or had their tongues cut out.

In the darkness of early morning, May 15, the *Alfhem*, a 4,600-ton freighter of Swedish registry, made an unscheduled stop at Puerto Barrios. Guatemalan troops immediately closed off the dock to everyone, including the ship's agent. The cargo was listed as "steel rods, optical glass, and laboratory supplies." A week later the actual contents—$6 million worth of military equipment from Czechoslovakia—was hauled 150 miles to the capital in 119 freight cars. Much of it was still in the original World War II crates marked in English but overprinted in Russian and Polish.

Chartered to a Swedish national, the ship was paid for in London. It was loaded in Stettin, Poland, and sailed on April 17. Once on the high seas, it changed destination four times. Its first destination was given as Dakar, the West African port capital of French-ruled Senegal. On April 23 it changed course in mid-Atlantic for the Caribbean island of Curaçao, Dutch West Indies. On May 7 it changed course in the Caribbean to Puerto Cortes, Honduras. On May 13, forty-eight hours after receiving its fourth and most crucial change at sea, the zig-zagging, slow-moving *Alfhem* steamed fifty miles past the Honduras port at night and ducked into the Guatemalan harbor.

Once off-loaded, the ship left immediately under ballast, mission accomplished.

No Communist nation had ever before made such a bold move into the hemisphere. Guatemala now had enough weapons to arm all its worker militias, who stood ready to march on Honduras—and beyond, if all went well.

The panic bell clanged madly in Washington. President Eisenhower described the situation as "disturbing" and expressed concern at the prospects of an armed Communist dictatorship in the hemisphere.

A State Department announcement, according to the May 18 *New York Times,* stated, "Because of the origin of the arms, the point of their embarkation, their destination, and the quantity of the arms involved, the Department of State considers this a development of gravity."

U.S. Navy and Coast Guard ships began stopping and searching all vessels in American waters sailing from Iron Curtain ports, regardless of registration.

And in New York, U.S. Customs officials called Julian in for questioning about the controversial shipment. Not only was he still listed as Guatemala's official arms purchasing agent, but British papers like the London *Daily Mail* stated without reservation that he had arranged the shipment of arms from Poland.

After a closed meeting with the customs people, Julian told newsmen that though he was not directly involved, he knew all about the order. "It was paid for through an agent in Europe," he said. "The agent is a Swiss firm of which one official is an American." The shipment was an outgrowth of a smaller order with the same firm he had negotiated a few years ago, he noted in order not to be left out of the action completely. As long as the United States maintained relations with the country, Julian insisted he would continue to deal there. In fact, he announced, he was already negotiating to buy seventeen American-made Mustang fighters for Arbenz from Sweden.

When one reporter asked if he leaned toward the left, Julian shouted, "I'm not a Communist sympathizer, I'm a Roman Catholic."

Julian sailed for Europe in early June. His country-hopping activities kept the State Department working overtime trailing him. Once he left Sweden, the United States Embassy informed the government that filling any of his orders for Guatemala would be considered most displeasing to Washington. That killed the Mustang deal.

When he arrived in Paris on June 14, he was immediately taken by French security agents to the United States Embassy, where he signed a sworn statement that he wasn't in the pay of Guatemala nor seeking any military equipment. At that moment, it was technically and physically true. Hours later the United States High Commission office in West Germany signaled Washington that six tons of Swiss-made antiaircraft shells destined for Guatemala had just been located at the port of Hamburg.

When Julian arrived at New York's International Airport from Paris on an Air France flight at 7:30 AM on June 17, his passport was seized by Federal authorities.

Four thousand miles away Castillo Armas' American-armed counterrevolutionaries beat Arbenz to the punch and attacked Guatemala. An air force of four P-47s flown by American mercenaries hit key petroleum storage positions and an ammunition depot without encountering antiaircraft fire. Guatemalan resistance along the fighting fronts collapsed almost instantly, and sometimes rather noisily, when *Los Sulfatos* passed overhead.

Julian returned to Harlem a stateless person. In his mail he found a letter from the Justice Department's Foreign Agents Registration Section chief, Nathan B. Lenvin. It announced that his license as an arms dealer was "being terminated as of May 21, 1954." He had been so busy shipping arms that he had forgotten to renew his dealer's permit. It certainly was one of his more unpleasant days.

By the following morning, however, his martyr complex was in high gear. He threatened to renounce his citizenship, or at the very least to stand outside the White House gate until the President gave him a hearing.

"If I am deemed *persona non grata* around here, then I want to know why," he told the *New York Herald Tribune*. "I tried to get John Foster Dulles on the telephone today, but his secretary said Mr. Dulles was out. So now I'll try to see the President himself."

Ten days later Arbenz fled the palace for political asylum in the nearby Mexican Embassy. One of his companions-in-refuge was Ernesto Ché Guevara, who was taking his political internship under Arbenz.

In early August, when things had simmered down, Julian was summoned to Washington by the State Department. During a lengthy meeting he promised to avoid further business with Communist regimes. In return he was granted a new passport.

To show his good faith, he sent Armas, who had recently been sworn in as Guatemala's new president, a cable of congratulations. He told him he was ready to serve him in whatever capacity necessary. Armas cabled No thanks, noting he found his country already well stocked with military hardware.

Julian was in bad need of rest and repair. In disrepute in his own nation, he decided to find comfort in the place where his adventures were always more appreciated.

He arrived by ship in London on July 14. His spirits recharged swiftly as he took up his place as a popular favorite among a press corps that delighted in covering intriguers. With a Fleet Street entourage, he headed straight for Savile Row. Entering the Cyril Castle, Ltd., establishment, he ripped off his jacket and stomped on it.

"Give it away to someone," he cried, "and make me a couple dozen decent English suits. I've just been talking to someone wearing one of your suits. He made me feel badly undressed!" After being measured, he left for a nap.

The press found him again the next morning at his country hotel in Surrey, lounging in pajamas of gold brocade with dressing gown to match. While munching a bacon sandwich, he reminisced about his Latin experiences and plugged Black Eagle Enterprises, Ltd.

"Yes sir," Julian said to Noel Monks of the *Daily Mail*, one of Fleet Street's most respected foreign correspondents and an old chum from Ethiopian war days, "only a sucker would buy arms from behind the Iron Curtain, sight unseen. Guatemala did just that and they lost the war. For the big shipment of arms they got from Poland—cash on the nail just before the balloon went up—turned out to be duds. A lot of rusty old junk. At my rate, which is 30 percent, I could have cleared three million bucks on the deal. Sure, sure I'm in the arms business. And I was doing all right until Washington gave me the works. They thought I was the boy shipping the Iron Curtain stuff. Brother, that made my British blood boil. Okay, so I do have a U.S. passport now, but I was born British and blood will tell. Anyhow I convinced them I was on the level, that I had bought my arms on the up-and-up in Switzerland, and they gave me a brand-new passport. Whoever runs Guatemala now owes me a hundred thousand berries—and I don't mean bananas."

He handed Monks a copy of his calling card, which noted his line of work as "Arms, Military Equipment, Ammunition."

"See," he said, "nothing hidden there. I'm in the arms business. I deal only with sovereign states."

Then he mused, "Say, what's this about Germany re-arming? Do you know I wouldn't handle that for all the money in the world! No sir, not after what they did to London. But brother, someone is going to pick up a pile of dough on *that* deal."

19

The Flimflam Man

Rumors, rumors, rumors! Christopher Columbus!
THE BLACK EAGLE *when arrested as a* triple *agent* *Havana, February, 1960*

IT ONLY appeared that Julian took a pounding in the Guatemalan affair. Actually, he came out of it well ahead in bank deposits and press clippings. And the future looked even brighter for his craft. Increasingly, rulers and revolutionaries alike were realizing that military hardware was best supplied by independent munitions dealers such as Black Eagle Enterprises, Ltd. They produced what was wanted, when it was wanted—and without attaching political strings.

After renewing his dealer's license, Julian began a careful study of the Caribbean scene. He knew it well. The three principals he watched most carefully were Fulgencio Batista, the stenographer-sergeant who had seized control of Cuba in 1952; Rafael Trujillo, the Dominican health nut who practiced self-perpetuation by presenting bonuses to parents who named their sons after him; and Fidel Castro, who was determined to free all the Americas from the likes of the first two. Julian did business with the lot.

While on a sentimental journey to his Trinidadian birthplace in August 1955, he heard reports that one of the principals was about ready for servicing. The talk among West Indian politicians whom he chatted with while in Port of Spain dealt with a band of young revolutionaries and agrarian reformers planning to overthrow the Cuban government. The information tied in with similar reports he had heard in Guatemala City from Cubans-in-exile who had come there to learn the revolutionary trade firsthand.

It seemed worth a closer look.

He flew to Havana and went straight to the American Embassy, where, since he was now well known in diplomatic circles throughout Latin America, he was given a briefing. But it was done reluctantly, for his reputation preceded him, and his arrival anywhere was like that of a gunslinger suddenly appearing on the main street.

At the briefing it was quickly stated, of course, that his information was wrong; all was well in Cuba. In fact, the commercial attaché pointedly noted, Cuba was receiving all the military equipment it needed through United States Mutual Defense Pact and Mutual Aid Act programs.

Julian wasn't so sure. He decided to check with the Cubans themselves and arranged a meeting with several Defense Ministry officers.

They were cautious at first. But after he explained—with his inimitable and disarming charm—the way he worked, the goods available, and his high respect for strongmen like the Dominican Republic's Trujillo and Haiti's Duvalier, they suggested he keep in touch with the Ministry through its overseas embassies. They admitted that there was always the chance that a twenty-eight-year-old troublemaker named Fidel Castro Ruz might try something again as he had in 1953. If that happened, they might need certain special equipment faster than the United States government could or would provide it.

Leaving a handful of calling cards and price lists, Julian promised quick service on whatever they might need, and left.

This time there wouldn't be the problem of special shipping orders. Cuba's president was the type of dictator considered safe by the State Department; registered arms dealers could do business with him. He represented no threat to American democracy. Or, more exactly, he was not Communist-inclined.

When Julian arrived back at his Harlem office on September 21, stacks of urgent cables from troubled capitals around the world greeted him. One had come from Juan Perón's Ministry of Defense a month ago requesting he fly down immediately. It was too late for action, however; the Argentinian dictator had been deposed on September 19. Julian was sorry about that. It would have been a short but fat account.

Several days later, when he read of the devastation Hurricane Janet was spreading across the islands of Grenada and Trinidad, he dropped all business plans and got to work raising relief funds with all the efficiency, flamboyance, and energy he mustered up for an arms deal or a press conference.

Reports claimed 750 killed and countless injured. Vehicles to transport the injured, the dead, and medical supplies were urgently needed. By December Julian had donated at his own expense a 1949 Cadillac ambulance, two hearses, and several tons of clothing.

His efforts brought him numerous letters of thanks from the islanders as well as organizations like the Ford Foundation. One, from George Solomon of the Registrar's Office on the island of Grenada, said, "I can assure you, Colonel, that I vouch for the sentiments of each and every Grenadian in saying that never in the annals of West Indian history do we find that any one man has done so much for his people."

No stories on this activity were carried in the American press. Julian the humanitarian didn't have quite the fascination of Julian the wheeler-dealer.

The arms business is a waiting game. Revolutions and coups, while often appearing to happen overnight, usually are in planning stages for months, even years. Julian never put all his energies into one developing situation. He kept a dozen projects around the world under surveillance until the time was right to service an account—be it the attacker or the attacked. By 1956 he was selling everything short of pocket battleships to a drove of client-nations from Pakistan to Portugal. He now performed as well by phone and cable as by personal appearance. At the same time he offered Israel 500,000 rounds of 50-caliber U.S.-made ammo at $325 per thousand (rejected), he also offered Egypt 25,000 Mausers at 50¢ apiece (accepted).

Once Castro got a foothold in the Sierra Maestra in December 1956, Batista's men activated their account with Julian. The U.S. was still providing Batista with military equipment—he was the better bet to protect American business investments, which totaled a whopping $800 million—but Congressional pressure was slowing down the flow. The bearded young freedom-fighter's cause was proving successful despite Batista's terrorist tactics among the peasants. Important newspapers like *The New York Times* had begun to champion Castro's *26 de Julio* movement, and popular support for him in America was growing.

The United States' changing policy and Castro's rising international image caused Trujillo to rush to his fellow dictator's assistance. Florida wasn't the only place ninety miles away from Cuba: the island's eastern tip lay seventy-five miles from the Dominican Republic.

Julian began buying for Cuba indirectly by working through Dominican representatives in New York. He quickly located ten thousand 37-mm shells for Batista's medium tanks. Grenade launchers and napalm were next. Throughout 1957 he was kept busy filling Batista's growing needs and scouting for goods in London, Paris, and Rome.

At the end of March 1958, the United States suspended all shipments of arms to the Cuban government. Julian's business immediately increased. Guatemala had taught him the risks involved in delivering arms to hot spots, so he helped the Dominicans devise a safe routing for Cuba-bound purchases. They were shipped from European and United States ports with Ciudad Trujillo marked as the final destination. From the Dominican capital they were transshipped directly into the fortified capital of Havana by an almost daily air shuttle service of unmarked planes.

Batista's desperation peaked in December. The smoke of burning sugar-cane fields that wafted through the once-sparkling playland was a death signal for his regime. In a last-gasp effort Trujillo sent Julian to Europe with his personal munitions coordinator, Enrique Garcia Hijo. Their orders: Fly in all the Browning 30- and 50-caliber machine guns available for the civilian defense of Havana.

In Geneva they hastily inspected and purchased 150 of them from the Montgomery Equipment Company at 13 Quai de l'Île and chartered two Constellations for the emergency airlift. But on December 23, with the crated weapons ready for shipping, Garcia disappeared from his suite at the Hôtel du Rhône with the checkbook. Both the party mood and the *mañana* bug struck him at the same time, and he forgot to leave Julian his Paris number. (He did not forget to pay his hotel bill, but he might as well have—his check for $365 later bounced, and Julian had to make good for it.)

After furious cabling to Ciudad Trujillo, Julian reorganized the airlift directly into beleaguered Havana for New Year's Day.

The planes were paid for, loaded, and ready for takeoff when the news flash came. The guerrillas under Ché's command were marching into Havana unresisted. Fidel Castro had won, and Batista had fled.

Long before Castro was born, Julian had learned to balance on the wings of abrupt change. He finished a hasty re-routing of the loaded planes to the Dominican Republic (where the client had gone), then sent a cable of congratulations to Cuba's new leader. He already had a good contact in the Castro camp: he'd met Guevara several times at Guatemala's National Palace. Also, he'd been too busy lately to hold a major press conference, so the word was not generally around about his Trujillo-to-Batista operation.

He decided not to come on too strong, however, until the thirty-two-year-old *Número Uno* showed financial responsibility.

In December 1959, on his way back to the States after a shopping trip for a Middle Eastern client, Julian decided to present his credentials to the new Cuban Ambassador to the Court of St. James's in London, Señor Rojas Santamarina. It was also a goodwill gesture. At a July press conference in the Cuban Embassy, Santamarina had listed Julian as a munitions agent for Trujillo.

At the meeting in the embassy he knew so well from pre-Castro days, Julian explained to the Ambassador that while he at times had met with Enrique Garcia, who was serving Trujillo, the dictator was certainly never a client of his. When Santamarina didn't press the point, Julian refreshed the diplomat's memory about his work for Arbenz and produced a copy of the congratulatory cable he had sent Castro in January.

Santamarina bought the story, mostly because Julian had something to offer he knew his leader could use: ten North American AT6-Gs for immediate delivery. The single-engine jet trainers, Julian explained, were suitable for strafing, bombing, and pamphlet seeding.

The Ambassador advised Julian it would be worth a trip to Havana, then sent a Telex message to the Cuban Air Force Chief of Staff, alerting him to their discussion and noting that Julian had a reputation for delivering what he promised.

Julian's London visit was well timed to a Cuban need. Neither cold war side was supplying Castro with military equipment of any great importance. Western nations were apprehensive of him; Iron Curtain nations were still analyzing his loyalty and usability.

Julian arrived in Havana on January 3, 1960. At the airport he spotted Castro getting out of a DC-3. He had just arrived back from an aerial tour of agricultural development programs in Oriente Province.

Disregarding the armed guards, Julian marched right up to the Premier, introduced himself, and explained his urgent business.

Surprised by the approach and the man, Castro smiled shyly as they shook hands. He then introduced Julian to his brother, Raul, and Ché Guevara.

As a translator swung into action, Guevara noted to Castro that he recalled Julian's work for Arbenz during his Guatemala days.

Castro smiled again and appeared more interested. He shook hands again with Julian, and as he walked away, called back with a wave, "*Bienvenido.*"

It was enough of an introduction for Julian to be at his demanding, name-dropping best in getting to see the top officers in the right ministries. After three days of hard bargaining with the Ministerio de las Fuerzas Armadas Revolucionarias, he had worked out a deal. Commandante S. del Valle Jiminez, the chief of the Air Force, handed him a signed contract in Spanish.

> The Cuban Revolutionary Air Force agrees to purchase, subject to inspection from a member of the Air Force, 10 (ten) North American AT6-Gs at the fixed price of 150,000 U.S. dollars, plus two complete aircrafts of the same type in spare parts, for which the freight and insurance will have to be paid by the Cuban Air Force. . . .

It was marked "*firme e irrevocable*" and dated "6th of January, 1960, the second year of our revolution."

The transaction was worth $30,000 to Julian and his Swiss supplier. He flew to Rome where the planes were in storage, and after inspecting them and arranging for shipment, went to the Regina Hotel to await word from Cuba on who would inspect the planes.

The word came on February 15 by cable:

THIS IS TO ADVISE YOU THAT BY ORDER OF THE MINISTER OF ARMED FORCES ALL CONTRACTS ISSUED BY US TO YOUR FIRM ARE HEREBY CANCELLED STOP CAPITAN E. FERRER INSPECTOR.

Julian was furious. For ten days he tried to phone through to Jiminez from Rome. Unsuccessful. He flew back to New York and tried again, still without luck. There was now nothing left to do but fly to Cuba and straighten out the *commandante* in person.

Accompanied by Jon Kraker, an old friend and student of Latin American affairs who spoke good Spanish, Julian departed for Cuba on February 28. On the one-hour flight from Miami to Havana he prepared for his act by playing high-stakes poker with Kraker for wild sums that were kept on paper. The game was conducted with such dazzlement that the plane dragged most of the way over the straits of Florida; few passengers could resist watching the rear-lounge action.

Once through customs, they took a taxi to the Capri Hotel, checked in, then headed for Air Force headquarters.

When Jiminez heard that Julian and an unidentified American were in the building, he ordered them brought to his office. Once they were led in, he closed the door and locked it. He coldly motioned them to stay standing.

"How dare you come to Cuba after selling arms to Trujillo?" was Kraker's translation of Jiminez's tirade.

Julian's eyes bulged with surprise. He protested it was all a mistake, it was not true. "Rumors, rumors, rumors! Christopher Columbus!" he said over and over, shaking his head.

Jiminez demanded he prove it. Julian rose and promised it by first light. He stormed out of the office, shooting Jiminez his most indignant look.

That evening in the hotel room Kraker cautioned Julian that they were both in deep trouble if he couldn't come up with something. He noted that no proof was needed in Cuba to send accused traitors to their deaths.

Julian listened and plotted.

The next morning he drove to the American Embassy. In front of a Foreign Service officer, Hugh Kessler, he swore in a written statement that at no time had he supplied military equipment for the Dominican Republic.

Once the red seal was placed on the document, Julian rushed to Jiminez's office and presented it to him.

The *commandante* seemed if not impressed at least pacified. Julian left feeling relieved, even confident.

Later in the day Jiminez spoke to Castro about the matter. A former junior diplomat in the pre-Castro Embassy in London was called in and shown the document.

Throwing it aside, he insisted that he had seen this man at the Embassy coordinating a munitions deal for Trujillo. In fact, he said, some of the weapons ultimately made it into the hands of Batista's troops.

Castro made a decision.

That night, before Kraker went out to inspect what was left of Havana cabaret life, Julian insisted he call up not the waiter or the maître d' but the chef himself. In a victorious mood, he was hungry and wanted to feast on a specialty of Caribbean origin: chicken cooked in beer and served with rice and slices of fried plantain. Kraker detailed Julian's gourmet instructions to the chef, who appeared delighted to have a little touch of the old opulent days return to his drab existence.

Shortly after midnight Kraker arrived back at the hotel. He picked up his key at the desk and walked through the empty lobby toward the elevators. A young Cuban in green khaki fatigues stepped in front of him and identified himself. He was from G-2, Cuba's intelligence sector.

The Cuban asked Kraker to accompany him to headquarters. Kraker hastily explained he wished to first check to see if his roommate was all right. The agent impatiently explained that *su amigo* was already outside.

There, in the back seat of a long, darkened car sat Julian in pajamas and silk robe, surrounded by soldiers armed with submachine guns that he thought looked vaguely like a Czechoslovakian make he had bought for Batista in the old days. He was in a very foul mood because his sleep had been interrupted. Also, his slippered feet were cold, he told Kraker.

At G-2 headquarters they were both photographed, fingerprinted, and handcuffed. Then they were taken outside and put in a shed with a corrugated tin roof and iron bars for walls.

Julian decided this would never do, not even for what was left of the night. Rattling the bars, he commenced a bellowing protest about the accommodations.

As Kraker winced, the guards appeared and nervously discussed among themselves what to do—such a roar in the quiet of the night was bound to awaken their leader. To silence him, they hastily took them back into the main building, moving them along with kicks and hard jabs of their rifle butts. Julian and Kraker spent the rest of the night in the library on hard benches, nursing their bruises.

The next morning the local *cantina* opened at the first cock's crow, and the two prisoners were allowed to buy morning coffee. As they sipped the brackish liquid, a sergeant marched up to them.

He announced that they were to be deported. He regretted, he added as he looked up from his orders, that it was not the firing squad. Julian's nocturnal commotion had indeed disturbed his sleep.

Allowed to get their belongings and pay their hotel bill, they were driven to the airport in a car filled with armed guards and Julian's luggage. As they moved along a narrow road at high speed, Julian suddenly shouted, "Stop!"

The two guards swiftly swung their weapons at his head, clicking off their safety latches as they moved.

Kraker nervously translated his friend's command. Finally the guards shrugged at each other. One of them told the driver to stop and back up to where the prisoner was pointing.

Followed by the two soldiers with guns at the ready, Julian got out and trotted over to the huddle of small stores. In a few minutes he reappeared wearing a triumphant grin and holding up two large mason jars.

"Hard to get at home," he said to Kraker. Then he waved the driver on and began a dissertation on the rare experience in store for his palate when he got home and into the mangoes preserved in ginger.

At the airport they were locked up in a windowless G-2 office. When they were finally ushered out to the tarmac toward an Aerea Cubana DC-3 headed for Miami, Julian stopped short and refused to board the plane.

Kraker translated, hesitantly this time, his announcement: "We came here by Pan American, we go home by Pan American."

Now utterly frustrated, the guards argued among themselves until after the plane's hatch was closed and it taxied away and took off. Julian and Kraker were marched back to the G-2 office, again accompanied by kicks, shoves, insults, and jabs of rifle-barrel noses.

An hour later they left—by Pan American.

On March 14, 1960, Julian sent a letter to Jiminez:

Cmdte. S. del Valle Jiminez
Fuerza Aerea Rebelde
Ministerio de Defensa Nacional
Havana, Cuba

Dear Sir:

Thanks very much for your cordial reception and for the embarrassing incarceration I suffered after departing from you with the assurance that I was to proceed to Europe to complete the negotiations. As you well know, I was arrested at midnight by G-2, taken to headquarters with my associate, photographed, fingerprinted, and interrogated without any charges being preferred against us. We were taken to the airport and put on a plane for the United States without even being permitted to telephone our embassy or call you.

It is the privilege of your government to cancel any contract they have given to a firm who is duly licensed by the U.S. but a "firme e irrevocable" contract means precisely what it says—firm and irrevocable. Therefore, I submit to you the cost of said cancellation is 20% of the plane deal or $30,000 for which I do hereby demand full restitution. Failing to receive the necessary reimbursement within ten days, I have no alternative than to bring legal proceedings to recover said damages.

Very truly yours,
BLACK EAGLE ENTERPRISES
Col. Hubert F. Julian, *Pres.*

The mangoes would have tasted much better if he had received an answer. That he was lucky to have gotten out with his life never crossed his mind for any length of time. He was much too annoyed for sobering thoughts and chose, instead, to rise above it all.

20

Our Man in the Congo

> Why if I had the inclination I would buy a plane, hire a crew, and fly off to Switzerland without waiting for the regular flight.
>
> THE BLACK EAGLE *on being refused entry to France Paris' Orly airport, May, 1960*

CONGO. THE WORD rumbles with the impassioned moods of Vachel Lindsay's poetry and Joseph Conrad's prose. It beats of Stanley's exploring and Livingstone's converting. It pounds with the pulse of Africa.

Congo speaks of lush rain forests and misty mountains where blue gorillas and pigmy warriors are sentinels. It is the moon gate to a whole continent that is dark with people, 350 million strong.

On June 30, 1960, freedom came to the Congo. Belgium's gift to fifteen million blacks after seventy-five years of colonization was twenty-one college graduates.

At the celebrations in the capital of Léopoldville, Belgium's King Baudouin grew nervous under the hot African sun that was never kind to foreigners. The Republic's first Prime Minister, an ex-postal clerk named Patrice Lumumba, heatedly reminded all assembled of the "contempt, insults, hangings, and shootings" under Belgian rule. He spoke in French so there could be no misunderstanding. The words were not a particularly auspicious omen. Most of the two hundred invited guests, including the white king in horn-rimmed glasses, were anxious to board Sabena jets and fly away as soon as diplomatically possible.

Five days later, on July 4, black troops of the Force Publique mutinied against their white officers. Within a fortnight the Congolese returned Belgium's gift in cruel kind: 15 Europeans were killed and 251 women raped. More than 30,000 Belgian *colons* fled. They could sense the night of the long knives coming.

Black troublespot and black troubleshooter became acquainted on an early May day in 1960 in the transit lounge at Paris' Orly Airport. Immigration officials had just refused Julian permission to enter the Fourth Republic. The French, according to a *Chicago Daily News* dispatch, had heard rumors he was on a mission for the Algerian FLN (Front de Libération Nationale) to buy weapons for the revolutionary organization. They were wrong. He was shopping for a few Sherman tanks for Haiti.

Turned back at the entrance gate, Julian paced in mock fury.

"Why," he protested, "if I had the inclination I would buy a plane, hire a crew, and fly off to Switzerland without waiting for the regular flight." He then stomped off to the lounge, where he selected a comfortable chair to catch up on his reading while waiting for the next scheduled flight to Geneva.

The Congo's approaching independence was major news in the French-language press. Editorials were darkly warning what was about to happen.

Julian was amazed to learn that the new nation—the size of the United States east of the Mississippi—had not a single African pilot. Perhaps, an inspiration coaxed, he might be of assistance in getting an air force started. Changing his flight plans to Africa, he got off a cable to Duvalier informing him that no tanks were now available, but if he could put off the planned military parade for a month or so he'd find something. He didn't wait for the answer.

After landing in the Congo's capital of Léopoldville, he

checked into the Memling Palace Hotel, then telephoned the Prime Minister-designate's office.

He met with Lumumba the next day and discussed his cadet-training plan in French. It impressed the bespectacled Congolese leader as much as the sharply pressed blue military uniform, which, Julian told Thomas Kanza, Lumumba's aide, he had had tailored "while on a mission in Finland." He didn't mention the date, and it fit as if it had been made the week before.

Lumumba recognized the prestige value of Julian's offer. After independence, due in a week, he was determined to send most Belgians in the military packing.

At the same time, in the nearby American Consulate, Consul Clare Timberlake received word of Julian's arrival and meeting. He cabled Washington for instructions, and the answer came back swiftly: Under no circumstances let Julian get involved with the Congo, or vice versa.

The next day Timberlake conveyed these sentiments to Lumumba, who at the time leaned toward the United States for both guidance and assistance in preparing for freedom. Lumumba reluctantly sent a handwritten message to Julian's hotel informing him the cadet deal was off.

Julian shrugged off the note, bought a few African wood carvings, and returned to Harlem, convinced he would eventually find something of value in Congo affairs. This kind of patience he had plenty of. If you had seen one African leader, he figured, you hadn't seen them all.

Once home, Julian was quick to let the press know he had been updating his African portfolio. Shortly after the enlightenment in early 1961, an executive of International Broadcasting System, Inc., contacted him on participating in an elaborate African scheme. The New York-based firm wished to pitch newly independent African nations, now numbering more than thirty, on handling their publicity campaigns.

Julian wasn't too impressed with the plan or IBS, but

he was eager to make it back to Africa. He joined as an account executive and chief charmer.

Within the week he was parading through UN corridors looking more important and sounding more diplomatic than many of the real delegates. He was a constant host at elaborate luncheons and dinners at the Waldorf and "21." Between acts he kept his eye on the Congo situation, which was worsening because of a breakaway province called Katanga.

Located in the southeast sector of the Congo, Katanga contained 8 percent of the world's copper reserves and produced 50 percent of the Congo's revenue. The provincial President, Moise Tshombe, had watched the post-independence happenings in the Republic and decided to secede in July 1960.

Lumumba immediately requested UN intervention. The world organization entered reluctantly because the scene was so complex. Negotiations, cajolings, conferences, promises, broken promises, and finally threats went on for a year. But Tshombe would not relent. The UN, already deep in debt because of the Korean War, running sores in the Middle East, and a host of deadbeat members, ran out of patience.

On August 28, 1961, a battalion of blue helmets representing Sweden and India seized Elisabethville's airport, post office, and radio station. The UN police action eventually turned into a two-and-a-half-year war.

Round one of the shoot lasted twenty-three days. It ended with a cease-fire order on September 20, 1961.

Using white mercenaries, Tshombe had broken even on the fighting field but lost the propaganda battle. A major factor in this loss was Dag Hammarskjöld's death in a fiery plane crash on September 18 just over the Katanga border.

In late October, IBS President L. Nicholas Dahlman assigned Julian to seek out Tshombe, then in Zurich for medical reasons, which included checking the health of his numbered account at the Banque de l'Indo-Chine. On November 4 Julian called the Katanga leader's suite in the

Baur-au-Lac Hotel and received an appointment for 4:30 the next afternoon.

The IBS package proposal included producing a propaganda film on Katanga for distribution in the United States. The film, plus the coordinating of Katanga's "total and world-wide daily publicity" for one year, would cost $500,000, Julian explained to Tshombe.

The former president of the Elisabethville Chamber of Commerce bought the whole program. Money was not a problem, he said. "What I need now is to be understood."

Julian placed a transatlantic call from Tshombe's suite to Dahlman in New York and put the two presidents on the line to work out details. He did the translating.

Before leaving, he obtained a $1,000 advance from Tshombe and written authorization to collect a round-trip ticket to Katanga on Belgium's Sabena Airlines. Tshombe told him to be at his residence in several weeks ready to start work.

Julian flew back to New York to pack his long-stay bags and to find out how to use a tape recorder.

He arrived in Elisabethville in late November 1961, stepping forth to challenge Africa in peacock splendor—striped pants, double-breasted pearl-gray vest, formal coat, spats, bowler hat, furled umbrella, and monocle.

A young American diplomat, Terry McNamara, waiting to collect his arriving wife and children, spotted the splendid figure. He asked if by any chance he was American.

"Actually I'm British," Julian said to McNamara in his best Oxonian accent, handing him his IBS engraved calling card, which read in part: "Colonel Hubert Fauntleroy Julian, Vice-President and Director of African-Asian Affairs," and in the right-hand corner, "The Black Eagle."

McNamara, who was an African affairs specialist, nodded recognition. He told Julian he had been reading about his adventures for years. Julian smiled benignly and replied it was kind of the "Consul-General" to personally meet him at the airport. The diplomat's polite but firm explanation that he was not the Consul-General and that he was there for family reasons produced no response that indicated Julian had heard him.

"In fact, the President's car is supposed to meet me," Julian said as he looked about impatiently, "but it hasn't arrived yet, I see."

Julian paraded over to the customs office in the faded peach-stucco administration building to find out about the delay. Inside he ordered a fat little Belgian to dial President Tshombe's office for him. The flustered civil servant snapped to and rang through to Madame Vermeulen, Tshombe's European secretary.

"*Bonjour, madame,*" was as far as he got when Julian grabbed the telephone receiver.

The IBS executive explained in French to *madame* that he was at the airport "*avec le consul-général*" and would leave with him if the limousine did not arrive in five minutes.

Madame apologized profusely and begged him to wait, for the car would be right out. Julian then put the phone down. The Belgian sighed with relief when he said he had no further calls to make at the present.

Out in the hallway Julian met with the American diplomat's wife and children. He kissed the lady's hand, saying, "*Mes hommages, madame,*" scooped up the two children in his enormous arms, and humming a Strauss waltz, danced around the main lobby of the airport as if it were Roseland. Traffic in the building stopped as all eyes riveted on the sixty-three-year-old grand-teddy bear.

Tshombe's limousine arrived in under five minutes, and Julian motored to town in style. After settling into his room in the red-roofed palace on Boulevard Reine Elisabeth with a view of the city park, zoo, and tin-roofed American Consulate, Julian attended the cabinet luncheon his host had just invited him to.

Everyone was there—Defense Minister Godfreid Munongo, Foreign Minister Everiste Kimba, and a brace of Belgian advisers. Julian got right to work taping everything that was said. After that he went on a tour of the city with Tshombe in the President's new royal-blue Lincoln Continental.

Their path was cleared by the palace guard mounted on silvery Harley-Davidsons and sporting outfits that resembled those of a regiment of light dragoons—complete with shiny, pointed hats that looked like souvenirs from a Prussian officers' mess.

The chauffeur was kept busy avoiding unseated dragoons left scattered along the winding route as their machines roared off, out of control, like wild mustangs.

Tshombe produced the first installment of $50,000 and an envelope packed with round-trip tickets for a ten-man IBS film crew, and Julian made plans to return to New York to organize the operation. Just before his flight took off, Julian and Tshombe held a secret discussion in the back seat of the Lincoln. The Katangan leader explained he was having trouble buying munitions through normal channels. Though the Belgians wanted to help, they could not chance getting directly involved. He invited Julian to run some guns to him.

Julian could hardly control his excitement. Tshombe was the kind of client most arms dealers only dreamed of. Katanga was in the best of all possible situations. It had an income of $80 million annually, not a *centime* of which now went to the Central government, and a tough little army bolstered by white mercenaries who were veterans of Algeria, Dien Bien Phu, the Foreign Legion, and both sides of World War II. It seemed destined to be a lengthy war. All Katanga needed to keep going and perhaps even succeed was equipment—the best money could buy.

When Julian reached IBS headquarters in New York, he found Dahlman waiting to relieve him of tickets and check. However, he parted with only two tickets and told Dahlman he was holding the money until the camera crew actually took off.

On December 5 shooting erupted again in Elisabethville.

To Dahlman it was good enough reason not to send the camera crew. He tried to convince Julian that they had best cash in everything quickly and forget about Katanga for the time being.

Julian didn't agree. He was sure Tshombe would make it. Also, he was not about to blow the bigger deal.

Only after cabling Tshombe to stop payment on the check did he turn it over to Dahlman. And though IBS consisted of no stations or profits, Julian's December 7, 1961, wire of resignation made it sound like NBC.

> IT IS WITH DEEPEST REGRET I HEREBY TENDER MY RESIGNATION TO TAKE EFFECT IMMEDIATELY AS OF TODAYS DATE AS VICE PRESIDENT AND DIRECTOR OF ASIAN AFRICAN AFFAIRS FOR INTERNATIONAL BROADCASTING SYSTEM STOP I AM MOTIVATED IN THIS DECISION BY THE UNHUMANITARIAN ACT OF THE UN WITH THEIR MERCILESS BOMBING OF THE CIVILIAN POPULATION IN KATANGA STOP I AM THEREFORE GOING TO THE ASSISTANCE OF MY FRIEND THE PRESIDENT OF KATANGA TO BE MILITARY ADVISER SO THAT I CAN ASSIST HIM IN GETTING HELP FROM ANY POWERFUL COUNTRY THAT WILL HELP THEM FIGHT AGAINST THE SAVAGERY AND BRUTALITY DISPLAYED BY THE UN IN MY PRESENCE WHEN I WAS THERE STOP IF AFTER THE TERMINATION OF THESE UNFORTUNATE HOSTILITIES AGAINST KATANGA CULMINATES TO THE SATISFACTION OF ALL CONCERNED AND YOU DEEM IT PROPITIOUS FOR THE RETURN OF MY SERVICES TO YOUR ORGANIZATION I WILL BE MOST HAPPY TO DO SO STOP PLEASE CONVEY TO THE BOARD OF DIRECTORS MY SINCERE THANKS AND AGAIN THANKING YOU PERSONALLY FOR THE HIGH ESTEEM IN WHICH I WAS HELD BY YOU AND YOUR ORGANIZATION I BEG TO REMAIN COMMA HONORABLE SIR COMMA REGRETFULLY YOURS COLONEL HUBERT F (FIGHTER) JULIAN THE BLACK EAGLE.

Julian got out just in time. While he went over to Katanga, IBS went under for good.

Throughout the second round of shooting, Julian again resided at the palace, often touring the battlegrounds on an English bicycle borrowed from the Presidential garage. He soon became a well-known figure to the growing international press corps that found the war as confusing as the black-market currency-exchange rates.

It was a weird shootout. UN forces, some 6,000 strong, ringed the capital. Defending it were 3,000 Katangan troops and 250 white mercenaries. The fighting was furious, but only in sporadic bursts. UN and Katangan forces usually observed the 4:00 PM tea break, and both sides (except for the Gurkhas, who only did one thing well) used weekends more for drinking than fighting.

The local brewery was hit only by mistake. When a stray mortar shell knocked it out, the shooting in the brewery's vicinity usually stopped until repairmen could get the suds flowing again. With Irish-born diplomat Conor Cruise O'Brien present and calling the UN's shots, the restoration of the brewery's operation was always given priority. Both sides agreed that Simba beer was worth an unofficial cease-fire.

All sorts of wheeler-dealers arrived: diamond smugglers, big-game hunters, double agents, Parisian prostitutes. A doctor by the name of Victor Lionhearte-Reichardson caused a stir for a while. He was a Welshman who came with academic credentials from UCLA, yet thought nothing of asking American reporters, "What's it like in the States, mate?" His true identity as a former waiter in a British railway dining car was uncovered only when he asked a wounded mercenary, "Is it okay to cut penicillin with water?"

Tshombe was concentrating on exploiting alleged UN atrocities against allegedly innocent Katangan civilians. He pelted Western journalists with photographs of bombed-out hospitals and blister-faced children.

He also officially announced that he had retained the Black Eagle to search the world for doctors and medical supplies. In an attempt to win the support of African nations, among whom he was distinctly unpopular because of a label as a Belgian pawn, Tshombe instructed Julian to hire only Negro MDs.

Julian headed for the Caribbean authorized to offer one-year contracts for $8,000 plus transport and housing. His fee was $1,000 per delivery.

In the midst of interviewing in Martinique, he received word that a second cease-fire had been arranged. The agreement was the awaited signal—buy up everything and get it into Katangan hands before the next round started and UN security again tightened up.

Moving with haste around Europe, displaying official documents listing him as Katanga's "Ambassador-at-Large," Julian quickly assembled an enormous arsenal. He was assisted, unofficially, by France, Belgium, and Portugal.

While accountants in Brussels did the final paper work on the shipping orders, Julian made a quick trip home to Harlem with a surprise: a first-class ticket for Essie aboard the *Leonardo da Vinci*, sailing for a rendezvous planned in Naples for the end of April. By then, he reckoned, the equipment would be on the high seas from a Belgian port, he'd be paid, and a victory celebration would be in order.

He arrived in Brussels on April 14 to meet with the shipping agent handling the convoy, and left for Elisabethville on April 18 after the most successful single shopping spree of his life—$18 million worth of equipment for a profit of 10 percent of the deal.

For the first time in a bold career that spanned half a century, he thought of retiring. The temptation dissolved, however, when he scanned the international dateline stories in his copy of the Paris *Herald Tribune*. There were, he concluded, just too many appetizing prospects.

21

Jugged Mercenary

That, my boy, is because I neither drink nor smoke and try to take a maiden a day. That's what keeps one young.

THE BLACK EAGLE *to a United States diplomat in a Congo jail*
Elisabethville, April, 1962

ON HOLY THURSDAY morning, April 19, 1962, the macadam runway of the Elisabethville airport was a clutter of blue-and-white DC-3s taking off, landing, and unloading stacks of supplies flown in from Léopoldville. Indonesian and Gurkha soldiers handled cases of canned food, cartons of Plymouth gin, and knotty pine coffins.

Tshombe had just been forced to turn over the airport's control to UN forces—at least for the length of the second cease-fire.

The secessionist President had no choice. Most of his Air Force personnel were mercenaries. Yet in order to get and keep the cease-fire, which he needed in order to replenish his dwindling munitions stockpile, he had promised to dismiss them. The pilots were now restlessly waiting for Julian's shipment to arrive, as were the ground-force mercenaries. All the hired swords were "in hiding," which meant out of camouflage and burgundy-colored berets and into civilian clothing.

Looking out his window as the Sabena 707 jet made its final approach, Julian spotted the UN action below. He jabbed the overhead call button. When the Belgian stewardess arrived, he asked what had happened to the Katanga Air Force.

The girl shrugged and told him about yesterday's agreement.

Julian leaned back, his stomach muscles tensing. He didn't like it at all. But as the jet touched down smoothly, he relaxed. There was nothing else he could do.

At the bottom of the first-class ramp he was greeted by a Pakistani officer of the UN wearing well-starched green fatigues and sporting a handlebar moustache. In pukka English he invited Julian to join him at the customs building he pointed to with his swagger stick.

Inside, he offered Julian a drink.

"Water," the Ambassador-at-Large said weakly, looking around for friendly faces. There were none.

The officer ordered tea, and they chatted amiably while waiting for the other passengers to clear customs. The officer mentioned he had just heard over a BBC news broadcast that Julian was involved in collecting badly needed medical supplies for the civilian population. He praised this humanitarian effort and hoped he had been successful enough to bring some supplies with him on this trip.

"The need is very urgent," the Pakistani said, shaking his head sadly.

"Yes," Julian mumbled as sweat began to bead on his brow.

Drinks finished and the crowd diminished, they walked over to the baggage-claim section.

"I must inspect your luggage," the UN officer said, embarrassed in polite fashion.

The formality proved embarrassing only for Julian. Once he got below the silk shirts, linen handkerchiefs, and paisley dressing gown, the Pakistani officer's face showed astonishment. He shook his head slowly as he picked up a battle helmet, a set of puttees, and, in a corner under a pair of shorts, a gas mask. He looked at Julian.

A large package was brought in by an African porter, who looked at Julian, smiled, and said, "*Jambo bwana.*" As the officer asked if the package was his, Julian wished he had never seen the porter.

"Well," he said, seeing his name clearly inked on it as the sender, "in a way it is and in a way it isn't." He explained that in fact it was a surprise gift for his good friend the President.

"I picked it up in a sporting-goods store just before I boarded the flight," he said with labored nonchalance.

In fact, the whole scene was a bad mistake. The package was to have been collected out on the airstrip by a Monsieur Marachel of Sabena and taken directly to the palace without ever going into the public baggage-pickup area or through customs.

Apologizing for delaying a man of Julian's diplomatic rank, the officer took out his pocket knife and began cutting the thick string tied around the heavy corrugated-cardboard box.

After much careful slicing and snipping, he finally opened the package. And then the box's top.

They both stared—one amazed, the other aghast—at the sight: three pearl-handled 45s in a velvet-lined container, a Sten gun in handsome carrying case, and 400 rounds of the appropriate ammunition.

Within minutes of the Pakistani's whistle, the customs section was packed with UN military and civilian personnel —Indians, Swedes, Gurkhas, Irish, Canadians, Ethiopians (who came with bayonets drawn), and Indonesians. In trotted intelligence experts, translators, and the inevitable crash of the curious.

"What are you trying to do?" Julian bellowed out with fury. "Make a federal case out of this?"

The hastily summoned U.S. Vice-Consul, Terry McNamara, advised Julian to cooperate.

Eventually, when things quieted down, Julian produced a receipt for the guns. It showed that he had paid $510 to E. J. Binet & Fils of Brussels for them. He again insisted they were gifts for his employer and friend, Tshombe.

A UN official, a civilian, said Julian was lying. They were samples from a renowned arms-supplying firm, he insisted.

Julian pretended not to hear. He started giving flip answers to questions.

"The Sten gun," he said, "is an excellent weapon for elephant hunting, you know."

No one present laughed or smiled.

"Well," he tried again, "the Sten is a gift for Tshombe's bodyguard."

The other equipment taken from his luggage was brought forth. What about the gas mask, the puttees, and the steel helmet? he was asked.

The gas mask and helmet, he explained, were samples for a business presentation he was scheduled to make before executives of Union Minière, Katanga's giant copper-mining company that was Belgian-owned. Both were excellent protection for African miners. The pair of puttees, he said, was a demonstration model for a planned province-wide safety program.

"They are very useful for the natives as protection against snakebite," he said.

Finally, he was asked to explain a Binet & Fils letter dated February 12, 1961, taken from his briefcase. It was addressed to him and stated: "*Nous nous engageons à exécuter cette commande au plus tôt.*" Stapled to it was an enormous order for guns and ammunition organized by the sporting-goods store that did indeed happen to be one of the biggest munitions suppliers in Europe as well.

Julian had had it. "Shoot me," he snapped. "I refuse to answer any more of your confounded questions. What do you want me to do—lie?"

UN Telex lines linking Elisabethville, Léopoldville, and headquarters in New York ran late and hot with messages on the Julian affair. This was the break the world organization had been waiting for: the secessionist leader's chief arms procurer caught in the act. Julian happened to arrive on the same day the UN had uncovered the secret plan to smuggle $18 million worth of arms and munitions into Katanga.

U Thant had suspected Tshombe would try to use the cease-fire for such an arms buildup (which was what the UN was using it for, too). However, he had had no proof. Nabbing the key man was sure to kill the enormous deal. No company, no nation—even Belgium—wished to be caught openly violating UN resolutions. And without the equipment Katanga couldn't last another round.

Julian was driven under heavy guard from the airport to UN headquarters in a villa outside Elisabethville, where he was formally arrested.

Security officers took his wallet with $335 in it from him, along with the wardrobe that he had planned to wear on his Neapolitan holiday with Essie. They made him sign the checklist of the possessions they were holding: forty white handkerchiefs, seven white shirts, two pairs of silk pajamas, one pair of gray gloves, two Sabena napkin holders, one gold-plated Swiss twenty-five-jewel watch, nine Christian Dior neckties, four suits, one pack of playing cards, nineteen assorted pieces of toilet articles, and one paisley dressing gown.

Jailed and under guard, Julian's only contact with the outside world was through Vice-Consul McNamara, who bought him a bottle of Rose's lime juice because it was the only way Julian could take the local water.

The next day, Good Friday, Roman Catholic Julian raised a great roaring clamor when the Sikh guard, a Hindu, brought him pork chops for lunch. McNamara was called and quickly arranged a menu change to canned pilchards.

On Easter Sunday the diplomat brought Julian the overseas newspapers, which were thick with stories about the consequences of the Congolese cease-fire. There was no mention, however, of the Julian affair.

The next day the diplomat noticed Julian appeared despondent. He hardly looked up; his shoulders were hunched; he mumbled responses. The guards were also concerned. They feared a suicide attempt.

Finally McNamara felt compelled to discuss it with him. During his afternoon visit, as the brooding Julian sat on a wooden stool in rumpled gray pin-stripe pants and slightly soiled undershirt, McNamara told him of his fear.

"Are you mad, my boy," Julian suddenly roared, eyes flashing for the first time since his arrest. "Don't you realize that I have a fourteen-room mansion overlooking the Harlem River to which I certainly want to return? I have no intention of doing anything so foolish."

McNamara was relieved. He started to leave, then paused and turned around.

"You know, Colonel," he said, "you're a remarkable man for your age." He smiled admiringly.

"That, my boy," said Julian warmly, "is because I neither drink nor smoke and try to take a maiden a day. That's what keeps one young."

McNamara left and went to the post office with a cable Julian had asked him to send for him. It was to Essie, now sailing to Italy.

DUE TO PREVIOUS ENGAGEMENT MUST
MISS NAPLES LOVE HUBERT

Caging the Black Eagle in a foreign land created enormous problems for the United States government. The State Department had to let Julian be jailed; pulling superpower rank would only further alienate a developing nation that already was convinced big nations ran everything on the double standard.

Washington's worry, however, was what America's black population would do when they heard that one of their own was locked up. The double-standard charge was a potential danger at home, too. Chances of black rioting across the nation were unnerving to many officials.

"We were walking on eggshells," said a top American diplomat stationed in Léopoldville at the time.

While State Department officers in Washington made numerous phone calls to black leaders in major American cities, Julian's arrest was kept quiet. But once the consensus showed that Julian wasn't a current power among young militants, it was announced.

On Monday, April 23, Julian was officially charged with violating Security Council resolutions pertaining to doing business with an illegal regime. The UN claimed he had negotiated the whole $18 million munitions order. It included, the UN announced, 2,000,000 rounds of ammunition, 200 120-mm mortars, 200 60-mm mortars, 320 machine guns, and 200,000 rounds of mortar ammunition.

While Julian kept protesting his innocence, Tshombe attempted to help by announcing that the arms dealer had no formal connections whatsoever with his government. The UN, however, didn't believe either one of them. As far as the Congo experts were concerned, they were two of a kind.

After the Easter holidays Julian was flown in a DC-3 under armed guard to Léopoldville. There he was placed in the maximum-security section of le Royale, UN headquarters in a partially finished modern high-rise building that was to have become a deluxe hotel until post-independence events killed off, among other things, tourism.

Intensive interrogation began immediately. The UN had great expectations that Julian would tell them Presidential palace secrets: How many mercenaries were really employed? Who was paying the big bills? What foreign powers were secretly helping? But first the Binet & Fils letter was gone over and over again. After several days both the Swedish interrogators and Julian showed signs of fatigue.

Finally one afternoon Julian breathed a heavy sigh, stretched loudly, and said he'd cooperate and explain what it was really all about. Yes, there was a shipment of arms headed for nearby Angola, a land both friendly to Katanga and possessed of a seaport.

Why Angola? they asked eagerly. The interrogators were nervous with anticipation. They were getting close to the kill.

"Well, you see," Julian answered in hushed tones, "the arms were really destined for the Bahamas for people trying to overthrow the Communist regime of Castro . . ."

Angola, the Bahamas, Communism, Castro! It was all too much for the interrogators. Cursing in Swedish, they paced the room in frustration.

"Have me shot," Julian growled at them. "I don't care. Under penalty of death I will answer no more of your questions." The day's questioning was ended abruptly.

At the next day's session Julian, fresh from a good night's sleep, was prepared to thicken the plot.

"When the Chinese Communists came to Elisabethville," he said, "now that was something."

"What?" said an incredulous UN voice. A guard was sent running to buzz the intelligence department.

"Oh yes," said Julian, wincing at the recollection. "Fifteen of them in one night at two AM."

"Where did they stay?" his questioner pressed as the room filled with puffing brass trying to be quiet about their entry.

"At the residence," he said, taking the whole scene in. Then he clammed up. He refused to say another word.

At this point the UN decided to terminate the interrogation of Hubert F. Julian in the interest of maintaining its sanity. The world organization didn't get what it wanted, but Julian did.

The official UN report entitled "The Case of Mr. Hubert Fauntleroy Julian" simply recorded, "The documents found on Mr. Julian and the statements he made to ONUC officials established clearly that he had been dealing in arms, ammunition, and military equipment on behalf of the Katanga secessionist authorities."

22

Over But Not Out

> The Premier sent a car for me today and assigned me a captain as my personal aide-de-camp. That shows you how *persona grata* I am around here.
>
> THE BLACK EAGLE *to the press*
> *Léopoldville, Congo, July, 1964*

THE CASE OF the UN, the U.S., and the Central government of the Congo against the Black Eagle was made even stronger—as if that were necessary—on May 12, 1962. At airports in both Chicago and Newark four B-26s destined for Katanga were seized by FBI agents. They were listed on Black Eagle Enterprises, Ltd., purchase orders as "executive aircraft."

Such evidence created an added headache for the State Department. How could they have Julian deported without going through a Congolese trial? The way jurisprudence was handled in the African land, if a trial were allowed to start it would almost certainly finish with a public hanging in the soccer stadium before a cheering cast of thousands. Premier Cyrille Adoula was so infuriated by Tshombe's artful dodging of the conference table that he was out for blood. Executing a friend and confidant of his most hated enemy was one way of getting at least partial revenge while quieting ambitious members of his cabinet who felt they could run the whole show more efficiently.

Julian, who knew he wasn't in the best of positions even with guards protecting him around the clock, started his own campaign for survival. With UN permission he composed cables to President John F. Kennedy and to Ralph

Bunche, who was the UN's chief troubleshooter in the Congo. He felt he had a chance only if he kept his name in the news.

When he exhausted his list of people to cable, he started writing letters to key Congolese officials pleading for leniency. In a letter on UN stationery to Adoula, he noted that if released, "I assure you, sir, that under no circumstances would I ever return to the Congo." He was also shrewd enough to transmit letters to his wife through the Embassy. They carried heavy praise for the President (Kennedy, not Tshombe), the State Department, and the UN.

On May 19 Julian suddenly collapsed in his room. It appeared to be a heart attack. Now the UN was also worried. If their prisoner succumbed in a land where political prisoners rarely died of natural causes, there could be trouble. UN doctors quickly moved him to le Royale's best corner suite and assigned around-the-clock nurses to his side.

With Julian ill, U.S. Ambassador Edmund A. Gullion asked Adoula, in the way diplomats say please, to release him, promising to ship him out of Africa for good. Ralph Bunche also recommended release.

Adoula, who had softened somewhat when Julian was stricken and the guns never actually arrived, discussed the matter with his cabinet at various periods between May and August. At first most of them said no. But when he reminded the stubborn ones of the UN's massive aid program in their land, they finally relented.

On August 20 Adoula told the UN, "My government has decided to request Mr. Julian's expulsion." The next day a State Department official told Julian, who appeared to have made a full and remarkable recovery, that he would be put on a plane on August 23. A formal letter to Julian from John R. Clingerman, the Vice-Consul, noted, "The Embassy arranged your release without trial only by assuring the government of the Congo that you will depart the Congo immediately and will return directly to the United States."

That morning, packed and ready to go, Julian had a last-minute visitor. Robert Gardiner, one of the new Africa's leading diplomats, was in charge of UN operations in the Congo. The Ghanaian entered Julian's room and stared hard at the prisoner, who was packing.

"Are you Colonel Julian, the Black Eagle?" he asked.

"Yes," Julian answered. "You are Mr. Gardiner of the United Nations?"

"Yes. This is one of the saddest days of my life," Gardiner said with emotion. "When I was an undergraduate, I worshipped you as a hero. You were reported to be fighting as a Negro pilot with the forces of Emperor Haile Selassie to help maintain the territorial integrity, dignity, and sovereignty of an African state. I meet you in person for the first time, today, as a mercenary willing and ready to deliver lethal weapons to persons who care nothing for the lives of Africans and seem determined to enslave us again."

Julian squeezed his eyes closed and shook his head. "No, Mr. Gardiner," he said. "Those are harsh words. I was misled—"

"You are too much a man of the world and too experienced to be so easily misled," Gardiner interrupted. "Do you not see in Katanga a betrayal of faith of abolitionists, philanthropists, and missionaries like Dr. David Livingstone? When you get home, tell our people in America and the Caribbean of your agonizing encounter."

That evening Julian was driven to Léopoldville's Ndijili Airport by an American vice-consul in an unmarked car. Two UN security men in civilian clothes went along for protection. Pan American Airways' Flight 151 was already boarding passengers. It was headed for New York via West Africa.

Julian was checked through with more speed and efficiency that the Congo airport had shown since independence. His passport was immediately turned over to the flight's purser. There were no good-byes, no crowds, no recognition.

Once the big Boeing's wheels were up and locked in the bay, though, the old spark ignited. Julian looked around the cabin to find the configuration unfamiliar.

He suddenly realized what was wrong. He was not in first class. He sat back in a roil of indignation, unable to recall ever flying tourist before.

At the plane's next stop, in the Liberian capital of Monrovia, he located the ticket agent, produced an air travel card, and selected a first-class seat.

As the plane once again nosed closer toward home, Hubert Fauntleroy Julian relaxed with a glass of mineral water while his mind got cracking on an immediate project: the inevitable press conference at touchdown in New York.

When the captain shut down the giant jet engines, Julian got up, tilted his homburg back on his head, and began to hum a French love song. He twirled an umbrella as he came down the ramp to drop in on the Congo once again. After a twenty-five-month absence he had returned—this time without guns. Instead, he packed pillows for the uneasy head of the Congo's new Premier. By one of those enigmatic quirks of African fate, the Premier turned out to be none other than Moïse Tshombe, two years ago an archvillain, but now the new boss charged with putting the *whole* Congo back in financial shape.

"My wife didn't want his head resting on the same pillows as Adoula's," Julian told members of the press, whom he received in his suite at the Memling Palace Hotel while he prepared for a nap after the all-night flight from Paris.

"As to business," he said, "I have a hundred million dollars with me from a European bank, and I'm authorized to go up to five hundred million to help resuscitate the economy here. Now that's confidence for you."

He displayed a slight limp. Asked about it, he said, "I go through five wars without a scratch. But coming down here in a plane, a Coke bottle falls off the stewardess' tray and wrecks my knee."

He delighted in describing his present status in the Congo. "The Premier," he said, "sent a car for me today and assigned me a captain as my personal aide-de-camp. That shows you how *persona grata* I am around here."

The protean adventurer looked around as if searching for someone who should not be listening. Then he confided, "I've actually come to collect a bet from Moise. When I saw him this winter in Madrid, I bet him he would be Premier of the whole Congo within three months after the United Nations troops left. Well, he beat the deadline by plenty and now I want my money. That'll give you a little idea of the powers of The Black Eagle. You could call me a clairvoyant."

The press conference was interrupted by a phone call. It was Julian's aide-de-camp. He just wanted to let the Colonel know that the limousine was out in front, ready whenever he wanted it.

Allons! For there is no ending to this story. He's still at it, somewhere. Right now. In fact, if you're reading this on a plane, look around. He may be aboard.